# COMMUNAL DISCERNMENT
## A Lamp for Our Synodal Journey

Edited and with an Introduction
by Brian Grogan SJ

Foreword by Arturo Sosa SJ
Superior General of the Society of Jesus

Published by Messenger Publications, 2024

Copyright © Brian Grogan SJ, 2024

The right of Brian Grogan SJ to be identified as the author of the Work has been asserted by him in accordance with the Copyright and Related Rights Act, 2000. All rights reserved. No part of this book may be reproduced or utilised in any form or by any means electronic or mechanical including photography, filming, recording, video recording, photocopying or by any information storage and retrieval system or shall not by way of trade or otherwise be lent, resold or otherwise circulated in any form of binding or cover other than that in which it is published without prior permission in writing from the publisher.

Scripture quotations are taken from the New Revised Standard Version Updated Edition. Copyright © 2021 National Council of Churches of Christ in the United States of America. Used by permission. All rights reserved worldwide.

ISBN 978 1 788126 663

Designed by Brendan McCarthy
Typeset in Garamond Premier Pro and Cormorant Garamond
Printed by Hussar Books

Messenger Publications,
37 Leeson Place, Dublin D02 E5V0
www.messenger.ie

# Contents

Preface .................................................................. 5

Foreword by Arturo Sosa SJ ................................. 7

Introduction by Brian Grogan SJ .......................... 9

## Part One: The Setting

The Art of Making Wise Choices ........................ 19

The Esdac Vision ................................................ 24

## Part Two: The Heart of Decision-Making

Spirit-led Conversation ....................................... 37

Discernment in Common ................................... 43

Personal Prayer ................................................... 48

The Small Groups ............................................... 53

Plenary Session ................................................... 60

Fostering Group Energy ..................................... 68

The Personal Review .......................................... 74

Authority in the Group ...................................... 79

Making a Decision Together .......................................................... 88

## Part Three: Consensus

Fostering Consensus on Who We Are ........................................... 97

The History Line Deepens Consensus on Who We Are ............ 103

Fostering Consensus on What We Are Called to Do ................. 113

Fostering Consensus on How to Respond to the Call ............... 122

'What Wind Blows My Boat Along?' ........................................... 128

Group Sadness or Desolation ....................................................... 138

## Part Four: Facilitation

Facilitation of Groups ................................................................... 145

Team Aspects of Facilitation ........................................................ 156

Recognising the Spirit's Signature ............................................... 165

## Appendices

Appendix 1: Negotiating and Planning a Workshop ................. 173
Appendix 2: A Sample Workshop Schedule and Timetable ...... 182
Appendix 3: Prayer Sheets ............................................................ 185
Appendix 4: Discernment Journeys of Diverse Groups ............. 215

Acknowledgements ....................................................................... 250
Bibliography .................................................................................. 252
Index .............................................................................................. 255

# Preface

The French book adapted here for English speakers is titled *Pratique du discernement en commun*, edited in 2022: it was written by a team of six: Michel Bacq, Jean Brasseur, Sandra Chaoul, Jacques Fremiot, Michel Ulens and Véronique Croizé. In French, 'Esdac' stands for 'Spiritual Exercises for Communal Apostolic Discernment': its logo is a feather or quill within a circle. In this English adaptation the name and logo of Esdac are retained, to indicate the resource group to which one can apply for its services (www.esdac.net).

This book has many uses:

- It will help those who are already engaged in communal discernment.
- It can be usefully read privately by anyone interested in the dynamics of group discernment. It is rich in wisdom gained through patient experience, and will throw light on what is going well or badly in groups in which one may be involved, be they Church-associated, NGOs, business associations or other.
- A group looking to run their meetings better might read this book together and learn many useful ways of approaching their task.
- Christians grappling with developments within the Church will be enriched by the book which brings synodality down to earth and shows it to be workable.
- Groups seeking outside help in communal discernment can read this Manual and then contact Esdac for assistance.

Since this is a Manual for busy practitioners, capitals are occasionally used (e.g. Manual; Workshop, Prayer Sheets). The language is as inclusive as possible, and repetition and cross-references facilitate access to the various topics.

*Preface*

For immediate practical help you can go straight to Part Two: The Heart of Decision-Making. To see how communal discernment works in practice, go to Appendix 4: Discernment Journeys of Diverse Groups.

Quotations from the *Spiritual Exercises* are from Louis Puhl's version except where marked 'Ivens'.

# Foreword to the French Edition
by Arturo Sosa SJ, Superior General of the Society of Jesus (abridged)

While discernment in common is a treasure of the Church and part of the tradition of the Society since its beginnings, today it needs to be put into practice more explicitly. Spiritual conversation should be the ordinary way of sharing among Jesuits and within its apostolic works ... Other groups, communities and ecclesial institutions also feel the call to progress in this practice, and in other concrete ways of living out synodality.

Pope Francis has often insisted on the importance of spiritual discernment for the whole Church. For example: 'Today, the ability to discern has once again become particularly necessary ... Without the wisdom of discernment, we can easily become puppets at the mercy of the trends of the moment'.[1] The pope has especially asked the Society of Jesus to contribute to the spread of discernment in ecclesial life. The habitual use of spiritual discernment, as an instrument for seeking and finding God's will ... should lead to a revitalisation of our mission and life.

The conviction that God is at work in history and communicates with human beings is the presupposition for common discernment. So we must seek the conditions that allow us to be guided by the communicating Spirit ... True discernment presupposes that we first try to become interiorly free of disordered attachments, helped by the practice of the examination of conscience, so that as a group we become 'like a balance at equilibrium' (*Spiritual Exercises*, 15). It also implies a shared desire for union of minds, since it is the whole group that is called to

---

1 Pope Francis, *Gaudete et Exsultate*, 167.

choose how best to contribute to the proclamation of the Good News and to the world's transformation in this time of profound change.

I am deeply grateful to all the apostolic teams who authentically communicate the art of discernment in common to the many groups who are anxious to 'recognise the concrete means that the Lord predisposes in his mysterious plan of love, so that we do not remain only with good intentions'.[2] I welcome in particular the rich contribution of experience and skills that the Esdac team has been offering for more than two decades in this area. It is thanks to such contributions that we hope to advance towards the ideal that discernment in common may become the normal way of making decisions in the life of the Church.

21 October 2021

---

2    Pope Francis, *Gaudete et Exsultate*, 169.

# Introduction
## by Brian Grogan SJ

This morning I was taking a break along the nearby Grand Canal when I was addressed by a man who was showing the wear and tear of the night before. With nine expletives deleted, his message was crisp: 'World's gone to hell ... Hopeless! ... Those guys up there should be shot! ... Only hope is to put a woman (named) in charge!' He stopped to assuage his thirst, while I bleated a few forgettable remarks and walked on, wrestling with possible titles for this book. Communal discernment is demanding, because as my friend said the challenges facing our world are enormous. From Adam and Eve down to the UN and in our own lives, human decision-making has shaped for good or ill the history of our planet and ourselves. So what are the elements that well-intentioned people, of whatever background, need to observe in order to make wise decisions? Are there rich traditions – the wisdom of the ages – to draw on? In this Introduction I want to draw attention to some key elements which can help us in making choices for a better world.

### *Who's at the table?*
This Manual offers a progressive path through challenging terrain: not only are the issues around good decision-making difficult to grasp, but each of us comes to the table with our unique background, culture, store of knowledge, personal philosophies, preferences, blind spots, prejudices. Each of us sees things from our own perspective, be we poor or rich, black or white, educated or illiterate, gay or straight. You may think in circles, I may think in squares; you have a good hand in clubs, while I have spades. We are a motley group as we sit around the table of decision, eyeing one another!

Let me illustrate with a thumbnail sketch of myself – the person you'd have to negotiate with if we were making a discernment together. I'm tall, male, white, Irish, from a lower-middle class family; as a child I survived World War Two because Ireland was neutral. I'm a priest, and a senior member of a religious order in a beleaguered Church. I have taught theology most of my life, became a writer by accident, and am grateful to a world of authors of good books. I have a passion to share the faith that has nourished me with those who feel the Church has served them a thin diet for too long. I'm celibate, I own nothing; but my needs, whatever about my wants, are provided for; unlike many people I have health-care, with security around my final years and my burial. Many years in administration have given me insights on how good decisions – and bad ones – are made by well-intentioned people.

I've learnt something about tolerance with others and with myself, and I try to soften tough moments with a touch of humour, so I describe myself as a burnt-out perfectionist. I have my own unique history of God's relationship with me: I've made innumerable decisions over the years, some more in line with the promptings of the Good Spirit, others less so. But I take great comfort from Pope Francis' comment: 'When everything is said and done, we are infinitely loved'.

## *And you?*
Enough about *me*! I invite *you* to take space at this point to reflect on yourself and what *you* bring to the decision-making table; then consider the others at your table, and finally marvel at the mystery that such a disparate group of individuals could decide *anything* together! Ask yourself why would God go to the trouble of gathering a group like this to listen and discern and finally arrive at decisions which they believe are pleasing to God. We come just as we are, carrying the burdens of the years and of the day – a relative sick; aches and pains; a recent tiff or shortage of money; but also, hopefully, a level of inner peace and a desire to please God. We bring our gifts, our life-experience, wisdom and energy, strengths and limitations, and our common desire to do something that will make others happy. Some of us enjoy group dynamics, others dread meetings. We don't arrive as disembodied

spirits; we're the people divinely tasked with decision-making; we work with limited resources, in a situation not of our choosing, while facing into a future that is hidden from us.

Yet we're God's chosen workforce, exemplars of divine humour, and are not meant to take ourselves too seriously. Our main resource is a God who is patiently present, bidden or unbidden, and who engages helpfully in our decision-making. What do you bring to the meeting table? What does God expect of you? Let's explore this question!

### *The cook and his lord*

Somewhere in Ignatius' writings there's a reference to a cook who has to prepare a daily meal for the master of the house. Let's imagine him on a given day wondering what the master might prefer for his evening meal. He explores his pantry: fish, venison and fowl are there, but fowl was the choice yesterday, and the master likes variety. That leaves 'surf or turf' as a chef might say today.

The cook listens to the chatter of the kitchen staff on the matter, but opinion is divided. No amount of discussion will sort things out: there's only one thing to be done, so the cook lays the salmon in one dish and the venison in another, tidies his hair and then tramps off upstairs.

He kneels before his lord with laden hands. Now it won't do for him simply to keep his eyes on the dishes: he needs to search the face of his master until one item or the other gets the nod and perhaps even the smile. He exits down the stairs gingerly but happily: the work of the day is focused. He will please his lord today!

This humble image offers a central insight into what we mean by discernment. We rightly prepare evidence and arguments on the topic in question, but the heart of the process is the encounter with the Lord. While we rightly dialogue with one another and within ourselves, the main dialogue partner must be God, and explicitly so. The 'smart folk', the inquisitive, the proud, the self-assured fall short here, as in the parable of the Pharisee and the tax-collector (Lk 18: 9–14), whereas the humble, the fallible, the poor, the tentative, drop on their knees and ask God, 'Show us what you want done!' To hear the 'still small voice' that came to Elijah on the mountain requires what is termed 'cardiac listening', and is founded on the belief that God is engaging with us as we search for the wisest and most loving thing to do. In this way our group meeting can become contemplative as we try to notice in which direction God seems to be drawing us. Ours is an engaged God who decides to send us to support those who are under pressure. As I write, Sisters in India are protesting publicly against the cultural ill-treatment of women; they are paying the price of peaceful resistance, but they believe God is calling them to do so, whatever the consequences.

### *Who speaks for Wolf?*
A gem of wisdom from the Amerindian world comes from a tribe that moved camp, only to find that the new location was inhabited by wolves. Sitting in a circle in the meeting tent they debated whether to kill the wolves or move camp again, and they decided on the latter choice. But they agreed that in future meetings, someone would be delegated 'to speak for Wolf'. Wolf stands for the outsider, the one who has no voice, or who is not consulted, but who will be affected by the group decision. The excluded voice may be that of the marginalised or the poor; Gandhi's recurring question before any decision was: 'How will this affect the poor?' It may also be the voice of the Holy Spirit, who speaks through us for the unwanted and marginalised!

Innumerable groups and individuals are disregarded in today's world. In a third-world country those in power decided to flood a large valley in order to build a hydro-electric dam which would 'service new industries and make our nation prosperous'. Those who had lived in the valley since time immemorial protested, not only for their own sakes but because their ancestors' tombs would be buried forever. They were driven off to meagre land elsewhere: the government however launched a 'Save the animals!' campaign because the animals were a tourist attraction, whereas the poor villagers had no commercial value. Who spoke for Wolf?

Pope Francis in *Laudato Si'* laments the fact that 'some committed and prayerful Christians, with the excuse of realism and pragmatism, tend to ridicule expressions of concern for the environment'. They need, he says, 'an ecological conversion, whereby the effects of their encounter with Jesus Christ become evident in their relationship with the world around them. Living our vocation to be protectors of God's handiwork is essential to a life of virtue; it is not an optional or a secondary aspect of our Christian experience'.[3] Is the voice of the Spirit often ignored even by 'good Christians'? Is care of the planet not raw material for corporate discernment? We need to do more climate storytelling, demand more climate justice, speak more truth to power, be more prophetic and more organised, more intentional and more strategic in our climate action.

### *Called to be prophets*
We may wonder if discernment should be a rare event, connected only with choosing between good and better ('Shall we build a parish centre, or organise a pilgrimage to a holy place, or renovate the church or erect a statue to a local saint?') But what about challenging the local community to accept the presence of migrants or offer a meeting point to LGBTQ+ people in vacant premises?

From our baptism our task as Christians is to be prophetic, to speak out for Wolf, to stand against all forms of domination. This can be dirty and indeed dangerous work, as it was for St Oscar Romero or Dorothy Day. But it was the agenda of Jesus: he set himself to bring good news to the poor, to free captives from every sort of domination. His table-companions included those who were 'sinners' in the eyes of the Law; he defended women, outcasts, foreigners and children. He challenged the rich and powerful, liberated the blind, the deaf, the crippled, stood by the poor, freed those possessed by demons, raised Lazarus and others from the domination of death and promised eternal life to all humankind. He spoke endlessly for Wolf!

The raw material for discernment is all around us, wherever Wolf may be found! We need to pray for eyes to see what's going on, and then wisdom to see what we can do about it.

Communal discernment is indeed laborious work: it demands generosity of heart and a pure desire for the truth. it makes demands on our concentration and our capacity to negotiate with others who may think very differently from ourselves. Further it may threaten our inner defences, our prejudices, our preferred and protected way of being and acting in the world.

---

3   Pope Francis, *Laudato Si'*, 217.

It is however a process that brings conversion, however painfully. In a Workshop about the rights of the First Nations in Australia, one speaker spoke up aggressively: 'The first question is, "Who owns this continent?" Now let's face it, it only began to be civilised about 1780, when the first consignment of convicts arrived from England. So let's start there!' The instant reaction forced him to see differently: he learnt that some 500 indigenous groups had lived there for over 50,000 years before the European settlers arrived.

Communal discernment requires openness to the truth, however unpalatable. But in that truth we meet God, and are set free to work constructively for justice.

*Are we deists?*
Each of us starts a discernment process with our own image of God, more or less refined. This may appear chaotic but God doesn't seem to mind so long as a person is willing – at whatever cost – to adopt an image of God that better fits the God of Jesus Christ.

It's said, not without some truth, that many of us carry a streak of deism: that is, we hold that God indeed made the world but then went away, leaving us to get on with the task of managing the planet and our lives. In this view the world is slowly winding down, and eventually the Great Clockmaker will return to see how things have gone for humankind. As one well-educated person said to me when I asked about his image of God: 'I don't bother God much, and God doesn't bother me!' This is deism: God is irrelevant to daily decisions.

A graffito some years ago ran: 'God is alive and well, but working on a much less ambitious project!' *But is God a sleeping partner?* Within a discerning group, are there enough members who believe in a God who is dynamically active, who holds all things together, and who moves the universe forward, though so mysteriously, towards a glorious culmination?

Time spent on checking out the initial images of God in the group is not wasted. In the Hebrew scriptures we learn that in fact Yahweh is constantly at work, planning for the good of the Chosen People, enabling them always to follow his leading – as in the metaphor of the pillar of cloud by day and the pillar of fire by night.

In the Christian scriptures the God revealed by Jesus is likewise working in all things, and Jesus lives by 'always doing what pleases him' (Jn 8:29). St Paul speaks to the Athenians of the God 'in whom we live and move and have our being' (Acts 17:28), the God who sustains and directs our lives. In the Acts of the Apostles the Spirit is busy, orchestrating all decisions, such that the Christian community can round off its momentous debate about the admission of pagans with the confident phrase, 'It has seemed good to the Holy Spirit and to us ...' (Acts 15:28).

The twenty-one Councils of the Church were also an exercise in communal discernment, led by the Spirit. Sixty years ago Vatican II was a revelation of how God could lead the Church when the bishops exercised their freedom, and listened to one another, to the Spirit, and to the needs of the world around them.

*A working God!*

How much does God engage with us when we experience calls to build a better world? Ours is no absent Being, good-willed but ineffectual, lamenting the chaotic state of the world. Instead God is totally present to creation in every detail, and unwavering in care for our world and ourselves. God is always trying to catch our attention, 'to lure us into the wilderness and to speak to our hearts' (Hos 2:14).

Thomas Merton, hermit and writer, is unequivocal about God's continuous engagement with us: 'Every moment and every event of every person's life on earth plants something in their soul'. This infers that the action of God in us is, dare we say, relentless and totally comprehensive. Karl Rahner concurs, saying that God communicates to us all the time: whether or not we accept or reject what comes to us, it remains true, he says, that God is present in the office, in the school, in the kitchen.

Ignatius of Loyola believed that God is to be found *in all things*, and his insights, scattered throughout this book, enable us to explore how in our personal and unique experience God is at work in our moods and feelings: this is a huge gift to contemporary spirituality. We can check the touch of God by looking inward and noticing our consolations and desolations.

Philosopher-theologian Bernard Lonergan says that God orchestrates each event in history by orchestrating all events, rather like city traffic managers who organise each particular bus by overseeing the whole fleet of buses. How God does this, while respecting human freedom, is for us an unfathomable mystery. But somehow God can manage! The Internet, which transmits knowledge instantly and globally, gives me a clue: I don't understand its workings at all, but I depend on it every day and it enriches my life immensely. Mystery, then, doesn't have to be understood before being relied on!

While God is sheer Mystery, God is also joy to work with! Ignatius writes: 'God works and labours *for me* in all creatures upon the face of the earth' (*Spiritual Exercises*, 236). In communal discernment we in turn labour with God as valued members of the divine workforce. The Son tells us: 'My food is to do the will of the One who sent me; to complete his work' (Jn 4:34). He adds that in eternal life he as sower and we as reapers will rejoice together. The Spirit will show us how to move forward in graced decision-making. So we have the three divine Persons working with us, and thus 'God is able to accomplish abundantly far more than we can ask or imagine' (Eph 3:20).

We can read the Bible in various ways. For our purposes it helps to think of it as the Divine Lesson-book for Good Decisions'. Decisions, good and dreadful alike, are dotted across every page. God's intentions for humankind and the planet are made abundantly clear, and Jesus shows us how we are to go about things: 'I have set you an example, that you also should do as I have done to you. ... You are blessed if you do this' (Jn 13:15–17).

## *A health warning!*
Communal discernment brings you close to the Holy Spirit, closer than you initially might wish to be. Be prepared, for the Spirit leads us by new paths and makes unexpected demands: life becomes a risk, but a beautiful risk, as the Greeks saw. Watch closely what happens to no less than the Son of God, the One who first lived wholly by the Spirit and calls us to do likewise. Yet this is the path to true and unending happiness.

This marvelous prayer of the Church could well be prayed throughout a discernment process and indeed throughout our lives:

> Direct, we beseech you, O Lord,
> all our actions by your holy inspirations,
> And carry them on by your gracious assistance,
> so that every prayer and work of ours
> may begin always from you and by you be happily ended.
> We make our prayer through Christ our Lord. AMEN.
> – Collect for tenth week in ordinary time

# Part One: The Setting

## The Art of Making Wise Choices

*The signs of our times*
The thirst for participation in the decisions that affect us is today more acute than ever. Those who wield power because of their exclusive knowledge are being challenged. School-goers are taking to the streets to demand from politicians urgent action on climate change. This thirst to be listened to is expressed at all levels of society, regarding dignity, equality, climate and justice issues, politics, prices, sexuality, violence. People want to be free subjects rather than passive objects: they want to have a say in their own lives.

A massive vacuum of energy results from ignoring the thirst for genuine participation. Across the world a huge majority feel unwanted and ignored, some of them within the Christian community. Populations suffer from 'democratic fatigue' – they are disengaging from democracy as currently presented, because of its failure to meet their human needs. Other forms of government fill the vacuum, many of them leading to the repression of minorities. *To remedy this, how can relationships be built instead on mutually shared power?*

Across religious organisations and civil societies is the burning thirst for more honesty and truth. There is less and less tolerance for the unspoken, the cover-up, the lies, the fake news, the situations of abuse, control, deviance, manipulation and perversion. *How can we work towards greater authenticity and honesty in relationships?*

We thirst for truth, at least in what concerns ourselves. When we are given truth we experience it as setting us free, as Jesus promised it would (see Jn 8:31). Thus it is that the deep desire for discernment emerges from the distorted situations that face us: many of these are unprecedented and require us to think 'outside the box'. This makes deep demands on us, as became abundantly clear within the Catholic Church during discussions in the 2016 Roman Synod on *Love in the Family*, particularly with regard to so-called 'irregular situations'.[4] And while the Second Vatican Council opened the door to collegiality, that is, to greater participation in the leadership of the universal Church, this has been only partially internalised as yet. *How can the discernment required at the universal level be synchronised with that required at the local level?*

Pope Francis is convinced that the way forward is through 'synodality'.[5] This term, derived from the word 'synod', means 'to walk together' or 'to cross a threshold together'. 'The only method of the synod,' he says, 'is to open ourselves to the Holy Spirit, with apostolic courage, with evangelical humility and trusting prayer, so that it is the Spirit who guides us'.[6] 'A Church of dialogue is a synodal Church, which listens as a community to the Spirit and to that voice of God which reaches out to us through the cry of the poor and the cry of the earth'.[7]

Synodality is not only about meetings of the pope with bishops, or gatherings of diocesan delegates with their bishop: at its broadest it is about any meeting of a community, Christian or other, with its leader. How can we implement discernment in common at all levels, including those of families and couples?

We ask: *'Couldn't Ignatian spirituality provide a clue if we practise communally the dynamic of Ignatius' Spiritual Exercises rather than restricting it to one-on-one encounters?'*

This brings us to the identity and mission of Esdac and the present Manual.

---

4 Pope Francis, *Amoris Laetitia*, 296–300.
5 Pope Francis, 'Address of his Holiness Pope Francis Commemorating the 50th Anniversary of the Institution of the Synod of Bishops' (speech), 17 October 2015, https://www.vatican.va/content/francesco/en/speeches/2015/october/documents/papa-francesco_20151017_50-anniversario-sinodo.html.
6 Pope Francis, *Introduction to the Synod on Love in the Family*, 5 October 2015.
7 Pope Francis, 'To the National Council of Italian Catholic Action' (speech), 30 April 2021.

*The genesis and history of a dream*
Esdac is the French acronym for 'Spiritual Exercises for Apostolic Discernment in Common'. This acronym is used internationally to designate a team-led process which enables groups to make good choices. Esdac teams, usually composed of two or more trained members, accompany groups – parishes, institutions, communities, businesses, couples, teams, students, young adults, etc. – to help them discern the action of the Holy Spirit within their group, so that the decisions they come to may free them to build a more just world.

The dynamics of the Spiritual Exercises of St Ignatius Loyola (1491–1556) underpin the Esdac project.[8]

Its process for communal decision-making is not simply a recent addition to contemporary management literature. It is instead based in the Gospels, in the practice of the early Christian community, and in the Spiritual Exercises of St Ignatius.

- In the Gospels Jesus is constantly urging his listeners to interpret their experience: 'Why do you not know how to interpret the present time? Why do you not judge for yourselves what is right?' (see Lk 12:54–57).
- The Acts of the Apostles are accounts of moments of communal discernment.
- The Spiritual Exercises of St Ignatius, with their one-to-one approach, have helped to transform the lives of innumerable individuals over the centuries. More than 5,000 editions of the *Exercises* exist, they have been approved by the Church, and are drawn on by millions of people searching for how to manage their lives better.

Esdac presents the Exercises in a form adapted to groups, in the belief that the Holy Spirit is as much at home when working with groups as with individuals. This use of the Exercises has been tested and proven across the world since the 1970s when a group of North American Jesuits first pondered the insight that *it is the decisions of groups rather*

---

[8] For more on Ignatius, see B. Comerford SJ, *The Pilgrim's Story* (Dublin: Messenger Publications, 2017); Brian Grogan, *Alone and on Foot* (Dublin: Veritas, 2008). For the Spiritual Exercises, see J. Munitiz and P. Endean, *Saint Ignatius of Loyola: Personal Writings* (London: Penguin, 2004).

*than individuals that shape the world today.* They went on to harness the power of the Exercises to transform group decision-making, in response to the challenge of Vatican Two that Christians must work together for justice in the world. Hence they developed 'Ignatian Spiritual Exercises for the Corporate Person' of which the acronym was ISECP.[9]

In 1999 Cobble and Elliott wrote *The Hidden Spirit: Discovering the Spirituality of Institutions.* These pioneers had the audacity to combine a personal spiritual journey with group dynamics. At the time, the word 'synodality' did not exist, but it describes well their approach, and Pope Francis, himself a Jesuit, would have approved of this innovation. A dialectical thinking of 'individual/collectivity' inspired these innovators: on the one hand, they said, 'each person is an expert in their own experience', and on the other hand, 'if in the past it was individual persons who changed the Church, tomorrow it will be corporate persons that will change the world'.

## *Esdac*

A group of five Belgian Jesuits was interested enough to go to the University of Scranton, Pennsylvania to learn the skills behind ISECP. On their return in 1995 they decided to organise discernment Workshops for groups: they themselves became a team by living out the Exercises together. Thanks to the Workshops and the accompaniment provided, some participants were encouraged by this mission and felt called to engage with it.

In 2009, following a session with some eighty participants in Rome, the Esdac team became international. This global-oriented focus is now part of its DNA: as at the first Pentecost (Acts 2:1–13), the Holy Spirit seems to take pleasure in ignoring the walls that separate languages, cultures and mentalities. Thus Esdac's recent international assembly in 2021 was attended by 45 participants from 16 countries. And given that contemporary society is deeply marked by secularisation and

---

[9] See the bibliography under 'Borbely'. Note that the term 'corporate person' was used in the development of ISECP in the 1970's, not in any legal sense but as indicating the bondedness in a group that decides to work as a body for the common good, led by the inspiration of the Holy Spirit. Today 'corporate' and 'corporation' are in some circles less acceptable terms than they were, so the word 'body' is substituted, the term St Paul uses to refer to the people of God; Ignatius in turn refers to the 'body' of the Society of Jesus as its members work together in the service of the world and the People of God.

pluralism, the question as to whether non-Christians can engage fruitfully with the process was answered in the affirmative. Experience has shown that since all human beings are called to make wise choices as best they can, any person or group of goodwill can be accompanied to make wise and loving decisions. We will pick this up later regarding the role of conscience in decision-making.

In 2006, the Belgian leaders of Esdac had tried to capture their dream in a Manual, *The Practice of Discernment in Common*.[10] This Manual was completely revised and updated in 2022, with the addition of the following dramatic piece of history from the origins of the Society of Jesus in 1539. Ignatius, searching over many years for clarity on what God wanted of him, had gathered nine like-minded companions; these spent considerable time together and found that they had much in common: each had made the Exercises individually, each had personally dedicated his life to God. Strong bonds of mutual support united them such that they called themselves 'friends in the Lord'. In 1539 they asked themselves whether God was calling them to become a religious order. To arrive at a decision, over three months they followed in group form the pedagogy of the Spiritual Exercises, as described below.[11] The Jesuits of today had discovered the genesis of their dream! What had emerged in North America a half-century ago had in fact originated in Italy almost 500 years earlier and is now alive and active in the twenty first century. Esdac has a strong pedigree.

The French edition of 2022 takes account of the links between spirituality and psychology and the complex emotional factors that influence group dynamics and play on the human heart in decision-making. As the prophet Jeremiah soberly acknowledged 2500 years ago: 'The heart is devious above all else: it is perverse – who can understand it?' (Jer 17:9). Those who enter together on the path of discernment find this to be true, firstly perhaps about their companions, but then about themselves: I notice in myself prejudices, false assumptions, preferences, evasions of truth, like everyone else! Hence the value of the psychological insights embedded in the book.

---

10  Edited by Michel Bacq, Jean Charlier and an Esdac team: *Pratique du discernement en commun* (Bruxelles: Fidélité, 2006).
11  See Appendix 4: Discernment Journeys of Diverse Groups.

# The Esdac Vision

### *The Holy Spirit is offered to all*
We have indicated the historical origins of Esdac. Now we outline its vision and the theological framework for communal discernment. You may find this chapter demanding reading, but if you can stay with it, it helps you to gain a better sense of the main dialogue partner in our discerning, the Holy Spirit who engages with us at every hand's turn in our labour!

The emphasis is on God's gracious presence to the group setting out on the path of discernment. God is closer to us than we to God; God is in our neighbour, and our basic conviction is that *in order to speak to us, the Holy Spirit can choose a person whom we might never have thought of.* It is God who freely engages people in the task of discernment, no matter how ill-prepared they may feel! God is the God of small things and small people as well as of the cosmos. What we contribute to the great scheme of things is indeed tiny, but God wants us small people to play our part in the growth of the kingdom of God. It is a nameless slave girl who points out that Naaman, the great Syrian commander who has leprosy, needs only to bathe in the Jordan to be cured (see 2 Kg 5:1–27); it is the small boy who offers his five loaves and two fish who is behind the feeding of the 5,000 in the desert (Jn 6:9); it is the poverty-stricken widow with her two coins who puts more into the Temple treasury than anyone else (see Mk 12:41–44). Like these unnamed persons, each of us, small as we are, has a role to play given to no other person. As Newman puts it: 'God has created me to do him some definite service. He has committed some work to me which he has not committed to another. I have my mission. I may never know it in this life, but I shall be told it in the next. I am a link in a chain, a bond of connection between persons'.

God delights in doing new things (Is 43:19; Rev 21:5); God knows us personally – better than we know ourselves – and engages us in bringing these fresh surprises about. That is the context for all our discernment. God is the main player, and we have essential, if minor, roles in the development of the kingdom of God.

Since God can choose anyone as an intermediary to speak to us, our conviction is that we must listen to everyone with respect; women and men, young people and adults, marginalised as well as central, believers, searchers and alienated. As in the tale where the Indian tribe is asking, 'Who speaks for Wolf?' it may be my task to listen to those who have no voice, to get to know them, and then to speak for them. It may also be God whose voice is missing from most of contemporary discourse, so I need to get to know God better too. Let me not grieve the Spirit by being closed to divine promptings (see Eph 4:29). The abandoned and unwanted carry a message from God. But do I care, do I risk speaking for Wolf?

After his resurrection, when the doors were locked for fear, Jesus showed himself to his frightened disciples as being fully alive, embodied in a new way. He breathed on them, saying, *'Receive the Holy Spirit'* (Jn 20:22; Acts 2:1–13). And he continues to do this, generation after generation. At Vatican II the successors of that first handful of Christians dared to say: 'We must hold that *the Holy Spirit offers to all, in a way known to God, the possibility of being associated with the paschal mystery'*.[12] Note the words 'The Holy Spirit offers to all' because this phrase includes not alone us but all humankind! Since this is so, we pray the radical prayer, 'Give us, all of us, your Spirit!' In the paschal feast at Easter we celebrate the miracle that from death springs life, and that our discernment can bring life to a situation that may appear to the human eye to be dead. I have in mind a friend who can't bear to throw out even exhausted flowers. 'You never know …', she says.

## *The signature of the Spirit*
How do we recognise the Spirit? It is enough to follow the traces of loving service in any human life! During his public life, Jesus had worked to make his little band of disciples into a body for the service of the world. Peter was given his task: *'Strengthen your brothers and sisters'*

---

12  *Gaudium et Spes*, 22.

(Lk 22:31). As he does today with our group, Jesus had to work on the relationships within the individuals he had chosen; like us, they had their various psychological complexities, their strengths and limits. So when the Twelve had disputed among themselves as to who was the greatest, Jesus had said to them: *'The rulers of the Gentiles lord it over them, and their great ones are tyrants over them. It will not be so among you: whoever wishes to be great among you must be your slave'* (Mt 20:25–26). Jesus had set them the example of loving service by kneeling down to wash their feet (Jn 13:5–7) and had left them a mark by which all would recognise them as being living members of his community, that is, by the love they would have for one another (Jn 13:35). This image of loving service is to characterise our relations with one another.

Jesus had taught the Twelve to ask for the Spirit, the gift of divine love: *'If you know how to give good gifts to your children, how much more will the heavenly Father give the Holy Spirit to those who ask him!'* (Lk 11:13). So on the day of Pentecost *'all of them were filled with the Holy Spirit'* (Acts 2:4). To their amazement they experienced that each of them was a carrier of the Spirit, uniquely chosen and missioned to serve the world. Less dramatically but no less truly, our group too and each of us uniquely are empowered and missioned for service.

The Early Christians were inspired by a collegial mode of discernment and decision-making based on God's love for them. In their earliest days they felt that the office abandoned by Judas should be given to another, so they proposed two candidates, prayed and said, *'Lord, you know everyone's heart. Show us which of these two you have chosen'. They cast lots for them, and the lot fell upon Matthias; and he was added to the eleven apostles'* (Acts 1:24–26). The Spirit led their communal decision-making. Again, we have noted that when around AD 50, a sharp division arose as to whether or not to impose Jewish religious observances on Christians of non-Jewish origin, the apostles and elders met in Jerusalem to discern the issue. Given that the process of synodality was their normal way of decision-making, the group had the audacity to write to the churches saying that the Holy Spirit had signed off on their decision! (see Acts 15:6–28). No less than the Early Church, our group today is a privileged place where the Spirit of Truth and Love is active.

## Transformative interactions

If asked 'What is a group?' the person in the street will spontaneously answer: 'A group is a collection of individuals who have come together for a common purpose.' In this perspective one instinctively starts with the individual in order to build the group. This can be true, but there is a broader perspective. Since the end of the 1940s, researchers in the human sciences have looked at what happens in 'training groups' – small groups that enable participants to get to know each other through free interaction. Psycho-sociologists led by Max Pagès concluded that what happens in a group gives meaning to what goes on within its members. In other words, group interactions can transform the members. Likewise what happens in a plenary group gives new meaning to the small groups contained within it. Otherwise the latent potential of a group, whether large or small, remains undeveloped as merely an aggregate of individuals.

This is an important insight – that an aggregate of individuals can undergo *an affective transformation* when they experience a quality relationship between them. When they are welcomed in their vulnerability, respected, listened to respectfully and loved, they are stimulated to give the best of themselves to the others. Individual and group growth occurs, out of which the members come to commit themselves to a common project, even if demanding, because they experience a sense of solidarity. In any group you work with, you can ask whether its potential is being fully realised, and if not, what can you do to help?

At the end of Vatican II in 1965, the Jesuit theologian Karl Rahner proposed that the Ignatian tradition should create, for the 'times to come', a new kind of spiritual exercises, complementary to the traditional ones, which would be communal rather than individual. He believed that such group Exercises would bring about a real revolution in the way we think about spirituality and how we practise decision-making in the Church. Esdac exemplifies this revolution and more than a half-century on, Pope Francis has endorsed this primary insight by emphasising synodality.

Often, at the end of a discernment process, people discover the power of sharing so strongly that they say they have had 'a real retreat', one which has deeply transformed their relationship with God and with others. In a sense they have experienced in a short time what the Twelve experienced with Jesus – a common life that transforms both the individuals and the group to which they belong.

> - *Loving service is the hallmark of the Spirit*
> - *'Where two or three gather, there I am among them' (Mt 18:19–20)*
> - *So Jesus is a member of our group*
> - *Transformative growth occurs in a Spirit-led group when their relationships deepen*
> - *Something new is born in the group, because in respecting one another, Jesus can come in to bring new life to all (Jn 10:10)*

### We top God's agenda

A child asks, 'What does God do all day?' A simple and true response is that the divine Persons spend their time talking about us! Our sorry plight led to their consensus that one of them had best become human to show us what our lives are meant to be about. The incarnation of the Son was, in the broad sense, the fruit of a divine communal discernment! They work endlessly at the task of inspiring us and getting us to collaborate in their dreams for our happiness. Their call to us to be discerning is not occasional but persistent. It is the 'still, small voice' that Elijah heard on the mountainside (see 1 Kg 19:13). They are trying to teach us from within how to make good and wise decisions that resonate with the designs of God and the well-being of the world. Our task is to tune in to this small inner voice!

The graced consensus that exists between Father, Son and Spirit is available to us through our efforts at discernment. God works to orchestrate our human hearts, trying to win us over to harmonious relationships and good decisions. Ignatius tersely observes that *'the love that moves and causes one to choose must descend from above, that is, from the love of God'* (*Spiritual Exercises*, 184). Rather than simply getting through an agenda or making sure that we ourselves will not be discommoded by decisions made, we aim to discover what 'the Father of lights' wants of us. Consensus is our goal, a consensus that includes God and is inspired by divine love.

## The term 'GOD' today

In our current culture, the word 'God' creates difficulties; fewer now believe that the goal of right human living is, in Ignatian terms 'to praise, revere and serve God'.[13] But good-willed people seeking a truly human consensus are driven by a thirst for unity, truth and justice, and for whatever is best for all those affected by the decision taken. When at our best, we want to ensure that no one is treated as 'a waste product, surplus to requirements'. So while Ignatius' declaration may go unheard, *the thirst for belonging, for creating human community,* can be the basis for consensus between believers and others. Indeed, when misunderstood, belief in God can alas be a source of scandal, exclusion and war. Jonathan Swift's comment has its truth: 'We have learned enough religion to hate one another, but not enough to love.' Non-believers are spared this obstacle.

God is active, even if often *incognito*, in every heart. Note the startling assertion in Vatican II about conscience:

> Deep within their consciences men and women discover a law which they have not laid upon themselves and which they must obey. Its voice, ever telling them to love and do what is good and to avoid evil, tells them inwardly at the right moment: Do this; Shun that. Their dignity rests in observing this law.[14]

This appeal to unity and good conscience, however basic it may seem, makes it possible to progress, step by step, towards the fulfilment of Jesus' prayer to his Father: *'I ask that they may all be one'* (Jn 17:21). Humanists and others find this goal of unity in action acceptable.

## From individuals to collaborators

For a group to become fully alive, the primary challenge for its members is to move from being isolated individuals to community as far as possible, while remaining true to themselves. This is the task of the Holy Spirit who labors to 'make us grow in love'.[15]

---

13 It is with this 'First Principle and Foundation' that Ignatius begins his Spiritual Exercises. See *Spiritual Exercises*, 23.
14 *Gaudium et Spes*, 16.
15 See the Second Eucharistic Prayer, former translation.

However, inter-dependence does not come easily to us: we like to think and act out of our own ideas and desires, and so in group work we may interpret the views of others as an obstacle to our freedom. The Spirit has much work to do in a group whose members may hold principled but contrary positions, as Catholics do on the issues of women's ordination or liturgical changes. The members need to keep their eye on the three divine Persons throughout the discernment process, even by simply praying silently the 'Glory be' and by imagining the Three as present in the room.[16]

- *Every group matters to God. Each decision shapes or spoils the kingdom of God*
- *Divine wisdom respects and elevates the work of the members*
- *Even if incognito, God labours with every group, trying to win each member over to harmonious relationships and so to the common search for truth*
- *For Christians, graced consensus has its source in the communion between the divine Persons*
- *Conscience is the divine action on every human heart, saying 'Do this' or 'Shun that'*

### *Divine love is compassionate: ours must be too*
The three divine Persons long to share their love with all human beings: *'Let us make humankind in our image, according to our likeness. So God created humankind in his image, in the image of God he created them; male and female he created them'* (Gen 1:26–27). This compassion for humankind is the source and the measure of our compassion for our neighbour; it is the origin of the gift of self to others. It recognises that every person, however their situation, is infinitely loved by God and

---

16 Prayer for one another builds a deep sense of common purpose. Each can be invited to link with random prayer-partners during the discernment process.

will always remain so. Pope Francis states this clearly: 'When everything is said and done, we are infinitely loved'.[17] This is the basis for our hope that the discerning group may become one, welcoming life from each member (Jn 10:10) and becoming free from what blocks this fullness of life (Jn 15:2). Our love for one another is to be self-giving and compassionate, as God's is.

Max Pagès observes that every good human relationship is affective. It is a sensitivity to the other, a concern for and support. He holds that the purpose of a common action – such as communal discernment – is not only to unite a group for an agreed goal, but to witness to the *compassion* that they feel for one another. As was said in surprise of the early Christians, 'See how these people love one another!' Communal discernment, then, goes beyond hard-headed decision-making or majority vote: it grows into a communitarian experience and its focus is altruistic and in no way self-serving.

### 'It is the Lord!'

After the resurrection, when the disciples were trying in vain to land a catch, the disciple whom Jesus loved cried out to Peter: 'It is the Lord!' (Jn 21: 1–7) This is an example of good discernment: because he was close to the Lord in his heart this man could recognise the voice of Jesus who was giving helpful instructions from the shore.

Discernment goes beyond human planning: it means recognising the presence of the Holy Spirit in the situation. But the Holy Spirit is not the only influence we experience: contrary voices make themselves heard, so how can we know which is the right one to follow? Recognising this challenge, the Spiritual Exercises have as their purpose 'the conquest of self and the regulation of one's life in such a way that no decision is made under the influence of any inordinate attachment' (*Spiritual Exercises*, 21). Experience of the Exercises helps communal discernment.

Partnership with the Lord is needed for inner freedom, '... which is an affective space within which the movements of the Spirit can be sensed, making possible an unconditional listening and thereby a wise

---

17  Pope Francis, *Evangelii Gaudium*, 6. See also his encyclical *Fratelli Tutti*.

decision'.[18] The conversion experience of Ignatius which follows here illustrates the inner journey involved.

### *Link moods with God!*
We have already hinted that the approach in this Manual is based, not on a theory, but on a historical experience that occurred to a wayward but sensitive and perceptive person in the sixteenth century. We are fortunate to have his own account of what went on between himself and God.[19]

During his convalescence, when Ignatius contrasted his wasted years with the life of Jesus and the apostles and saints, he discovered a remarkable fact: that some thoughts, day-dreams or plans gave him temporary pleasure, but were followed by sadness and dejection. Other dreams and thoughts, however, gave him lasting joy and stimulated his vitality and dynamism. He slowly realised that God was educating him through these contrasting moods: he interpreted that the joy that faded was not from God, whereas the joy that lasted was of divine origin. God wants our happiness and draws us to divine joy. 'Enter into the joy of your Lord' (Mt 25:23).

Ignatius became ever more attracted by the project of giving himself completely to God with all that this entailed, and over the years he developed ways of interpreting the differing experiences of sadness and joy, energy and weakness. He found he could help people who were struggling with contrasting inner thoughts and feelings to spot the difference between one dynamic and the other. He called this the discernment of spirits, or the capacity to make distinctions between passing joys and the deep down ones that bring lasting peace and joy. He invited people to bring to consciousness their attractions and resistances, and to notice what thoughts and moods accompanied either feeling. He would have them ask themselves, 'In what direction am I being led – towards loving service of God and others, or toward self-centred concern?'

Such reflection or 'discernment of spirits' is the art of distinguishing between the spirit that leads to communion and truth on the one hand and the spirit of division and deception on the other, so that with the

---

18   Michael Ivens SJ, *Understanding the Spiritual Exercises*, p. 32, hereinafter referred to as *Ivens* in text.
19   Ignatius, *Personal Writings*, pp. 3–64.

beloved disciple on the lakeside we can say of one spirit rather than the other: 'It is the Lord!' The habit of living in familiarity with the Lord is a great help here, as is a sensitive conscience; life becomes a partnership between two friends, one of whom is divine. Often the 'small people' in a group live this intimacy spontaneously, so they have more to offer in the discernment process than the powerful and the 'important'.

## *From good to better*

Discernment is about recognising or unmasking evil, but also about choosing, among options that are good in themselves, whatever will bring *more* life to a particular situation.[20] Thus the Parish Pastoral Council might ask itself: '*What best* can we do with our resources? Build a community center open to all, or create a facility for refugees?' Another might ask: 'How can we reach out to the alienated?' Or: 'What does evangelisation mean for us in today's multi-cultural world?'

The freer the members are within themselves and with one another, the more easily will they sense the attractiveness of one option over another, so that the drawing or tug of the Holy Spirit will tip the balance (*Spiritual Exercises*, 1, 23, 179, 184). To enter the discernment process with a closed mind is not unusual, but unless a working level of inner freedom is achieved through prayer and life-giving group interactions, a person will not become like 'a balance at equilibrium' nor be in a position to discern.

An illuminating example of what is meant by 'making oneself free' is given by Ignatius' 'friends in the Lord' who were to become the first Jesuits: they were asking themselves if they felt an inner call to obey any given member among them. They decided that, during the period of discernment on this issue, each one would work to *make himself free* in regard to either obeying or commanding. Page 219 and following shows how they did this.

## *Accompaniment*

When the discernment stakes are high, it is useful to have recourse to external help. Such help should be neutral in regards to the issue for discernment and the group members and leader. This *external* help brings a feeling of trust and security, whereas if group members are

---

20 Those familiar with Ignatian spirituality will recognise the concept of '*magis*' or 'greater', hence the motto AMDG meaning The *Greater* Glory of God.

entrusted with the task of leading the discernment, they may – rightly or wrongly – be considered both judge and jury, or may find it difficult to combine their personal discernment with that of the group.

Faced with a major obstacle or crisis, a group will need outside help both to question itself honestly and to allow itself to be 'reborn' (Jn 3:3–4 and 16:21). An outside support team can best set the framework for this birth. The team's confidence in the action of the Holy Spirit counterbalances the fear of change that stable organisations may experience: trust grows that something will emerge whose beginnings may already be hidden as seeds within the hearts of some in the group.

Esdac acts as a resource by making available to a group one or more trained facilitators, ideally a woman and a man. A large group may need more guides. Accompanying a group in pairs enables the facilitators to support each other in managing the group dynamics, in discerning which spirit is leading it, what stage it has reached and what exercises might be offered to help it move forward. If only one trained facilitator is available, as may often be the case, that person can be assisted by someone who has some familiarity with group dynamics.

Later chapters develop the roles and attitudes of the facilitators.[21]

## *Taking time*

Some groups open themselves only slowly to the work of the Spirit, and discerning together proceeds more laboriously if a group has not stopped for a long time to evaluate its action, or is rusty in the art of discerning together. Sorting out the inevitable tensions that arise when members are not yet 'at home' with one another can also take time.

Conversely, groups for which the art of communal discernment has become habitual can move through their agendas relatively quickly, as in the case of a Provincial leader and Council. A quality of joy emerges, and the Holy Spirit has a way of providing good surprises when the group has acquired a mutual knowledge of each other, born of love.

---

21 In this book the full Esdac event is called a *Workshop*, and its inner moments are called *Sessions*. The term *Facilitator* is used to cover the French terms *support group, accompanying team*. The term *Spirit-led conversation*, rather than *'spiritual conversation'* or *'conversation in the Spirit'* highlights the pre-eminent role of the Holy Spirit in the interchanges that are central to the group's work.

Communal discernment is sometimes criticised as cumbersome, to be used exceptionally. But with practice the facility grows whereby you can use it effectively, constantly and with brevity. Ignatius sets the bar high: he is said to have advised that we should make *no decision, however small*, without first seeking the counsel of God as a wise and loving Father. The more one engages with God, the easier does communal discernment become.[22]

When a discernment process is spread out – for example, over several weekends – the first weekend may end with some confusion or resistance. It is only by watching the process evolve over time that one can see how the group is maturing and how the Spirit is gaining ground – mutual acceptance and collaboration emerge. Moments of chaos, instead of causing disruption, can then become opportunities to think outside the box and to discover God in a new way. In his poem, 'God's Grandeur', G. M. Hopkins hints at the Spirit's abiding and loving activity in our changing world:

'The Holy Ghost o'er the bent / World broods with warm breast and with Ah! bright wings.'[23]

> - *The three divine Persons are always working with us.*
> - *God is to be the principal dialogue partner and focus in communal discernment*
> - *The group members are meant to grow in mutual acceptance and compassion*
> - *The closer the members are to God, and the freer they are, the greater their contribution to the discernment journey*
> - *Wise interpreting of moods and thoughts leads to good discernment*
> - *Even barely noticeable feelings can tug at your heart, making you happy or unhappy. Is something nagging at you?*

---

22 Pedro Arrupe led 36,000 Jesuits through sixteen turbulent years after Vatican II, making endless decisions daily. He could do so because Spirit-led conversations pervaded his waking hours. The Persons of the Trinity were his 'inner cabinet', while in his daily encounters his focus was always on what God might want done in each situation. See Brian Grogan, *Pedro Arrupe: A Heart Larger than the World*, pp. 1–14.

23 G. M. Hopkins, *Poems and Prose*, p. 27.

# Part Two: The Heart of Decision-Making

## Spirit-led Conversation

Having described Esdac's theological and spiritual vision, we will now explore how this vision can be put into practice in everyday life to enable communal discernment to impact for good in a situation.

*The key element to discernment in common*
Through their many years of experience, Esdac's facilitators have discovered that the key to communal discernment is 'Spirit-led' conversation, an interpersonal dialogue led by the Spirit. This is so important that Esdac now offers two types of training: in Spirit-led conversation and in communal discernment. Participation in the Spirit-led conversation training is a condition for being able to take part in the communal discernment training. It is in conversation that both the Holy Spirit and the forces that oppose the Spirit are active. During my review of my day, I'll ask myself: 'Was there some life in this or that conversation, and if so, to what action is it prompting me?' So for example, the local priest meets a parishioner who suggests the value of a Family Mass. That evening as the priest rummages back through his day, the notion of a Family Mass pops up. What will he do? Will he let the idea fade and turn on the TV or ask the Lord for guidance in the matter?

### *The Spirit as leader*

Synodality, properly understood, is something *to be experienced first of all in everyday life*. We negotiate with one another most of our lives, and this reality can be named as synodal if together we want to do what is best in any situation – in the sorting out of a family will, a family leisure trip, a menu for supper, a decision to go to the doctor.

The dialogue between Jesus and the Samaritan woman models a conversation led by the Spirit (Jn 4:5–42); each person listens carefully to the other and recognises in the other's words the Spirit's quiet voice.

Spirit-led conversation is then a practice that can be used widely: in the family, at work, during moments of relaxation or at meals ... It can be learned and perfected in small groups as well as in large assemblies. Whatever the details, the central person in such conversation is the Spirit.

Since it aims to discern the beckoning of the Holy Spirit, communal discernment relies centrally on Spirit-led conversation in daily life, a conversation led by the Spirit whose task is to lead us to the Father. Within a group the Spirit is the main Person, and is invisibly active. 'Let anyone who has an ear listen, not to the prophets of doom or to those who sweep all problems under the sanctuary carpet, but to what *the Spirit is saying* to the churches!' (see Rev 2:11). The Spirit speaks through the members' contributions, but someone must speak for Wolf – whether Wolf in the guise of the ignored, the neglected, the poor, even the disruptive and angry: our 'enemies' have much to teach us.

### *Conditions for Spirit-led conversation*

Any conversation, in the kitchen or on the road, can become Spirit-led. Jesus tells us: *'Where two or three are gathered in my name, I am there among them'* (Mt 18:20). Psychologist C. G. Jung had inscribed over his front door the phrase, 'Bidden or unbidden, God is present'. This can transform a room into a sanctuary.

- The kernel of Spirit-led conversation is attentive listening and truthful speech: it can be found in anyone of goodwill. Openness to the real is the critical factor.

- At least one speaker (as in a couple or small group) is needed who is seeking to discern in the words exchanged what is inspired by the Spirit of harmony and truth and what is opposed to it.
- The ground rule is accepted that the words of another must not be discounted without a sensitive and empathic effort to reveal the truth in them. The listeners in the group try to put a good interpretation on what another says, or by intervening, try to facilitate the emergence of a more acceptable formulation.

This is vintage Ignatius! He lived in an age no less troubled than our own, due to the turmoil of the Reformation. Speaking of the relationship between the giver of the Exercises and a retreatant, he says:

> 'So that they may the better help and benefit each other, it must be presupposed that every good Christian should be readier to justify than to condemn a neighbour's statement. If no justification can be found, one should ask the other in what sense the statement is to be taken, and if that sense is wrong the other should be corrected with love. Should this not be sufficient, let every appropriate means be sought whereby to have the statement interpreted in a good sense and so to justify it' (*Spiritual Exercises*, 22; *Ivens*, 23).

Ignatius' presupposition is as important today as it was 500 years ago, even with our differences of theology, our relativism and our world-outlook. Mutual respect and trust grow in this two-way dynamic, with speakers and listeners helping one another to arrive at the truth.

- We can recognise that a conversation is Spirit-led — whether named as such or not — when it promotes life, energy, joy, dignity, freedom, communion, truth, happiness. Such are the fruits of the Spirit, and they should be obvious. The contrary qualities that emerge when the Spirit is stifled are also all too obvious: disagreements, strife, jealousy, anger, quarrels, a sense of dead ends and apathy … (See Gal 5:16–23).
- When we adequately express what the desire for communion and truth inspires in our hearts, we share in the gift that the divine Persons make of themselves to human beings: we inhabit the world of grace in which we truly find ourselves at home.

The nuances of Spirit-led conversation will be elaborated below, but in essence it is a state of mind that can be nurtured anywhere, even in a busy group. Before each item on a Board's agenda (well communicated in advance), you can, in the privacy of your heart, invoke the Good Spirit, asking 'Come, Holy Spirit!' and spend a moment in reflection. This increases your sensitivity to the Spirit, who, as we repeat, is the big player and the main dialogue partner.

Attention to the Spirit can shift from notional to real by the group agreeing to reserve a good proportion of the hours of the Workshop for private reflection and prayer. In a wordy Workshop I created dismay by proposing that we'd spend as much time in prayer and reflection as we were giving to 'shooting the breeze'. Ignatius advised the general of the Jesuits to divide his day as follows: time for discussion with others, time for private reflection, and time to meet with God. Endless discussion, no matter how engaging, leaves no time for silence and for the Spirit, and misses the whole point of the discernment exercise, which is to listen – with our hearts – to God.

## *Conversation with the Father*

Before formal Spirit-led conversation in the group, we need time for conversation with God, and Jesus is the exemplar. Although fully human, he lived in conversation with his Father and the Spirit, and so we can and must enter into his basic attitudes. While he did not debate his daily choices with his disciples, he had, as someone said, a hot line to God that was always open: see especially his prayer in Gethsemane and on the cross. The Spirit led him constantly; Mark tells us that after his baptism in the Spirit, 'the Spirit immediately drove him into the wilderness' (Mk 1:9–12). The wilderness may be understood today as the unformed or chaotic scenario in which the action of God is not evident.

Jesus helps us to have the right dispositions by revealing that the Father and the Spirit were his primary consultants. He sees himself as always open to the call of the Father, who missions him, and he can do nothing by himself (see Jn 5:17–30); he summarises his life-stance in the words: *'The one who sent me is with me ... for I always do what is pleasing to him'* (Jn 8:29).

Spirit-led conversation, then, is not a recent invention or a passing fad: it originates in the Trinity and is revealed in the life of Jesus; and so we try to be drawn into its dynamic, even though this is demanding of us.

### *Sitting in a circle*

Since in a group the Holy Spirit can speak through any person, it is critical to organise the seating so that it connotes the equality of the members. This is no small step, because it runs counter to prevailing hierarchical and patriarchal structures.

The arrangement of sitting in a circle was devised early on by the indigenous peoples of North America and Australia. The Esdac logo is heir to this tradition: it is comprised of a circle and a feather. The circle symbolises that all those present are equal in dignity; this reduces the temptation of authority figures to dominate, and the temptation on the part of others to subservience. The eagle feather is held in the hand of the person who wishes to speak. This is a sacred symbol of the authority and wisdom which the Great Spirit may be about to confer on any of the speakers. Today we might use a pen, a microphone, a crucifix …

The holding of the feather symbolises a person's desire to speak from their innermost being, as well as the wish to be listened to in this holy place where each is trying to be in touch with the Holy Spirit.

Daring to tell another what you really think and feel demands courage. And to do so with *everyone*, including perhaps the person who, statutorily, has authority both over you and the group, demands even more courage. However, at stake here is the quality of the evaluations and recommendations fed into the group.

Progress in psychological maturity requires a favorable climate in which every person perceives that they are valued by others as unique and precious: only so can they begin to value the different aspects of their own being, and become aware of what is going on within themselves, what they really feel and want. Then, as psychologist Carl Rogers affirms, they can begin to trust their experience to guide their behaviour and its expression. In turn they must communicate the same positive trust to others.

- *Communal discernment requires honest listening*
- *Any encounter can lead to a Spirit-led conversation*
- *All concerned must be seen as equals: hence they sit in a circle*
- *Each puts a positive interpretation on what others say by asking, 'What is the Spirit trying to tell me through another?'*
- *Conversation is Spirit-led when the primary concern is to sense the 'nod' of the Spirit*
- *A sense of ease, goodwill and expectancy begins to lighten the labor of the group*

# Discernment in Common

We look now at the inner dynamics of Spirit-led conversation, of which the components are prayer, sharing, listening and noticing in what direction the Spirit seems to be leading one's own heart and the heart of the group in regard to the given issue of discernment.

The process for a large group involves three stages: personal prayer, small groups and plenary sessions.

*Three stages of Spirit-led conversation*
**1 Personal prayer: Spirit-led conversation alone with God**
Private reflection and prayer around the topic for discernment is focused through the scriptural Word of God and/or on various supports such as foundational texts, images, poems, Prayer Sheets, etc. This silent time has a time-limit.

Then we move to small group sharing.

**2 Small-group sharing: Spirit-led conversation between 5 or 6 people**
This is done in three speaking rounds with a pause after the first round.

- First round. Each person in turn shares the fruits of their time of prayer, however humbling that may be (due to distractions, emotions, etc.) and also tries to listen carefully what the other members of the small group say. At most 5 minutes per person are given. It may help to write down some points. There are no interventions, unless for clarification.
- Pause. When all have spoken once there is a small pause during which each asks themselves: 'What has resonated or echoed with me in what the others have shared?' 'What particularly touched me, giving me peace, joy, confidence, energy, fear, sadness, confusion?' 'What has become clear to me?'
- Second round. Following on the pause, those who wish can share its fruit. These interventions enable Spirit-led conversation to begin.

'I was moved by what X said...' This moment helps to refine our listening to the Holy Spirit, who speaks through others in a way that is often quite different from how I may have heard the Spirit alone in my silent prayer. Attentive listening dislodges me from my certainties, my comfort and my self-withdrawal. My security becomes centered instead on the fact that God is leading us as a group, and will show us the way to go.

➤ <u>Third round</u>. When the second round has ended, the members share on whether an initial consensus seems to be emerging. Particular attention is given to the common points that emerge, and what they are grounded on. Those who feel led to do so can pray that they or the group be freed from a fear or resistance, or can express gratitude for the action of the Spirit. Finally the small group draws together what it wishes to bring to the plenary session which follows.

**3 Plenary session: Spirit-led conversation in the large group**
Next comes the plenary session, in which each group reports briefly, not so much on what was said, but on what the group *has arrived at*, and which it hopes will be helpful to the plenary. Ideally this will lead to an initial agreement or consensus – of which more will be said below (p. 84).

*From 'I' to 'We'*
This sequence of stages – personal prayer, small group sharings, plenary session – contributes to the convergence of individuals towards the others, while respecting and even reinforcing the singularity of each: from 'I' to 'We' and from 'We' to 'I'.

Throughout the discernment process, what is being exchanged, in small groups and in plenary, influences the next time of prayer and personal reflection, and contributes to the development of a shared feeling or consensus around the topic.

The principal criterion for discernment is 'consolation'. We will say more about it later (p. 128). Consolation is God's gift, experienced by each person in the intimacy of their hearts, and ideally by all through the interactions of the Spirit-led conversation. Progressively, what is a source of communion is felt and tasted internally by all, it is a shared joy.

What is going on here is subtle and can easily be missed: for some it will be a new language. Ignatius writes that 'it is not much knowledge but the inner feeling and relish of things that fills and satisfies the soul' (*Spiritual Exercises*, 2). He is pointing to a delicate felt awareness which involves the heart.[24]

We can speak of a 'funnel effect': little by little, what is really important and shared by all is felt as converging towards a 'pearl' given to the group. '*The kingdom of heaven is like a merchant in search of fine pearls; on finding one pearl of great value, he went and sold all that he had and bought it*' (Mt 13:45). Yet while the goal is to move from the I to the We – from personal to group integration – it may be useful at the end to return to the 'I' so that each comes to 'own' the 'pearl' given to the group, and commit themselves with determination to the group decision that this 'pearl' has generated.

## Spirit-led conversation is enriching

Through Spirit-led conversation there is born a framework which, while ensuring security and confidentiality in the exchanges, brings to light what is most alive in each person, and also what is vibrant, pulsating and invigorating for the group. This is a manifestation of the Holy Spirit. 'It is the Spirit that gives life' (Jn 6:63).

*So with Jesus:* Spirit-led conversation is what Jesus engaged in constantly. In all he said he was speaking for the Spirit. We see this in his conversations with Nicodemus at night, with the Samaritan woman at the well, with the disciples on the Emmaus Road, etc.

*So with Ignatius:* From the very beginning of his conversion, Ignatius enjoyed conversing spiritually with others. He found this activity of great benefit in helping them – and himself. Rather than preaching or lecturing, this was his preferred way of sharing the Good News and it was thus that he led many to God. He was a 'one-to-one' person, always ready to learn where the other was at and see where grace was beckoning.[25]

---

24 Ignatius uses the Spanish term *sentir* – that inner awareness which people have of being 'moved' as when, for instance, they know that someone important loves them or has been hurt by them. Consolation and desolation lie within this realm. Beginners need help to identify these 'inner feelings and relish' in their personal experience.
25 See *The Way*, July 2023, which is devoted to spiritual conversation.

*So with monastic and religious Congregations:* These regularly engage in Spirit-led conversations (see App. 4). As we have noted, the origin of the Jesuits derived from an extended Spirit-led conversation in 1539 between ten good men, each determined to serve God and the Church. Likewise, the monks of Tibhirine conversed spiritually together before deciding to remain where they were, though it meant their certain death.

Today, the Society of Jesus is rediscovering the benefits of Spirit-led conversation both for its own well-being and as a major resource in its apostolic work, as indicated in the Foreword to the French edition above (pp. 7–8).

*So in Synodality:* Its essence lies in ongoing Spirit-led conversations. 'What does the Spirit want us to do?' Synodality is not to be a set of isolated events in distant Rome, but the very life-blood of the global Christian community as it wends its pilgrim way to God's kingdom.[26]

### *Graced Action*

Having agreed on what God seems to be saying the plenary group asks itself the question: 'What are the important consequences of what we have just shared?' In other words, 'If we are to remain consistent with the truth that has been shown to us, what decision, what action should follow?'

Behind this question is the sense that, whether as a group, as a couple, as community, as friends, at work or in the hours of relaxation, divine power is guiding us to action. Discernment is an attitude of mind and heart which tries to detect in all emerging circumstances what the Lord wants of us. It concretises the petition in the Our Father: 'Your will be done!' It also emphasises the remark in the Exercises: 'Love ought to manifest itself *in deeds* rather than in words' (*Spiritual Exercises*, 230).

---

[26] In Spirit-led conversation where all members are seen as equals in their searching for God's will, the Spirit alone is the Teacher. We are to be like Ignatius who acknowledges that 'God was dealing with him in the same way as a school-teacher deals with a child, teaching him … Now, whether this was because of his ignorance and obtuse mind … it was his clear judgement that God was dealing with him in this way' (*Personal Writings*, p. 25). Human pride makes it hard for the 'high and mighty' to return to the status of ignorant pupils: to make progress they have to look out for the promptings of others and of the Spirit rather than rely on their own 'bright ideas'.

The group may have the power to make the decision itself, or may have to make recommendations to some higher authority.

In either case note that discerning is a step prior to deciding: it falls short if the proposed decision is not followed through: the group becomes inauthentic, knowing what it should do but not doing it. Bernard Lonergan remarks that it is decision that brings reflection to an end, not *vice versa*. No amount of reflecting makes even one decision. Possibility becomes actuality only when willed, not merely speculated about.[27]

**'Discerning together' therefore does not *necessarily* mean 'deciding together', because that step may not be taken.**

In monasteries and religious congregations, life is punctuated by Chapters which, at fixed times, implement a formal type of synodality, according to pre-established rules.

We will next consider each of these stages: personal prayer, small group, plenary session.

---

*The three moments of Spirit-led conversation:*

1. *Personal prayer on the issue*
2. *Small group sharing on what emerges for each, followed by sharing on what others have said*
3. *Sharing in plenary*

- *The Spirit is the Teacher: the group listens out for the Spirit's prompting*
- *With the Spirit's help the group discerns the wisest and most loving course of action*
- *This must then be implemented, else the group fades into a talk-shop and frustration follows*
- *A graced transition from 'I' to 'We' begins to emerge*

---

27  See B. Lonergan, *Insight* (1957), p. 612.

# Personal Prayer

Prayer provides the central dynamic for the whole process of discernment. By praying personally we come together as people who have just been meeting someone else, who is the Lord. Thus we are already initially bonded in the Spirit. In other words, before sharing with others, we place ourselves under the loving gaze of God, as revealed to us in the Bible, and in particular in the Gospels. Ignatius remarks that rather than overwhelming a retreatant with long instructions, the guide should stand back and let God take over. 'It is much better that the Creator and Lord in person communicate himself to the devout soul in quest of the divine will. Like a balance at equilibrium the one who gives the Exercises should permit the Creator to deal directly with the Creator, and the creature with their Creator and Lord' (*Spiritual Exercises*, 15).

Each person can rightly say: 'I am not here just to make up the numbers: I am the beloved of God' (Rom 1:7). This helps each of us to remain truly ourselves, independently of the gaze of others.[28]

Each of us can allow ourselves to experience in the cave of the heart that truly '*the word of God is living and active, sharper than a two-edged sword... It is able to judge the thoughts and intentions of the heart*' (Heb 4:12). We can learn that Jesus is risen and at work today in each person in the group, as he was in Palestine 2000 years ago and as he is in the lives of every individual and community. We may query whether prayer 'works' until we *experience* the subtle play of grace in what we are about. To prepare a talk with study and reading etc. is good, but to pray before and during the preparation provides an added 'something'. As one participant acknowledged: 'Things go better when I pray them!'

---

28  Pope Benedict is quoted as follows in *Laudato Si'*, 65: 'Each of us is willed, each of us is loved, each of us is necessary'.

*Prayer Sheets*
**Introductory Note**
The term 'Prayer Sheet' is not only for the use of persons who give time for prayer; they are wisdom sheets too. The scripture texts offered in a Sheet can be read as coming from Jesus, one of the world's greatest teachers of wisdom, and can be used for self-reflection and pondering by anyone of goodwill. When presenting Jesus on the cross, Ignatius proposes that 'I shall *reflect* upon myself ... and I shall *ponder* upon what presents itself to my mind' (*Spiritual Exercises*, 53). Elsewhere he speaks of *considering* the matter set before me. For him what is presented to my mind, with its accompanying feelings and emotions, may well be coming from the good Spirit. I am being addressed by Another!

**Structure**
To ease the anxiety of participants who may find it difficult to engage in sustained prayer, some Prayer Sheets, twenty-six in all, are provided in Appendix Three. They follow the pedagogy of the Spiritual Exercises and support our efforts to practise Spirit-led conversations. They bring us in our personal prayer face to face with key issues in Jesus' teaching that we need to integrate with our personal experience. They follow a simple structure which provides a group focus, and saves the prayer time from being haphazard.

The structure:

- *Title*
- *Grace to pray for*
- *The scripture or other text*
- *Helps for reflection and prayer*
- *Conversation with the Lord*
- *Harvesting*

**Title**
Each Prayer Sheet has a title that links it to a specific moment in the discernment process.

## Grace to pray for

Ignatius emphasises this: 'I will ask God our Lord for what I want and desire' (*Spiritual Exercises*, 48). We pray here, not just vaguely, but with a clear focus. In group work, if we are to live in communion with one another while being respected in our differences, we need two things: to share common desires and to ask God for the specific grace of the moment.

At each stage the request for divine assistance specifies the help asked of the Lord and his Spirit so that the group can progress. The grace asked for is chosen according to the stage reached by the group and the issue at stake. Each person must seek it if the group is to move forward in union of minds and hearts.

Following Ignatius, the request for grace expresses in the best possible way what the group 'wants and desires' (*Spiritual Exercises*, 48), with a view to its spiritual growth at this point. The impetus for the movement is given by the Holy Spirit, the retreatant and the facilitators all at once. Likewise the facilitators listen to the group and intercede with the Spirit to indicate the next step to be taken.

Specifying the grace to be asked for, adjusting it to the stage the group has reached, avoiding a 'one size fits all' formulation, will contribute greatly to saving the group from going round in circles. Throughout, the imagination is to be focused on what is central, rather than allowed to 'fool around the house' as St Teresa of Avila puts it![29]

## Text

Texts for prayer may be taken from the Bible or from a key group document, such as a mission statement or an inspiring piece of literature. NGOs, Hospitals, Academic Institutions, National Constitutions, together with ethically-focused businesses and organisations articulate their values publicly. The UN Universal Declaration of Human

---

29  I should note too my own particular needs for which I need God's grace, lest I become an obstacle to the Spirit. Others in the group may see a blind spot in me, but because it is second nature to me I will be unaware of it. Remarkably, that most sensitive man, Ignatius, refers to himself as 'nothing but an obstacle' to God's working in his own heart. He presses the point: 'I would say that nobody can calculate the degree to which people impede and undo the effectiveness of the Lord's influence on themselves' (*Personal Writings*, p. 161). He believed that God is always pressing in on us, hence his insistence on the review of life, and growth in interior freedom from disordered affections, so that the person is keenly in tune with the Holy Spirit.

Rights, 1948, is a milestone document on basic human rights and remains as valid and urgent today as when first written. It enshrines the rights and freedoms of every human being. The main focus of a scripture text is to show how the Holy Spirit can transform a difficult or tragic situation into a saving event.

**Helps for reflection and prayer**
There are two stages: I consider the text itself; then I look for ways in which it can shed light on my life and on the issue before the group. I *consider, ponder, reflect* on the text for itself, freely, allowing myself to be touched by what it provokes in my heart and mind.

Another suggestion is to contemplate a bible scene, i.e. to let one's imagination build a setting, a context, to 'put flesh and blood' into the characters of this scene, thus to sit next to Jesus, to climb the steps of the temple, or even to enter the skin of a leper, and to become aware of the feelings experienced during this movement of imagination. Becoming aware of all my perceptions, through sight, hearing, smell, taste, touch of the hands and feet etc, enables me to remain in the 'concrete' of the imagination. See Facilitation of Groups for more details.

**Conversation with the Lord**
The goal of prayer is not to get side-tracked by ideas, preferences etc, but to converse with the Lord, 'as one friend with another' (*Spiritual Exercises*, 54). Thus before engaging in Spirit-led conversation with the group, we do so with God, and this makes our efforts in the group easier and richer.

The 'conversation with the Lord' invites us to be totally honest about our particular situation, while trying to take to heart what the Lord is saying. It is a two-way experience. This conversation can grow from occasional moments to a daily and life-long encounter, which generates ever-deeper confidence in God as faithful. From there our decisions – often spontaneous – flow, as do those of someone deeply in love, who is set in all things on pleasing their partner.

**Harvesting**
A few minutes before the end of the prayer time, I notice what I experienced in my individual prayer:

- 'What helped me materially (place chosen for prayer, icon, candle, chair, relaxation)?' Becoming aware of this will enable me to progress in my way of doing things (*Spiritual Exercises*, 77).
- 'What has brought me consolation or desolation, and what thoughts have stimulated my vital energy or blocked it?' (see p. 140). In the light of what has most caught my attention, I make a brief note of what I wish to share with my small group. This allows me to listen more attentively to others, without being preoccupied either by what I am going to say or how I will say it. Moreover, through these notes I will be more faithful to the experience of my personal prayer time, without being influenced by the words of others.
- I don't share all the fruits of my prayer, especially if they are abundant: rather I sort out the fruits that seem more important for the progressive up-building of the group. **Choosing what to share is a first step towards communal discernment.**

The time of personal prayer can end with a formal prayer such as the *Our Father* or the *Hail Mary*, or with a psalm, or a well-known song that summarises the state of my heart. In this way, a transfer of meaning can take place between ready-made formulations and a new experience which emerges from my prayer and the session.

- *In communal discernment the focus of prayer shifts from personal to divine concerns*
- *The issue becomes: 'Lord, what do you want us to do?'*
- *Prayer time is now taken up by intimate conversation with God*
- *We inch our way along towards the ideal expressed by Jesus who could affirm, 'I always do what pleases my Father' (Jn 8:29)*

# The Small Groups

*The dynamic structure of small groups*
The fruits of the personal prayer before the Spirit-led conversation will be shared in small groups.

Firstly a large group is divided into small groups. Even if there are only ten or twelve people, it's better to start by conversing in two separate groups before joining together.

In a small group of five or six people, all can easily interact, review what is happening and learn from it. Proximity leads to trust, so that each can trustingly say, 'Here, I will not get lost; this is a safe place to open up in truth; here, I will have time to explain myself by thinking aloud without having to present worked-out ideas right away; here, during successive meetings, we can really become partners without the fear that the expressing of our differences will shatter our efforts to work together'. This creates trust within the small groups, and this trust will spread to the large group.

*Composition*
Ideally, a small group should not exceed five or six people. Sometimes it may be sufficient to let the groups form randomly by asking the participants to count themselves: 1, 2, 3, 4, 5 … 1, 2, 3, 4, 5 … But it is often better for the group leaders to form the small groups, if they know the participants well. They must discern whether it is better for a certain person not to be grouped with another, given their projected difficulty in communicating with one another, for reasons of sensitivity or history. The participation of the leader of the overall group and its board members must be clarified, according to the situation and the individual. The aim should be to ensure freedom of speech, expression of feelings, safety for all and confidentiality.

Note that the facilitators normally do not participate in the small group meetings, as they need time to exchange with each other and to agree on the course of action in the forthcoming plenary group.

It is fruitful to cluster those who least know each other and who differ in terms of age, sex, state of life, profession, convictions, psychological type and, if possible, language.

Why do this? Because this is a primary community-building exercise: the genesis of the 'team person' is here.

- Encouraging communication between women and men reveals how complementary or otherwise their points of view are;
- Bringing the different states of life – lay, single, religious, priestly, active or retired – into dialogue helps to show that all share the aim of giving life, each according to their specific vocation;
- It is enriching to bring together people who differ in their sensibilities or who do not share the same mother tongue, as long as they can sufficiently understand each other.

The facilitators will make known the clear and objective criteria with which the small groups are formed in order to avoid any suspicion of manipulation.

### *The small group meeting*
When the group first assembles, the members introduce themselves. A simple ice-breaker may be helpful (p. 247).

If the group has already worked together but not met for some time, a brief period is given to each person to share on anything important that has occurred since the last meeting.

**A timekeeper**, who will not act as a chairperson, is chosen in the group. Remember that usually the facilitators of the big group are not present in the small groups.

The timekeeper will remind the group what time the meeting will end, that there will be three rounds of sharing (as already mentioned), that each member has no more than five minutes to speak in the first round, and that a small hand signal will tell speakers that their time is up.

The quality of the small group sharing determines the quality of the plenary exchanges. The members must be enabled to speak without fear of being judged, hear each other with attention and respect, and most importantly, listen to 'the still, small voice' of the Spirit (See 1 Kg 19:12).

## *Guidelines for good communication*
### Good listening

- As long as a participant holds the symbol (crucifix, pen, feather … ) in their hand, you give that person your attention and seek to be touched by their words, their silences, their non-verbal communication. Much of human communication is non-verbal.
- Try to hear and to understand what the speaker wants to share, even if they express themselves awkwardly: often the tone of voice is revealing.
- 'Everyone is an expert in their own experience.' This is not universally true, but when someone shares their experience, listen to them without judgement. Believe that the Spirit can speak through that person. Recall the story of 'Who speaks for Wolf?'
- Do not be dismissive of anyone, neither yourself nor others. Try to put a positive interpretation on what you hear.
- Listen fully without being distracted by what you yourself intend to say.
- Do not put anyone on a pedestal.

### Speaking up

- To speak, take the symbol: others will listen in silence as long as you hold it.
- Speak as 'I' rather than 'We'. Share your experience, not your ideas; speak from the heart rather than from the head. Don't start with 'I think' or 'We all know …' but with 'I wonder' or 'I believe …' or 'I have found …' or 'It seems to me…'
- The group is not the place to impose your favourite ideas or to give a little homily.
- Neither is the group the place to solve individual problems, unless they relate to the group process. Don't say, 'What happens to my job if we do this?'
- Share what you can and want to share from your time of reflection and prayer and let the Spirit guide you.
- Speak briefly and clearly. Allow yourself a silence or silences.
- Respect what is confidential.
- *Whenever these guidelines are not being respected, the facilitator or a group member must dare to point this out appropriately.*

## Additional notes on the guidelines

The guidelines given above for Spirit-led conversation are fundamental. They provide the required framework for a conversation to take place which will lead to the best apostolic discernment of which the group is capable.

It may be appropriate to remind people of the reason for the guidelines. It can be pointed out, for example, that in order to enjoy a game, it is essential to agree to respect the rules and constraints. Group members will agree to become personally involved in the process only if they feel safe doing so, and these guidelines respect individual freedom while providing a framework within which all can interact in a mutually respectful way.

The guidelines can be elaborated as follows:

### 1: Equal sharing of speaking time

Every human being has a simple thirst for justice. It is therefore important that speaking time be shared equally within the group. The timekeeper has an essential if thankless role to play in this respect, seeming to appear fussy, especially in the early stages. With the group's consensus the timekeeper will set the amount of time to be given to each person by distinguishing between the three rounds of sharing. This framework may seem restrictive to some participants, but experience shows that, from meeting to meeting, when this framework is respected with tact and flexibility, it gradually helps participants to better prepare and to express themselves more concisely and clearly. This in turn leads to increased interest, energy and dynamism in the group, and the focus is ever more determinedly set on God and God's will.

The use of the symbol helps to maintain the agreed speaking time and avoids having more than one person speaking at the same time. It allows the speaker to grow silent, knowing that their silence will be respected. They can search for the words that will express painful feelings that may arise. An example: one day, in a talking circle, a husband heard his wife say something she had never told him. When he pointed it out to her later she replied, 'You never gave me time to express it'.

## 2: Not monopolising the floor

When a person monopolises the conversation or cuts across the person speaking, the others – including the timekeeper – may not know how to react. But as soon as participants observe that the rules are not being followed, it is up to them to point this out. This will take courage, because often a little voice will whisper: 'Who are *you* to dare to intervene? Besides, you're not the boss here'. It is important to counter this little voice as soon as possible and to ask the Holy Spirit for the necessary poise to intervene with tact. The abuse of power – even if unconscious – by one participant is made possible only because of the slavish submission of other members.

## 3: Starting well

If the small group is meeting for the first time, it is helpful to give everyone a short time to introduce themselves. When a group meets only at intervals, it is good to begin by briefly reviewing what has been important since the last meeting, even if it has nothing to do with the subject of the current meeting (e.g. a family death, the failure of a child at school, a birth, a new job or the smile of a passer-by in the street). These events matter in our lives and color our group mood. Recalling them makes us more present to each other and reminds us that we are here not primarily to solve problems, but to grow in 'being together'. God is always at work to gather the People of God into one community: 'I will draw all people to myself' (Jn 12:32).

## 4: Difficult individual situations

It may happen that a group member is going through something very painful. If we are not careful, all attention may be focused on them. Respecting the structure of the three rounds of sharing and the fair distribution of speaking time avoids this pitfall. The small group is not a therapy group in which to solve individual problems. These can best be worked through privately during free time.

## 5: The second round of sharing shapes inner freedom

The second round of sharing is different from the first: it is progressive. Each speaker now expresses what echoes with them in what others have said. This can only be done if all have listened carefully in the first round, and are not hung up on some point that they want to defend at all costs. In the second round of sharing, with God's help, the inner freedom required for authentic discernment is being shaped. This is seen in one's openness to being moved by the witness of others, just as in praying gospel scenes imaginatively we allow ourselves to be moved by what Jesus says, does or endures.

When a climate of trust and respectful listening has been established, it is not uncommon for the person expressing themselves to discover what has been hidden from their own eyes. Little by little, people are freed from their fears, their resistances, and from what might still be ego-centric in them. Each opens up to unexplored dimensions of their personal being and of their being together. Personal transformation occurs.

It is then important to identify and name what this second round has revealed to the group, and not to lose what has been given. This is a condition for progressing towards a common discernment. While this second round may be unexpected for many people, it is a decisive time. It is here, in particular, that the Spirit can communicate the specific grace of communal discernment.

The third round of sharing is characterised by the fact that it explicitly introduces the Lord into the conversation. 'What does the Lord want?' 'What ought I to do for Christ?' (*Spiritual Exercises*, 53). It is with him that the members of the small group now converse. In a way, they are repeating the experience of the disciples on the road to Emmaus; first they were conversing with one another: now conversing with Jesus their hearts burn, they are filled with joy, and their future path is revealed to them (Lk 24:13–33).

## 6: Confidentiality

Some people are reluctant to participate in the discernment process for fear that what is said in small groups and in plenary will be shared. It is therefore important, at the beginning of the session, to set out the boundaries around confidentiality and to agree on what can 'go out' from the group to the others.

Confidentiality in a group can be defined as the security agreement between people speaking in groups. Let us distinguish a few situations.

- At the end of a meeting, members of a small group will usually take a few moments to agree on what to share in the plenary group and how to communicate it.
- The person assigned to echo to the plenary the fruit of what has been experienced will not name members, unless by prior agreement.
- When assessing the governance of the leader, it is advisable that that person leaves the meeting briefly so that participants can speak freely. What has been said in their absence should be communicated to them tactfully when they re-enter the gathering, without specifying who has made a particular point.
- It may be useful, or even necessary, to feed back to the large group the fruit of a private discussion, when it concerns what is happening in the assembly. This requires the prior agreement of both parties.
- What has been shared in the session can only be reported outside with the prior consent of the participants, both in terms of the content and the form of the communication.[30]

---

- *In sharings, look behind the words to the non-verbals: cardiac listening*
- *Give others the gifts of attention, patience and time*
- *Ask yourself: 'Perhaps the Spirit IS TRYING to squeeze divine intentions into X's words?'*
- *Norms for speaking must be adhered to*
- *Speak out the truth, but in love, 'so that your words may give grace to your hearers' (Ep 4:29)*
- *Sharing is not a forum for 'getting stuff off your chest' but to enable the Spirit to have the 'mic'*

---

30   If the exchanges reveal the existence of reprehensible acts such as abuse, two or three people should be chosen by their peers to inform the competent authority.

# Plenary Session

When the small groups end, they come together in a plenary session where the Spirit-led conversation continues.

## *Function of the plenary*

The main accompaniment by the facilitators takes place during the plenaries that follow the small groups. The dynamics of these meetings parallel those between the giver of the Exercises and the receiver (*Spiritual Exercises*, 1–20), but note that in the plenaries facilitators and participants both give and receive. Given that there are at least two facilitators, one facilitates the exchanges, while another notes the participation of the group members, the general climate of the group and the affective and spiritual movements that develop.

Given that we have gathered because called by the Lord, we can believe that he is not sending us on a wild goose chase, so some consensus around the issue usually emerges, which can then be nuanced and lead to greater consensus or even to unanimity. All will need to remain free, open and flexible, because what someone or some small group has thought to be best will not necessarily be judged as such by the large group. The work of conversion to *what God wants* takes its own time which must be respected.[31] This need for inner freedom is sometimes referred to as the 'Uncertainty Principle' which proposes that no one should make up their mind on an issue till the moment when they have to vote.

---

31 The term 'will of God' is to be understood as God's gracious designs for us. It is not predetermined or unfeeling, but open. It carries the image, not of an architect's blueprint, but of the game plan of a football manager: guidelines are given but many factors will come into play that cannot be foreseen: on-the-spot creativity will be needed. The term *co-creating with God* is theologically doubtful, but it catches the idea of God and myself working along through a day and deciding what best to do. This is what discernment looks like from my side: God and I discuss our strategy, I interpret as best I can what God may want, and God accepts my decision even though it may be flawed.

At the end of the plenary some may wish to pray openly. This may consist of asking God to free them from a fear or resistance, or of expressing praise and gratitude for the action of the Spirit who has opened their hearts to what may be an unexpected call from the God of Surprises. A hymn, song or piece of music may be appropriate, to express group consolation.

If no consensus is emerging, a period of prayer on the issue is called for, with space for meals, socialising, resting, followed by new rounds of sharing. Think of a Papal conclave where successive rounds (four daily!) of voting for a new pope may precede the required two-thirds majority and the issuing of white smoke!

## *Facilitating the plenary sessions*

The aims of plenary sessions are different depending on whether you are at the beginning or in the middle of a communal discernment. The goal of the first plenary sessions is mainly to create mutual trust and community in the large group by setting up the guidelines for Spirit-led conversation (see p. 37). The facilitators invite those who wish to express what they feel is important to share, following on the times of personal and small group Spirit-led conversation. They can ask:

- 'How satisfied were you with the way you shared in the small group?'
- 'What factors contributed to this satisfaction?' (We do not ask closed questions such as: 'Are you satisfied with …?' because this invites a yes/no response).
- 'How did the proposed process help in listening to the Holy Spirit?'
- 'How did the Prayer Sheet help to foster depth of discussion?'
- 'How were you able to distinguish the three rounds of sharing?'
- 'How did the process generate trust in your group?'

When the facilitators feel that there is a climate of trust between the participants, they can start the work for discernment in common. It is good for them to remember the purpose of the plenary and its style, as reflected in the design of the prayer sheet and in particular the petition for grace. Following on from this request for grace, the plenary is set in motion by putting to the group *a carefully prepared leading question*. It should be precise so that it opens the door to what is actually *going on* in the group.

Over the course of a discernment lasting several days, the theme of the questions will evolve from one plenary to the next.

a) In order to elicit the 'internal weather' of the group – whether it is in consolation or desolation – one could ask:
'Now as you sit here in a circle, what feeling most stays with you after what you have experienced today?'
'What meteorological image do you associate with this feeling – rain, sun, storm, fog, etc.?' 'What brings this image about?'
Each can be asked to respond in two or three words, to the question: 'Here and now, what do you feel?' The aim is to check where the group's energy is at (see the Energy Cycle on p. 71). Is the group alive, stimulated, paralysed or asleep? (See also Spiritual discernment, p. 130). The truth, even if humbling, sets us free (see Jn 8:32). Often, at the end, a word from the facilitator will encourage the group.

b) To highlight the 'ripening fruits' one could ask:
'What points of convergence do you perceive in the group?'
'To what extent has the requested grace been obtained?'
'To what extent is the call of God becoming clearer? What signs of this do you see in your group?'
'What has become clearer on this or that question?'

c) To express the steps to be taken following on the decision, and the strength of common commitment, one could ask:
'What are the inevitable consequences of what we have agreed?'

d) The facilitators can also invite the members to move virtually outside the group to observe it, silently asking the question, 'What is happening here?' 'What energies are at work?' 'What tensions are latent?' This exercise is known as 'the view from the balcony'. During the subsequent round, suggestions can be made about what to do next.

*Written sharing*
In the plenary where the formal work of discernment starts, before the end of the small group meetings the facilitators will have given a flipchart to the small groups and asked them to write the conclusions of their conversation. Note that verbal sharing is richer than the summary

written on the flip-chart! At the beginning of the plenary session, these sheets are displayed on the wall and everyone stands and reads them in silence. Then everyone sits down and a representative of each small group will express how their consensus was reached. This procedure prevents the small group report from being technical, long or boring, as is the case when every detail is reported – often a sign that the sharing was 'heady' and less in tune with the Spirit.

After a while, members who feel that their contribution may help the larger group to move towards 'us' are invited to speak. They share what touches them most here and now. It is together that we deepen, unfold, and taste whatever arouses more inner feelings and movements of consolation and desolation (p. 140).

These sharings will be collated, written down and displayed on a flip-chart or large sheet of paper, or projected onto a screen. The points deemed to be of value to the group as a whole will be underscored. To encourage participation, we avoid asking the leaders of the requesting group to present the sharing of the small group.

After a period of silence, members are invited to identify the elements of an emerging consensus. It is important to spend time on this. There may be a temptation to move on too quickly to the next stage, but discernment implies going to the end of each stage by asking the question: 'What has become clear to the group as a whole? To what do we feel the Spirit is pointing us?' These elements of consensus should be retained, even noted and displayed; they can serve as a basis for the next step.

Usually the plenary will not exceed one hour, and can be shorter. This is the case, for example, with the 'REPETITION' style plenary that follows the small group sharing on 'My deep experiences of God' (p. 192).

On the other hand, the plenary may exceed an hour when it is a 'RESTART' of texts written within small groups, following a question put to them. In this case, it is wise after an hour or so of plenary to take a micro-pause before continuing, in order to get consensus on the future length of the session.

## *Facilitating the interventions*

- If necessary, rephrase an intervention so that nobody feels put down (*Spiritual Exercises*, 22) and nobody is praised. Help members to base

their interventions on observed facts, not on unverified interpretations. Help them to be attentive to each other's feelings (feelings, emotions, sensations – see p. 68) and basic human aspirations.
- When an intervention is short and to the point, indicate it as very helpful.
- If two or more group members are conversing together rather than addressing the issue of the plenary, the facilitator needs to intervene. 'The conversation has begun to focus on a new topic, which may be important: do you want to continue with it? If yes, who would like to speak to it?' In this way the group is respected, and takes ownership of the change of focus.
- If the interventions are along the same lines, ask: 'Does anyone want to express a different or even an opposite opinion?'
- Invite those who have not yet spoken to do so.
- Pay attention, not only to what is said, but also to what is happening in body language, tone of voice, attitudes, facial expressions, noises ...
- When mutual listening breaks down, and there is tension, stony silence, or aggression, what to do?
  - Try putting the participants in pairs or threes for a few minutes around a question: then each pair or trio responds briefly and humorously by speaking in the voice of one of them.
  - Or suggest that they express themselves through a drawing, an image, a symbol, a gesture. Or use the common symbol. Or offer a moment of silence.
  - Or take a full break (during which the facilitators can consult with each other).

### *Emergence of the team member*

The team member is much more than an individual in a casual gathering of persons who have at least a minimal common interest, but who lack a leader or helpful structures. In a public protest each person is primarily for themselves, with little care for others or for the wider good. The loudest and most forceful can prevail, as in Jesus' passion. 'Crucify him! Crucify him!' (Lk 23:21).

But think of a group which forms around a strong common value, such as a Neighbourhood Watch Group concerned with drug proliferation, or as 'The Mothers of the Disappeared' in Argentina, or Climate Activists. The members may have a wide spectrum of religious beliefs, or none, but they become a common body when they agree to work together, to engage only in non-violent protest, to allow everyone in the group to be heard, to choose a leader, organise a strategy, have regular meetings, identify needed resources, and provide mutual support, aware that their struggle for justice will be resisted. A transient community is being born – a mysterious bonding of individuals who share a common concern for justice and how to go about it, whatever be their talents, resources, or belief in a transcendent Being.

Behind the group stands the Lord of History, who works through everyone of goodwill to build the kingdom of God. This God may be known, loved, and appealed to, or be mostly *incognito*. The rich resources of the Christian and other faiths are available to the group, as are the ideals of the humanist. All these can be tapped into. Perhaps common prayer is a non-starter, but here and there in the group will be persons who 'carry the portfolio for prayer': they can intercede mightily for the group as Abraham did for the doomed city of Sodom (Gn 18:22–33) and discreetly enrich it from within their religious dimension.

## *The power of groups*

Today it is group decisions that change the world for good or ill. So however small our group, it carries in its own way something of world value! Christians are abandoning isolationism as they become more aware that they can and should support non-Christian groups with whose values they find sympathy. Humankind is beginning to take a long, loving look at our beautiful but wounded planet, and to respond together to its needs by uniting all individual resources.

Groups have played and still play main roles in human history.

➢ Think of the horde of slaves of 3000 years ago who amazingly escaped from Egypt and over many years and trials were molded into a single body as the Hebrew people, the People of God. Their impact on human history has been hugely significant.
➢ Think of the Pilgrims who boarded the Mayflower in Plymouth in 1620 and set sail for America, in order to live together in religious freedom. From them emerged the United States.

> Think of people across the world who participate in Freedom Marches, or who demand equality for women, for LGBTQ+ etc.
> Think of Pope Francis' call to all people to enter into dialogue about our common home. 'Faced as we are with global environmental deterioration, I wish to address every person living on this planet'.[32]

### *Each member is co-responsible for the whole*

In a communal discernment each member is co-responsible for the smooth running of the small and large group. Their profound goal is nothing less than to enable the Holy Spirit to be heard and followed. 'All who are led by the Spirit of God are children of God' (Rom 8:14).

Belief in the presence of the Spirit is the key to right decisions. It is not the group on its own that reaches a right choice: it comes from the Spirit through the members of the group. 'Every perfect gift is from above, coming down from the Father of lights …The wisdom from above is first pure, peaceable, gentle, willing to yield, full of mercy and good fruits' (James 1:17; 3:17).

Thus in the group there grows a contemplative quality in the sense that the members are looking out for indicators of the divine presence. Such indicators are humble and tentative interventions, mutual love, and an inner freedom which enables each to deal with their own unfreedoms, and with those of others. 'Give the Holy Spirit the mic!' was a dramatic call from a group member who felt frustrated by a bland conversation in which people were locked into arguing for their private ideas. Ideally each member should be trying to hear and express the wisdom of the Spirit, to offer possible 'news of God' rather than claiming to 'possess' God by their dogmatism.[33]

We have outlined the structure of the Spirit-led conversation which underpins discernment in common. The group is not a quasi-parliament, nor a debating group; it does not end in Win/Lose situations; it is not at the mercy of the prominent, the powerful or the noisy. It is a humble communal search for God. Each tries to listen well, and

---

32  Pope Francis, *Laudato Si'*, 3.
33  See Judith Roemer, *The Group Meeting as a Contemplative Experience*.

to see other speakers not as representatives of a particular position, but as trying to articulate what the Spirit might wish them to bring to the group's attention. Each is to cultivate a sense of gratitude for what the others may contribute, even if it demands a change in their own stance.

- *In all sharing the focus is to be on God's desires for this group*
- *Notice what's going on in the group as well as in yourself*
- *'Weather Reports' help: blue skies, beach weather ... or dark clouds, stay at home?*
- *Sense the power in the group: 'Our group is Spirit-powered'!*
- *Team membership is born through the group's humble searching for God*

# Fostering Group Energy

*Basic human longings*
In any group there is an energy that can increase or decrease in a discerning group according to the greater or lesser welcome given to the Holy Spirit.

The action of the Spirit can be discerned by our becoming aware of the feelings (sentiments, emotions, sensations) of the members. Briefly, we can say that the basic feelings are: joy, sadness, fear and anger (see p. 98).

Feelings are like warning lights that signal whether a basic aspiration or longing is being honoured or not. So, for example, fear of change signals that the basic longing for security is not being met. On the other hand, joy can come from the fact that the basic longing for mutual understanding is fulfilled.[34]

There is value in expressing oneself in terms of basic aspirations, as these are common to all human beings. They are fundamental needs and longings. Referring to them generates understanding and communion. Basic human aspirations are the various vital desires and necessities that motivate and mobilise human beings to action.

The following is a non-exhaustive list of longings or aspirations:

- *Communion:* I want to be in touch with God, with myself, with others and with all creation.
- *Belonging:* Relationships matter.
- *Freedom and differentiation*: I want to be truly myself.
- *Reciprocity:* I give and I receive.
- *Justice:* We are all equal.
- *Empathy:* We do not leave one another alone in suffering.
- *Honesty:* I say what I really think.

---

[34] The relationship between a feeling and a basic human aspiration is explored by Marshal Rosenberg, American psychologist, 1934–2005. See bibliography.

Other needs and aspirations include: listening, understanding, patience, love, friendship, self-giving, gratitude, experimentation, formation, meaning, collaboration, participation, creativity, boldness, security, trust, celebration, forgiveness and reconciliation, overcoming obstacles.

*Energy and Power*

Before his Ascension Jesus strengthened the disciples, 'See, I am sending upon you what my Father promised: so stay here in the city until you have been clothed with power from on high' (Lk 24:49). In the group, everyone, according to their capacity, *has the power* to contribute to the discernment of basic aspirations that are fulfilled or not fulfilled.

Many people underestimate the power they have in their groups. They say to themselves: 'Anyway, the boss – or the bishop – will decide.' This thought diminishes group energy. But the power of our thoughts is enormous, and becoming aware of this allows us to freely choose to replace negative thoughts with positive statements such as Margaret Mead's assertion (though its truth is disputed): 'Never doubt that a small group of thoughtful, committed citisens can change the world. Indeed, it is the only thing that ever has.'[35]

The discerning group proposes to change from its status quo to a new situation, under the prompting of the Holy Spirit, who *'renews the face of the earth'* (Ps 104:30). To do this, it needs to harness the energy within.

Jesus always emphasised the need **to act**: *'Go and do likewise'*, he said after relating the story of the Good Samaritan (Lk 10:37). *'Go, and do not sin again'* is his word to the woman accused of adultery (Jn 8:11). Similarly, Ignatius reminds us that 'love is found in **deeds** rather than words' (*Spiritual Exercises*, 230).

There is no hopeless situation, even if the decision taken is foreseen to end in failure. Think of Jesus in the Garden: he accepts his impending death—but only after adopting a graced attitude that saves the world. When we fall into despair over climate change, we can decide to trust the staggering divine promise, 'See, I am making all things new' (Rev 21:5).

---

35 Note too Saul Alinski's *Rules for Radicals* (New York: Vintage, 1989), on the power of small people to bring big changes with minimal resources.

## The Energy Cycle
The Energy Cycle simply puts into words what we do all the time: we decide to change something: so we ponder/discern what best to do; we decide on the best option, and then implement the change.

So I wake up, decide to get up, dress, make breakfast, let the dog out, kiss my partner goodbye, get the car-keys and drive to work. There are seven uses of the Energy Cycle here!

## The elements
Your Parish Pastoral Council (PPC) wants to decide whether or not to build a Parish Community Centre.

- *Status Quo*: The starting point is that there is no Community Centre, though various groups have proposed one.
- *Decision:* You agree to engage in a process of communal discernment to reach a decision on the issue.
- *Action:* The PPC sets up a Working Party which consults all interested bodies, co-opts help from experts, works out a ball-park figure, etc., etc. The Proposal is made as unambiguous as possible: 'What exactly do we want – a large or small building, etc.?'
- *Recommendation*: The Working Party makes a recommendation at the next meeting of the PPC.[36]

With all relevant data to hand, the PPC will discuss the project, and list the arguments For/Against. A Spirit-led conversation process is used, with attention to the consolation or desolation aroused. This precedes the emergence of consensus.

We come then to the point where we can take a decision.

- *Decision:* 'This, we believe, is what God is inviting us to do'.
- *Action:* Implementation is decided by delegation: 'Who will do what, when, how …?' This preserves the vitality of the process.
- *Confirmation:* The intended action may have to be submitted to a higher authority – perhaps the bishop – for final ratification.

---

36 The word 'recommendation' is used to reach all members of a group. It is to be taken in the strong sense that invites those in charge to make a decision. It is stronger than 'proposal' or 'suggestion' which only precede the actual recommendation.

Whether or not this has to happen, the group checks whether its consolation continues or fades.
- *Evaluation:* Later, the whole process is evaluated: 'Has this given us more life, dynamism, breath, impetus, drive? 'Has it helped to better satisfy the fundamental aspirations of those impacted by the action?' 'Did anything get in the way of the best decision being made?' 'How can we become ever more open to the Spirit?'

It is in the interest of all members to participate in the evaluation process and in the development of recommendations for future action. In this way, everyone brings to the group the lessons learnt from their experience. Thus all contribute to increasing the group energy. In other words, power in the group extends beyond the power of decision and it is not the sole preserve of the leader. This better ensures implementation.

Thus emerges the **ENERGY CYCLE**, which moves the group from its current situation into a new one which appears to be more in tune with the Holy Spirit's wishes. It is an ever-recurring set of phases which we use every day, even if mostly subconsciously. The power of an organisation cannot be coercive power, based on fear of sanctions for non-compliance. Nor can it be the power based on reward, which is conditional. Ultimately it must involve the kind of power that comes from people freely choosing to engage in a project. The power of free persons can be called commitment, and it is liberated through appropriate structures and attitudes, as shown above.

The **task** is to empower the members of the group to achieve its purposes. Beginning from the status quo, **agreement to change** is followed by **reflection and discernment,** leading to the possibility of **a new order of things;** this is **evaluated** and a **recommendation** is arrived at. This in turn leads to **decision** and then **implementation.** A new status quo thus emerges which in time will undergo the same cyclical process. But since power resides in each phase, if any phase is omitted the group will be dis-empowered. Think of a family planning a holiday: 'We need a break!' 'Where will we go?' 'What can we afford?' 'How about going to X or Y?' 'We all agree on Y!' 'Let's buy the tickets'. 'But we haven't the money!'

All discernment follows a path which, from stage to stage, progresses towards a choice. These stages can be experienced as 'spiritual exercises' that contribute to the gradual transformation of individuals and the group, just as physical exercises transform athletes (*Spiritual Exercises*, 1). Jesus says that he has come that we may have life, and have it abundantly (see Jn 10:10); when our group works well we can see, with happy surprise, the growth of this life.[37]

## *Organisational development and 'Theory U'*

Since their beginnings, both ISECP and Esdac teams have used strategies developed outside the religious world, for example the 'energy cycle'.

Given the changes in their environment and their internal life, more organisations, companies, administrations and institutions are being led to evolve their systems of power and to adapt the relationships between their members: this is known as 'organisational development'.

Ecclesial institutions and congregations must be open to the insights of the secular world: these 'bright ideas' come from 'the true light, which enlightens everyone coming into the world' (see Jn 1:9). Companies hire organisational development consultants to help them function better systemically. 'Theory U' as developed by Otto Scharmer enables Christians and non-Christians to work together in a respectful way. Recalling that we said at the beginning that 'The Holy Spirit is offered to all', this is particularly evident here.

Theory U invites the members of a group to reflect and dialogue by digging deeper and deeper to reveal the common ground on which they all stand, and to let the energy emerge which can renew the system of their relationships. They observe the reality around them as well as that within their organisation; they leave behind old patterns of thinking and enter unknown spaces; they allow themselves to be surprised by paradoxical situations, they follow uncharted passages, and trust that beyond preconceived ideas a world in gestation emerges.

---

37   The word 'life' can be written and understood with or without a capital letter. Using this word makes it possible to reach not only those who refer their existence to Jesus as the Way, the Truth and the Life (Jn 14:6 and *Spiritual Exercises*, 139) but those who spontaneously experience the joy of living and want their lives and those of others to further develop, in life, joy, happiness and love.

In this process of deepening, the members of the group successively go through three deepening levels of consciousness, leading to:

- The opening of the *mind* to observe systems, to solve problems, and to unravel complexities;
- The opening of the *heart* so that one is touched by senses and emotions, and can release trapped energy;
- The opening of the *will* to let go, to meet others beyond one's own certainties and to engage with them on unexplored paths.

The Theory U approach can be represented as a capital U, moving from left to right. Descending into the hollow of the U, we find ourselves in a space of silence from which the future will emerge. The 'Life–Death–Resurrection cycle' and the U theory evoke different levels of reflection: on the one hand, the 'WHO, WHAT, HOW'; on the other hand, 'INTELLIGENCE, HEART, WILL'.

For Christians, what reconciles the two patterns is their hollow, the moment when the seed falls into the ground to germinate. Jesus himself comes to take us from our graves so that we can join him in his resurrection: *'Unless a grain of wheat falls into the earth and dies, it remains just a single grain; but if it dies, it bears much fruit'* (Jn 12:24).[38]

> - *Group energy is linked to group desire*
> - *Can the group pray from the heart, 'O God, you are our God, for you we long' (Ps 63)?*
> - *Are we open to the Spirit's renewal of the face of the earth – here and now, in us?*
> - *The Energy Cycle drives our lives from the status quo to desire for change through discernment to decision and implementation*

---

38  Otto Scharmer, *Theory U: Leading from the Future as it emerges.*

# The Personal Review

**'He stopped to think'**
In his *Personal Writings* Ignatius tells us that at one point during his convalescence 'he stopped to think'.[39] It seems an unremarkable thing to do, but it was the beginning of his change of life, and lies behind the emphasis in Ignatian spirituality on reflectiveness, which parallels the wisdom of the ancient Greeks: 'Know yourself' and 'The unexamined life is not worth living.'

In communal discernment we stop to think, in order to find God. It is never easy to be aware of what is going on within yourself as it occurs. That's why it's good to stop periodically during a discernment Workshop to examine the ongoing conversation, in order to discover in it the action of the Spirit of love and truth, and to open up more to it, while also trying to detect what may be hindering the free play of grace in your heart. We have noted that Ignatius became so aware of how he could miss the promptings of God that he used refer to himself as a 'total obstacle' to the divine action.[40] We often wish others would 'catch themselves on' but in a personal review we try to do this for ourselves or with a helpful companion. In a group aside, one member said to another, 'You're a great acrobat! 'Why?' she asked. 'Because you're constantly leaping to conclusions'. The penny dropped!

This is what is meant by 'reviewing' – the habit of 'catching myself on' in order to notice what spirit is leading me, or to ask, 'What's going on in me?'. The younger son in Jesus' parable can help us here: having been *'in a distant country'* and away from his father for too long, *'he came to himself'*, faced his situation, and changed his life (Lk 15:11–32).

---

39  Ignatius, *Personal Writings*, p. 14.
40  Ignatius, *Personal Writings*, p. 161.

Reviewing allows us to preserve the joy of life, to intensify it or to restore it when it has been lost. The absence of joy indicates that my desire for more life is not satisfied. Jesus is the Living One, and his task is to give life and restore it where it was lost. He says: *'I have come that [all] may have life and have it to the full'* (Jn 10:10), and: *'I have told you this so that my joy may be in you, and that your joy may be complete'* (Jn 15:11). He was himself a deeply reflective character, and must often have asked himself how well he was conveying the love of his Father to his audiences.

## *Personal Review*

Reviewing helps us to pray our own lives as we would pray a page of the Gospel. Our daily life is in fact the raw material for meeting God who is present in everything, everywhere, always, and is calling us to be ever more open to the divine action. Reviewing helps us to face up to serious questions and encourages a healthy critical spirit. It allows us to learn by doing, rather than endlessly having the experience but missing the meaning, as T. S. Eliot puts it.

The personal review is variously named in the Ignatian tradition as the Examen of conscience, the Examen, the Review of Consciousness, etc. It can be short or longer. Centrally it consists in evaluating a slice of life – your day, or a part of it, a meeting, a conversation, or a period of time between group meetings, in order to

- prayerfully search for the action of the Holy Spirit, to detect at what moments your energy was in tune with the energy, strength, light, love offered you by the Holy Spirit,
- and to detect what may have been an obstacle to the Spirit's action, so that you may adjust appropriately.

In a discernment Workshop, the focus of the personal review may be on how you listen, how you speak, and how you try to keep your eye on God, as Ignatius advises when he asks Jesuits *'to keep God always before their eyes'*.[41]

---

41 Ignatius, *Formula of the Institute*, 1540, 1.

In my everyday life, two fruitful questions to ask myself are: 'What gives me life?' and 'When have I given life to others?' These questions help me to enter into myself (Lk 15:17) where the Lord dwells and works within me. Reviewing makes me an apprentice. Every experience, whether pleasant or unpleasant, successful or failure, can teach me something. By reflecting on my experience, I truly become 'an expert in my own experience'. Jesus must have been an expert in such reviewing: 'What was going on between Peter and myself today?' ''How can I get to Judas to help him?'

'As I grow in self-awareness I may discover how driven I have been by some compulsion or evasion, how unfree I have been. Perhaps I have taken on a side-activity with lots of goodwill but on re-viewing it I realise that this activity has ended up absorbing most of my energy. Or I realise that I am no longer doing things that are good (praying in the morning, keeping in touch with a close friend, begging God to free me from an addiction), or that I have started to do what I never chose to do (two drinks before a meal, arguing vehemently, arriving late).'[42]

## Summary of the personal review

1. *Time out:* I settle down, and then ask to be shown the action of the Spirit in my life.
2. *Consolation:* Do I feel in my heart life, joy, momentum, peace? If so, what fundamental aspiration (or need) has been nourished in me and/or in others? What concrete fact helped – an action, circumstance, or situation? (Example: 'Today I gave quality time to meeting God in personal prayer.')

    I thank God for what I learn.
3. *Desolation:* Conversely, do I feel sad, agitated, fearful, angry, guilty, powerless, cut off from God, from others and from my own interiority?

    If so, what fundamental human aspiration (or longing, need, vital desire) has not been fulfilled in me and/or in others?

---

42  J. A. Tetlow SJ, *'The most Postmodern Prayer: American Jesuit Identity and the Examen of Conscience, 1920–1990'.*

What concrete fact – an action, circumstance or situation impeded the flow of God's grace in me? (Example: 'A riot of negative thoughts about the celebrant dominated my attention at Mass)'.
4. *Forgive me:* I ask the Lord for forgiveness, that I may open my heart to his mercy so that joy and life may be restored in me. I ask for compassion for the person whom I was judging negatively.
5. *Be with me:* I ask the Lord to continue to help me, especially in whatever I will soon be doing, and I thank him for enlightening and strengthening me.

*Sharing personal reviews*
When the discernment concerns the group itself, the group can do a shared review and use it to evaluate its own way of working and to formulate changes and recommendations.

The shared review can be done outside a Workshop. Sometimes called *The Revision of Life/ Revision de vie,* this is appropriate for people who regularly come together to support each other in their individual commitments: they share their personal reviews of what has happened since they last met.

This sharing can follow the guidelines of the Spirit-led conversation. The review is preceded by personal prayer over the period being considered – a Prayer Sheet may help; next comes sharing, and finally a sharing of how one has been nourished by the others.

Such periodic sharing of personal reviews, or Revision de vie, is becoming more widespread, in couples, religious communities, student groups, parishes, CLC (Christian Life Community) teams, pastoral assistants, and secular work groups. It includes the review of events experienced in common. With the loss of institutions, more and more religious communities are becoming aware that their 'living together' only becomes an apostolic witness of community when Spirit-led conversation, personal review and common review are practised.

- *Do I 'stop to think' about the more important things?*
- *Do I often have an experience but miss the meaning? (T. S. Eliot)*
- *If the unexamined life is not worth living, what about the unexamined ministry?*
- *Ignatius would never want a day to end, no matter how humble or disastrous it was, without reviewing it in order to find his soul's desire, who is God*

# Authority in the Group

## *The notion of authority*

The word 'authority' has a bad press due to its recurrent misuse as being linked with domination. Etymologically, however, it includes the notion of 'originating' and 'making something grow': think of an author who creates a book by making an idea grow; think of God who is *the author* of all reality (Gn 1). Think of Jesus as 'the *author* and perfecter of our faith' (Hb 12:2). The Lord, of course, is a special kind of author; he enters the story he is creating, to keep it on track as in the Incarnation! The history of salvation is not scripted at a distance: it is self-implicating – it catches in God, ourselves, and all others.

In this sense authoring, when lived in a profoundly personal way, is a service intended to help the group and each of its members to develop their potential and accomplish their mission.

Jesus is the paradigm of servant-leadership (Mk 10:42–45; Jn 13:1–15).

The notion of 'servant-leadership' as introduced by Robert Greenleaf in 1970 is illuminating.[43] For him the servant-leader is first of all a servant. Leadership which prioritises serving is seen in the care the leader takes to ensure that the priority needs of those being led are met first. Jesus prioritises service and tells us to do likewise.

The criteria for good servant-leadership are as follows:

- Are the people who are being served transformed and growing as people? Are they becoming healthier, wiser, freer, more autonomous, more likely to be servant-leaders themselves?
- What is the effect of this transformation on the less privileged in society? Will they benefit or at least not be more disadvantaged?

---

43 See R. Greenleaf, *Servant Leadership: A Journey into the Nature of Legitimate Power and Greatness.*

## Who's in charge?

Who should exercise authority in the Church? We can touch here only on one important point. In order to develop the spirit of synodality, two fundamental recommendations can be made:

- Distinguish between sacramental responsibilities (held by clerics) and responsibilities relating to Church government (open to non-clerics). The current concentration in one person of both responsibilities should be critically examined.
- Strengthen the presence of the laity in general, and of women in particular, in all the decision-making spheres of the Catholic Church.

The generic term 'shared governance' encompasses a number of ways of organising a team or structure to reduce or eliminate the concentration of power in the hands of a few people, and to distribute it among those who actually do the work.[44]

## Formal and informal authority

Persons in charge receive *legal* authority by delegation from a higher authority: either a hierarchical body, or the group (by election, for example). Or they receive informal but *effective* authority from the group. This comes from their capacity, innate or acquired, to take advantage of the potential present in each member to promote the common good.

## Styles of authority

There are three main ways of exercising authority, according to the greater or lesser participation of the group members, and in the elaboration and making of decisions.

- **The Directive Style.** The leader prepares the decision, by evaluating the past situation and listing recommendations with the help of the group. Then the leader takes the decision alone.

---

44 These different forms of governance are based on trust in the ability of those chosen, to make wise decisions within their own sphere of action. The term 'governance' refers to the exercise of power, while the term 'shared' refers to the distribution of power among several actors.

- **The Consultative Style.** The leader prepares the decision (evaluation and recommendations) in consultation with the group members. Here again the leader takes the decision alone. This is usually the case in councils, commissions, synods.
- **The Participative Style.** The leader sets up and manages the process of preparing the decision (evaluation and recommendations) with the members of the group. The decision is taken by all members of the group.

None of these three styles is better than the others. Each style meets different needs that may vary during the same meeting. The person exercising authority should be sufficiently free from personal preferences to be able to change styles quickly according to the circumstances, the issues to be dealt with and the psychological and spiritual state of the group.

Whatever the styles of governance, any one of which may be appropriate in certain circumstances, the goal of this Manual is to help the group grow in communion and in mature decisions by the engaging of everyone in the exercise of power.

*Possible exercises*
➤ *Prayer Sheet 5: My attitude to the exercise of authority*
➤ *Prayer Sheet 4: Serving others but not being used by them*

*Who has the ultimate power?*
If a discernment process is used to decide an issue, it is essential that everyone is clear about who has both the statutory authority and responsibility to make the final decision.

- Is it the group which is making the decision? This may be the case in a religious community Chapter, a couple, a general assembly, a board of directors. 'We decided!'
- Or does an authority within the group make the decision? This is the case when a leader consults advisors, while reserving the power to make decisions. Here are some examples:
  o A synod in which the pope, having consulted the bishops in attendance, and after wide consultation with the people of God, makes his decision.

- o The parish pastoral council is consultative as of now, not deliberative, according to current Canon Law. Only the priest in charge has the right to make decisions.
- o The Board of Management where the principal consults with teachers, administrative staff, parents, or students, and then makes the decision. Or the Chair of the Board mandates the principal to act in a certain way.
- o An authority outside the group may make the final decision. This was the case when the first ten Jesuits asked the pope to approve their constitution as a religious order (p. 223). It is also the case in a religious congregation where the superior general, who is responsible, for example, for the sale of real estate, asks the opinion of the members before deciding.

The issue as to whether or not it is appropriate for a group leader who is the authority figure to participate in the sharing, because this can limit the freedom of speech of the participants, has been discussed above (p. 80).

### *The place of the leader of the requesting group*
By 'requesting group' we mean a parish, a religious community, an association … any group that wants spiritual accompaniment. The facilitators will make it clear that, during the Workshop, they will have authority over the group regarding the approach to each session and the facilitating process. They will consult if necessary with the leader of the requesting group, or their representatives. In the Chapters of religious congregations, such consultation is foreseen between the facilitating team and those statutorily designated to organise the Chapter according to the norms of the congregation.

If the ultimate decision is the responsibility *of the group as such*, it goes without saying that the leader of the group participates in the communal discernment as a member of the group, but without employing their leadership function.

If, on the other hand, the decision is the responsibility of the leader, it is preferable, as far as possible, that they participate in the Workshop or, at any rate, introduce it, be present at its conclusion, take an interest in its progress, and understand it well. Otherwise, they will not grasp what motivated the recommendations made, what resistance was overcome, what assumptions were made and what views ultimately prevailed. As a result, the leader may be tempted not to act, or to act only partially on the group's judgement. This would cause group frustration.

If a leader has to take a decision that is not in line with the recommendations of the group, the reasons should be explained, which can only be done properly with knowledge of how the discernment was carried out.

If the leader cannot be part of the discernment, this often means that there is a deeper problem that needs to be addressed before a Workshop begins.

What can be done when group members fear a lack of freedom in the leader? Either a small group, in which the leader would participate, should be composed of people who will not be negatively influenced by the leader's presence, or the leader should not engage in the small group but only participate in plenaries. This last hypothesis should be considered with caution, because the word of such a person, or even their silence, could carry unfair weight in the assembly, which would be contrary to the principle of communal discernment where every person's view is of equal value.

If the leader has vital information that cannot be communicated to the group, it is preferable that he or she make the required decision without prior consultation.

### *What power do delegates have?*
When an association has a large number of people, even if all of them have been consulted, there comes a time when only some are delegated to discern together what conclusions to draw from these multiple consultations.

Are these delegates obliged to defend the ideas that have emerged in their group, or are they called upon to act according to conscience?

The answer is clear. In a process of joint discernment, having studied all the reports from the sub-groups and shared them with the other delegates, *each delegate speaks in conscience, on their own behalf.* For in listening to the others, every delegate is open to other voices through which the Holy Spirit speaks.

This requires each delegate to be free both from their own convictions and those of the group they represent. The aim of the Spiritual Exercises is precisely to bring about such inner freedom.[45]

Before leaving the Workshop the delegates will decide how they will communicate the progress and fruits of their Spirit-led conversations to the wider membership.

### *Consensus*

The term 'consensus' means a 'common feeling/conviction'. It is therefore related to 'unanimity'. We will use it where there is a wide majority, but not necessarily everyone, in favour of the proposal.

The pressure that most groups feel to resolve a problem as soon as it arises often leads them to consider consensus as a value to be defended throughout the discernment process. Thus, when two different interpretations of the same event appear, the group will tend to seek immediate agreement, for fear of falling into chaos.

However, differences are riches, within which lies the potential path to an outcome that cannot be specified in advance. It is therefore good to maintain the tension between the forces that manifest themselves in chaos, without seeking to avoid them at all cost. It can be beneficial to enter the abyss, to descend into it together rather than to seek a premature pacification of conflicts.

This happened during the Amazon Synod of 2020: Pope Francis held off from a decision about the roles of women in the Church because of strong arguments for and against particular proposals: instead he invoked the idea of the 'overflow' based on trust that out of the chaos something new would slowly emerge through silence, prayer, reflection and discussion. The resolution would not be a Win/Lose situation but a new formulation which would incorporate the values in the conflicting options and bring consensus.[46]

Consensus does not require that all members of the group come to complete agreement about an issue. Some may feel strong resistance, yet recognise that there is consensus in the group and that they are

---

45 The classic commentary on Ignatius' view of inner freedom is found in John English SJ, *Spiritual Freedom: From an Experience of the Ignatian Exercises to the Art of Spiritual Guidance*.
46 This was Pope Francis' approach at the end of the Synod on the Amazon, *Querida Amazonia*, 102.

given the strength of the Holy Spirit to adhere to it, even at the cost of great inner struggle. Throughout his agony, Jesus adhered to the eternal consensus that motivated his incarnation, while in the Garden he felt strong resistance to the divine plan of love: salvation through the cross.

Psychiatrist M. Scott Peck defines consensus as follows: 'It is a group decision which some members may not consider the best but which they can all live with, which they support and which they agree not to question, taken without a vote, through a process in which the issues are fully exposed, where all members feel they have been properly heard, where everyone has equal power and responsibility, and where varying degrees of influence due to individual stubbornness or charisma are avoided so that all are satisfied with the process.'[47]

The deliberation of the future first Jesuits in 1539 illustrates the point: it ends with a somewhat triumphal accent: 'The conclusion was reached, not by a majority of votes, but by absolute unanimity.' But a few days later, one of the companions rejected a decision of the group, whereupon the group agreed that in all further questions to be debated, no matter what their importance, it was necessary to stick to the judgement of the majority.

*Unanimity*

The word 'unanimity' means 'one heart, one mind'. This is the sense in which it is used in the Acts of the Apostles: *'They were all of one heart'* (Acts 1:14). Today it means that all agree with the decision to be taken.

The criterion of unanimity for successful deliberation, when used as a starting point, risks distorting its outcome by depriving participants of the freedom of expression required for the whole process. This criterion can put pressure on consciences. As J-C Dhotel comments: 'The desire for agreement at all costs can run counter to the freedom of invention of the Spirit that one claims to be experiencing. If there is no unanimity, some will be tempted to pass immediately to a vote, but it is necessary to deliberate on this way of concluding. What would happen to a decision reached by a very small majority? Some decisions require a simple majority, others a two-thirds majority. It is up to the group to deliberate and decide. If a vote is used only "to get things over

---

47  M. Scott Peck, *A World Waiting to Be Born; Civility Rediscovered*, pp. 290–291.

with", it is simply a stopgap measure which will harden opposition and introduce power struggles.'[48]

So it is wiser not to go too quickly to a vote, but to explore all opinions so that, in the final formulation of the decision, account is taken of the constructive elements contributed by the minority who cannot, in good conscience, endorse the decision as formulated. The favorable interpretation of another's view as proposed by Ignatius (*Spiritual Exercises*, 21) suggests that this minority is also listening to the Spirit and has something worthwhile to say for the good of all. Patience is needed to refine the formulation of the decision, so that it becomes acceptable to an increasing number of participants and, finally, that the remaining minority indicates that it has come to equanimity and feels that it has now been sufficiently heard. 'However it's up to the minority to say this, not to the majority! It is better to delay the conclusion in order to reach this result with more certainty'.

When there remains no unanimity, another way of proceeding may be possible, especially within more structured and hierarchical communities such as religious communities or associations closely linked to the hierarchy: the group hands over the decision to the leaders. 'This procedure can only be truly understood in faith and according to the advice given by St Ignatius in the Exercises to "feel with the Church" (*Spiritual Exercises*, 352–370). We are Church and in the Church those in charge, even if elected, hold their authority from the Lord. But the group must have deliberated on this so that this procedure does not appear to its own eyes as a capitulation.'[49]

Think again of a papal Conclave: when the required two-thirds is reached, all the cardinals approach the newly elected pope and promise him their obedience: thus a 'negotiated unanimity' is achieved.

---

[48] For quotations in this section, see J-C Dhotel, *Discerner ensemble: guide pratique du discernement communautaire*, pp. 72–77.
[49] Dhotel, *Discerner ensemble*, pp. 75–76.

- *Authority is meant to bring life and growth in freedom*
- *Servant-leadership is Jesus' way: he acts as one who serves*
- *Delegates have power and can use it well if they are inwardly free*
- *Don't bypass differences: they are like mines that contain hidden treasure.*
- *Don't rush to unanimity: let it emerge by reaching out to the reluctant*

# Making a Decision Together

*Is change healthy?*
Life is change. Therefore, every human group necessarily goes through questioning. Ways of seeing and understanding change, as do ways of acting and behaving. What was taken for granted in the past is challenged today. Generational differences appear, in sexuality and also in liturgy. Within every group people age, new people arrive, older people die and some members choose to leave the group. The meaning of words change, as does the appreciation of what is moral and just.[50]

So, in order to remain alive, a group is called to change, to evolve. In Cardinal Newman's words, 'To live is to change, and to be perfect is to have changed often'. This does not require denying our current identity. We inhabit a universe that is endlessly evolving which requires us to innovate in order to remain faithful to our call to become the children of God (see Jn 1:12). This is creative fidelity. To renew oneself is to adhere more closely to the Creative Breath that carries the universe into incessant re-creations.

'The true newness' writes Pope Francis, 'is that which God himself wants to produce in a mysterious way, that which he inspires, provokes, guides and accompanies in a thousand ways [...]. The initiative comes from God; it is he who first loved us (1 Jn 4:19) and it is he alone who gives growth (1 Cor 3:7). This conviction allows us to maintain a spirit of joy.'

A group that does not evaluate its past actions and make recommendations for the future ends up dying, because its original ways of doing things are no longer adapted to the changed situation, nor to the new direction given by the Holy Spirit. *'New wine is not put into old wineskins; otherwise, the skins burst and the wine is spilled, and the skins*

---

[50] The latest description of contemporary life came my way recently, in the new word 'VUCA' which stands, apparently, for volatile, uncertain, complex and ambiguous!

*are destroyed. But new wine is put into fresh skins, and so both are preserved'* (Mt 9:17). 'Jesus Christ can break through the dull categories in which we try to enclose him and he constantly amazes us by his divine creativity'.[51]

## Attitudes to change

In the face of change, groups adopt different attitudes depending on whether they feel worried or stimulated by what is new:

- *Denial*: 'Nothing essential has changed; the current chaos is temporary; everything will go back to the way it was.'
- *Resistance:* 'Let's not change anything ... our way of doing things has proved itself. Hold fast to tradition!'
- *Generous openness to the new*: 'I am about to do a new thing ... Do you not perceive it?' (Is 43:19). We are to live within the ongoing paschal Mystery, the cycle of passion, death and resurrection.

The first two attitudes indicate the presence of anxiety, which needs to be sensitively handled by working within a more protective framework. Clarify the profile of the group: are there two critical masses, with some members leaning toward the past, others toward the future?

The third attitude sketched above is that of those capable of entering into the divine process that opens up the new. To a representative of the established order Jesus says: *'No one can see the kingdom of God without being born from above.'* Nicodemus replies, *'How can anyone be born after having grown old? Can one enter a second time into the mother's womb and be born?'* Jesus answers, *'No one can enter the kingdom of God without being born of water and Spirit'* (cf. Jn 3:3–5). Rebirth is built into the order of things.

Of course, a group may have run its course, and fulfilled its mission. It is also possible that its grace is now being offered instead to others: this is how life is transmitted. Or the charism of the group may no longer be needed today. Coming to these conclusions requires

---

51 Pope Francis, *Evangelii Gaudium*, 11, 12.

discernment, because the fear of change should not motivate an ill-thought-out termination.[52]

Change always entails a certain form of death, a mourning to be consented to, because what gave life in the past has passed away. A willingness to die to what is no longer life-giving is required in order to open up to a new form of life and to the promises of an emerging future. *'Unless a grain of wheat falls into the earth and dies, it remains just a single grain; but if it dies, it bears much fruit'* (Jn 12:24).

## Conversion

The journey of change and inner conversion follows the successive stages of the Spiritual Exercises of St Ignatius, where awareness of being loved by God is followed by acceptance of the purpose of our existence; then comes the First Week in which we experience our sinfulness, but also the joy of forgiveness. In the Second Week awareness of being called into deeper discipleship immerses us in the life of Jesus and opens up the world of discernment, the experience of making choices that are in harmony with divine designs. In the Third Week the contemplation of Jesus' Passion reveals the cost of discipleship, while in the Fourth Week the Resurrection and the Contemplation to attain Love bring joy and the commitment to love and serve in all things.

These dynamics enable each of our actions to become truly free. A group will not necessarily go through these stages as set out here but it is good that they are taken in some way as appropriate. Members must endure the pain of dying to what binds them to what is unhelpful and allow themselves to be filled with a joy that comes from above. At the tomb of Lazarus Jesus says, 'Unbind him, and let him go!' (Jn 11:44). The same applies to the group as a body.

The more theologically up-to-date the facilitators are the more easily will conversion take place. The point of arrival is that 'the love which moves me and makes me choose something has to descend from above, from the love of God' (*Spiritual Exercises*, 184, *Ivens*). With the help of the Spirit the group works to that point and the kingdom of God moves forward.

---

52 See Ted Dunn, *Graced Crossroads, Pathways to Deep Change and Transformation*, which deals extensively with these issues.

## 'Who? What? How?'

The goal of the discernment process is to make a decision together. In established groups such as religious communities and parishes the issue can be experienced at three different levels that correspond to the following three questions:

- Who are we?
- What are we called to?
- How can we respond to this call?

In a once-off exercise of discernment the main focus will be on the third question, but the two prior questions will be hovering in the background and need to be implicitly responded to in the final consensus. However demanding it be, all *relevant* questions must be faced.

## 'Who are we?'

This indicates the identity of an existing group, the grace that is proper to it, its reason for being, which differentiates it from other groups; included is everything that is specific to it: its charisma, its vocation, its mission.

For example, the Jesuits are described on the Internet as 'a Catholic male religious order, founded by St. Ignatius Loyola and his companions in 1540. We are priests and brothers who live in community and are called to imitate Jesus Christ, as poor, chaste and obedient men. We offer our lives to the Lord and he sends us into the world to help with his mission.' J. C. Futrell SJ puts Jesuit identity more succinctly, as **the service of Christ through the aiding of others in companionship.**[53]

## 'What are we called to?'

Given that life means change, and that everything within the group and its environment evolves, the Lord is inviting the group to discern what today it is called to change in its way of being and doing. What renunciations are needed for it to be open to the promise of an emerging future, to be reborn, and thus to renew its fidelity to its charism?

---

53  J. C. Futrell, *Making an Apostolic Community of Love*, p. 14.

> **Example:** *The current Jesuit General, following on a communal discernment process across the Order, announced four apostolic preferences which are to shape its work from 2019–2029.*
> *They are:*
>
> *1. Showing the way to God through Discernment and the Spiritual Exercises*
> *2. Walking with the Excluded*
> *3. Journeying with Youth*
> *4. Caring for Our Common Home*

### *How can we respond to this call?'*

When the group believes it understands better *Who* it is, and *What* it now needs to do, it moves to *How* to do it. What concrete means are needed in terms of persons, collaboration, finances, structures, methods, agenda, material, modes of communication …? The Jesuit Order is steadily working on *What* it is challenged to do, but not without hiccups! This is where regular group review becomes so important.

When there is disagreement about the concrete means to be implemented (*How*), it is appropriate to build on the consensus at the level of the call (*What*), or fundamentally at the level of identity (*Who*). If a struggling group has all the signs of having been formed in response to a call from God, it will be consoled to realise that a radical consensus still holds, but perhaps at a deeper level than it had imagined or hoped.

Of the three levels, the *Who* is the most intimate, and the *How* is the most external and concrete. '*How* to respond to this call?' is a form of INCARNATION of the fundamental level, '*Who* are we?' and it passes through the intermediate level, '*What* are we called to?'

The word 'incarnation' is chosen deliberately: the project of the divine Persons (the *Who*) became incarnate when, moved by compassion for humankind (the *What*), they decided that the Son would become flesh (the *How*) (Cf. *Spiritual Exercises*, 101). The Trinity might be imagined as using the Energy Cycle!

At each level of questioning, it is possible to evaluate past action, make recommendations and take decisions for future action. Renewable energy is the key requirement here!

The three levels of questioning and consensus are inseparable from each other. Their boundaries are porous. We discover '*Who* we are' by discovering '*What* we are called to' and '*How* to respond to that call'.[54]

## The 'Life–Death–Resurrection' cycle

All groups go through ups and downs. Questioning occurs, which may bring them to more life or may lead to decline and death. Given the right insights and the needed resources, resurrection may occur because the Spirit, 'the Lord and Giver of Life', invites us to 'Choose life!' (Dt 30:19). It can help to keep in mind the decline of the Church prior to Vatican II, followed by renewal and aggiornamento, and now, in our challenging times, the papal call to renewal carried by synodality. Life, death and resurrection are interlinked and cyclical. We oscillate between the pain of Good Friday, the emptiness of Holy Saturday and the surprised joy of Easter Sunday.

## Consensus

Consensus within a group can be questioned at three different levels: '*Who* are we?', '*What* are we called to?' and '*How* do we respond to this call?

- **Who?** Energy was generated when a few individuals got together for a common purpose and after some shared action paused to re-read that action together. Out of this they managed to formulate an identity for their group, the grace of its foundation (the *Who*), its call and mission (the *What*), and the concrete means to respond to it: teams, finances, structures, mode of governance ... (the *How*). Agreement at these three levels gives the group ever more energy and consolation.

---

54 The interaction between these three levels of questioning and consensus can be illustrated by the experience of the Esdac team: by acting together, by proactively offering Workshops (HOW), the pioneering team received a grace of communion (WHO) and felt called (WHAT) to share with others the communion they were experiencing among themselves.

- **How?** When problems, questions and conflicts arise, this often concerns the *How*. The group then moves to the downward part of the curve; it feels desolate and loses energy. In the discernment it is therefore necessary to agree together to let go of some of the means that formerly enabled the group to achieve its goals. They must see that attachment to those means today constricts their freedom to respond to God's calling. While this 'letting go' is a form of death, it is also a promise of resurrection.

  Jesus warns against using as means **wealth** (Lk 16:13), **power** and the **esteem** of others (Mk 10:41–45 and *Spiritual Exercises*, 142). Why? Any means that ensure comfort, ease, success and notoriety will gradually blind us to the situation of our fellow human beings who, at the door of our homes, are in situations of poverty and injustice unworthy of human beings (see Lk 16:19–31). Then there is no one who looks out for Wolf, or if there is, such a prophet becomes marginalised.

  It may be that the required adjustments are only about the *How*. If the group then develops recommendations and ensures that appropriate decisions are made and effectively followed up in action, it will be reborn, and move towards resurrection. Its energy will grow again.

- **What?** When the group has difficulty in reaching agreement on the *How*, Spirit-led conversations about the *What* should take place: 'Do we all agree on the Lord's call to us today?' If there is high consensus at this level, the group will be strengthened by this recognition of fellowship, and will experience consolation. It will find the energy and courage necessary to face the questioning caused by differences of views or by attachments at the level of means.

When questioning persists, it is advisable, in an atmosphere of prayer, calm and positivity, to discuss the primordial agreement which has been the basis of living together: '*Who* are we? Are we still called to unite our destinies?' The assessment made at this level of *Who* will be followed either by recommendations and decisions for resurrection, or by a conscious and reflective entry into the end of life and an irretrievable declaration of termination or completion, as illustrated in Ted Dunn's book already cited.

Why did the group come to question itself? Because things have changed either in the group *environment,* (the surrounding culture, the population, the standard of living, etc.) and/or the *internal composition* of the group – old members have left or died: no new ones have arrived, or if they have, new ideas and behaviour have appeared, etc. The means appropriately chosen in the past are out of place today.

This was an ongoing issue for Pedro Arrupe in leading the Jesuit Order after Vatican II: he used to warn that a recipe for irrelevance was to offer yesterday's answers to today's questions. In the middle of the chaos of saying goodbye to the past and searching for the new, he was frequently asked, 'Where is the Society going?' With a twinkle in his eye he would respond: 'I don't know, but I do know one thing, that God is taking us somewhere; we are travelling safely, with the Church that is guided by the Holy Spirit ... Our job is to follow!'[55] But this trust was based on divine fidelity, which led to another question, 'But does God know where he's going himself?'

In the case of a couple it may be that the partners are no longer called to live together: after consultation, it may emerge that the partnership is no longer a source of grace for one or both, or the physical or psychological integrity of one or both members may be seriously threatened.

---

55  Grogan, *Arrupe*, p. 87.

- *Appropriate change is the sign of true life in a group*
- *'Let God amaze us by his creativity!' – Pope Francis*
- *Change brings conversion and new life, but also death to the old ways*
- *We can interpret our changing situation through the cycle of Life, Death and Resurrection*
- *Consensus can be questioned at three levels: 'Who are we?', 'What are we called to?' and 'How do we respond to this call*
- *Chaos has its place: 'We must believe that God is taking us somewhere'! – Arrrupe*

# Part Three: Consensus

## Fostering Consensus on Who We Are

In this and the following chapter are exercises to strengthen each of the three aspects of consensus, so far as they exist. We begin by exploring *Who* we are.

*The founding experience of the group*
Telling each other personal stories and reviewing the history of the group is invigorating. In the context of the founding stories, current personal experiences are given light and breath, while the founding stories are given deeper meaning. The group appropriates these stories and makes them relevant and current, beyond their older style and vocabulary. Awareness of the origins brings out the originality of today's experience: a bridge is built between past and present.

God's grace for the group becomes clearer, because the radical energy in the group is freed from its non-essential cultural forms. But the new challenges can be so radical as to shake its very foundations. Treasured images and securities may crumble. This is the case when negative but hidden elements of a founder's history are revealed, or when early episodes previously considered unimportant are suddenly revealed as essential.

*Re-founding*: This new situation is sometimes referred to as re-founding the group. This does not mean that the group had been badly founded but that in the course of the Spirit-led conversations that punctuate a common discernment, the germinal grace of the group is revealed anew and can manifest its fruitfulness again.

*Experience:* Over time, interpretations of the founding stories and of constitutive documents diverge. What should be done then? It is unhelpful, at least in the first instance, to try to make a correct exegesis of the founding texts or the charter, because this would provoke a debate of *ideas*. Rather, the focus must be on *experience* since it is not in ideas disconnected from reality that consensus is hidden, but in experience. If people remain together, it is because an experience has united them and keeps them together. What must be shared is this experience that, even now, gives life, energises and mobilises the members. The authority of experience is strong. Eliot's line, quoted above – 'We had the experience but missed the meaning' – can strengthen our efforts to see where we are now.

Each person is rich in the gift they have received. The experience that energises the group is first and foremost that which each person is living today rather than that of the founder. Recall the challenge to witness to 'the good news *in the present tense*'. If the experiences of each person refer to that of the founder, this common reference is the source of their agreement, and gains from being reactivated.

## *Sharing our desires and dreams*

As we saw, fundamental human longings, aspirations (or vital thirsts, needs, dreams and desires) mobilise and set a group in motion. Every future action is motivated by a basic human aspiration, and every past action has also been motivated by such an aspiration.

It is fruitful, at the beginning of a Workshop, to ask the participants to name their thirsts, needs, dreams and desires, whether at the level of their life in general or, more specifically, at the level of the discernment process they are undertaking. This makes it possible to reach each person at the most intimate level. Psalm 63 can help at this point: 'O God, you are my God; I seek you, my soul thirsts for you, my flesh faints for you …!'

There is a great temptation to repress our desires, to censor them, often unconsciously, because we know that they contain elements of illusion; they appear utopian and over-ambitious; they are scary and threaten our comfort zone. But God has no other resource at his disposal in order to fulfil us than to arouse desires in us. As Saint Therese of the Child Jesus wrote: 'The Lord made me *desire* what he wanted to give me'. And as a convalescent at Loyola, Ignatius was daydreaming and he noticed that one of his daydreams gave him lasting joy. This realisation transformed his life. Martin Luther King's famous phrase was: 'I have a dream'. The wise saying: 'You will never realise the dreams you have not allowed yourself to have', could also be invoked.

➢ *Prayer Sheet 6: My deepest desires and dreams*
➢ *Prayer Sheet 7: My deep experiences of God*

Our history reflects how far our deepest dreams and aspirations have been fulfilled.

The sharing that follows the times of prayer and reflection nourished by these exercises helps the members of the group to get to know each other in depth and to respect their differences.

### *The personal 'name of grace'*

This exercise, devoted to the formulation of the personal 'name of grace' given to individuals and groups, pursues the same goal.[56]

Appendix One below indicates the journeys of various groups which either implicitly or explicitly refer to their 'name of grace'.

We use the term 'name of grace' to express the charism, the spiritual identity, the reason for being – raison d'etre – of each human person, when they have opened up to divine grace and allowed themselves to be guided by the Holy Spirit. Jesus is named 'Beloved Son' by the Father; St John speaks of the 'Beloved disciple'. St Francis of Assisi is known as 'the poor boy' – *'Il poverello'*. This is his name of grace. It is linked to his conversion: he became 'the little poor one' when, against all that had hitherto satisfied his senses in a selfish way, he gave a kiss to a leper and put on a beggar's clothes. He then allowed himself to be led by divine grace.[57]

---

56 See J. A. Borbely and others, *Focusing Group Energies*, p. 23; Herbert Alfonso SJ, *Discovering Your Personal Vocation: The Search for Meaning through the Spiritual Exercises*; Viktor Frankl, *Man's Search for Meaning.*
57 Examples of names of grace are: 'Child of God', 'Communion', 'Trust', 'I am with you', 'Patient love', 'Unconditional acceptance', 'Abide in my love', 'Simply gift', 'Divine goodness'. Thus, the name of grace can express the one who is called, as in the case of the 'Child of God';

Exchanges between the members about their names of grace help them to reveal and respect the identity of each other. A powerful experience of God, a spiritual event that gives meaning and direction to one's personal existence, is not just a private matter. It is a gift, a grace at the service of the community, of the couple, or of the body to which one belongs.

The name of grace becomes a touchstone against which to evaluate a proposed decision; it allows me to discern an issue quickly by asking myself the question: 'Is this option in harmony with my name of grace, that is to say, with my deepest and truest self?'

A group will be all the more alive if its members seek to act in accordance with their own name of grace and that of the others. It is the Spirit who enables this, for it is the same Spirit who dwells and acts in all. 'I have called you by name, you are mine' (Is 43:2).

Knowing one's name of grace well allows each person to remain profoundly themselves, different from the others, while being intimately united to them. In order to become more and more themselves, each will have to become free from a false, aggressive or depressive 'self', eager for the recognition of others. Each of us needs to face our fears, temper our excesses, tame the shadow and unloved side of ourselves. In a word, we will have to be converted.

➤ *Prayer Sheet 8: My name of grace*

### The 'name of grace' of the group

Like any person, a group also has a 'name of grace' that specifies its identity when it has reoriented itself towards God and opened itself to divine grace. This name also refers to its purpose and mission, if it hopes to remain together.

The members may feel clearly called by God to be one, to unite their individual destinies. This conviction underpins the energy and potential of the group. Its members experience being 'put together', as receiving a gift of the Holy Spirit, a grace, a name unique to their

---

or it can express the one who calls, i.e. God, named 'Patient love', 'Divine Goodness' and so forth. The name of grace can also be a biblical mystery such as the Incarnation, the Visitation … In the Irish language the term *'Duine le Dia'* is the name of grace for a person with profound intellectual difficulties. It means 'one who belongs to God'.

group. If they do decide to stay together, to live a common history, it is because they have experienced that the more they welcome this grace, the more they find themselves united, while being respected and even strengthened in their individuality.

A particular grace shapes the essence of a group.

Examples:

1. The name of grace given to the early disciples in Antioch was 'Christians' (Acts 11:26).
2. The name of grace of the monks of Tibhirine in Algeria can be considered to be: *'Christian men of prayer among Muslim men of prayer'*. You will find on page 223 the account of the process that led to this formulation. The 2010 film, *Of Gods and Men,* is based on the final stage of the monks' lives before their massacre in 1996.
3. On page 234 is the report of the Esdac team that accompanied the discernment of the name of grace of CLC (Christian Life Community) in 2018 in Buenos Aires. The three key words were *'Deepen – Share – Go out'.*
4. Some organisations formulate their name of grace under the terms of their Vision Statement, as in the following instances:
   - *'Making disciples who live out their mission with joy'*
   - *'Loving God, loving others and making disciples'*
   - *'Taking part in the re-evangelisation of nations and the transformation of society'*
   - (Among Jesuit educators): Men and women with and for others
   - (Across the Society of Jesus) see the four Apostolic Preferences mentioned above.
   - The identity of a group does not lie in written documents such as the Bible, Constitutions, Charter or Rule but in what is lived by the members. The Spirit-led conversation about these experiences develops a common feeling, a common language, a common culture, often even an in-house jargon!

## Part Three: Consensus

➤ *Prayer Sheet 15: The name of grace of the group*

- *The group is enriched by reviewing its founding experience*
- *Living experience is what counts: no war stories*
- *Desires and dreams carry great energy. When you cease to dream …?*
- *The name of grace of the group and its individual members expresses their raison d'etre and their call*

# The History Line Deepens Consensus on Who We Are

*The History Line itself*
The History Line is the group-history as told by the members and recorded on a long strip of paper with appropriate dates, where all can view it.[58] Sharing this history together is often a prerequisite for any discernment aimed at the group's future. Why is this? Because the common history sticks to the skin, motivates us from within, but if ignored will act on the group in an unconscious, unmotivating, anarchic or even sometimes destructive way.

The objectives of the following exercises on the History Line are:

- To share the great story.
- To recognise together the action of the Holy Spirit in the history of the group, giving thanks for what has thus far been brought into line with the divine action.
- To recognise together what *has not* been adjusted to the action of the Spirit, and to be open to God's forgiveness and mercy, which is always unconditional, undeserved and liberating. This leads to engagement in healing and reconciliation among members.
- To help each member to recognise their personal complicity with the 'collective sin' of the group, parallel to what the Lord is saying about the Churches (see Rev ch 2–3).
- To encourage the integration of new members who will learn from the group's past.
- To keep alive the unique grace of this group, its 'name of grace'.
- To help members to listen to the Lord's call to the group today, because the ongoing call is rooted in its past history.

---

58  Cf. John English SJ, *Spiritual Intimacy and Community: Ignatian View of the Small Faith Community*, pp. 59–89.

*Part Three: Consensus*

The line can begin with the date when the oldest member joined the group and can end in the present. However, it is important to leave room for milestones that preceded the first date and those that are in progress today or already planned for the near future. Example:

| 1985 | 1990 | 1995 | 2000 | 2005 |
|------|------|------|------|------|
| 2010 | 2015 | 2020 | 2025 | 2030 |

History Line exercises require time! The times and prayer sheets should be adjusted to the concrete situation of the requesting group, while keeping the sequence of events, feelings, graces received and resisted, and the celebration of mercy.

To detect the most important events in our history we begin with prayer:

➢ *Prayer Sheet 9: The story of our group: its events*

The following points are important:

- It is crucial to formulate the historical events in a way that is free from interpretation and judgement. Whether in personal reflection and prayer or in small group sharing, dissociating the event from accusatory thoughts or from a happy experience requires careful attention. Example: 'We closed a school in 1974' – Omit 'This was good/bad'.
- It is not a question of consulting diaries or archives: the most significant events are those that have remained vivid in group memory, because they have aroused strong feelings, whether pleasant or otherwise.
- The more that confidence has been generated through Spirit-led conversation, the more we will dare to speak to each other in truth and avoid the unspoken.
- If the facilitators are aware of important and painful events in the life of the group, it is best to let the participants relate these events themselves, first in the small groups, then in the plenary.

- When there are several small groups, in order to avoid confusion, ask that each small group reports to the plenary only three or four events they consider to be the most important. Making this choice together is an important step in joint discernment.

*Plenary*
- Each small group puts its points on the History Line. There is no need to be afraid of repetition, as this focuses attention on the essential.
- The participants are then invited to break up from their groups and to form pairs or threes (triads) in order to talk about the facts displayed on the history sheet: 'Are any missing? Which are the most important?' When these buzz groups end, a plenary Spirit-led conversation ensues; the symbol is passed from hand to hand. What is most important in this is not what is written, but what is happening between the participants.

*Expressing feelings about events on the History Line*
The exercise begins with a prayer sheet:

➤ *Prayer Sheet 10: The story of our group: the feelings*

Through the Prayer Sheet we gain courage:

- To dare to express to each other the feelings (emotions, sentiments, sensations, consolations, desolations) that currently affect the members of the group and that have coloured it in the past.
- To associate with these feelings the vital human needs, both met and unmet, such as love, communion, truth, respect, compassion etc.
- To take account of cultural differences: a brief statement on feelings may help, because expressing emotions is sometimes seen as a sign of weakness. Many participants are very judgmental about their feelings and sometimes cannot find the words to express them. They find it difficult to show their vulnerability. Often tensions and anger are brewing.
- To indicate the link between a feeling and a fundamental human aspiration. A painful feeling is a sign of an unfulfilled basic human

longing. What was it? Was it in the direction of more life to be given, to be received? The experience of the disciples on the road to Emmaus (Lk 24:21) can be evoked here: sad of heart they explain to the stranger who has joined them that they had a great desire or aspiration that was disappointed …
- At the appropriate moment, reference will be made to the guidelines for distinguishing the differing spirits at play (p. 130).

## *Plenary at the end of the prayer-time*

It helps to distribute three post-it notes of one colour (green) to each member of the group, and three others of another colour (red). The instruction could be, for example: 'On each green post-it, you indicate a pleasant feeling (joy, peace …) linked to an event that you consider to be important. Only one word per post-it. On each red post-it note, you indicate an unpleasant feeling (sadness, anger …) linked to an event that you consider significant.

Then everyone sticks their post-its next to the events concerned and reads them out aloud. Alternatively, groups of ten can be invited to come and silently stick their post-its next to the relevant events. When all are posted, the facilitators read them out aloud.

Then all silently contemplate what is in front of them. After a few minutes, the participants break into pairs or threes to share what they have observed and felt.

After five minutes, the facilitators invite them to share the fruit of these conversations, taking care to link the feelings expressed with the vital desires (fulfilled or not fulfilled) that they indicate. In explaining the purpose of the re-reading, point out that a feeling is like a pilot light that draws attention to a vital need (p. 68).

## *Points to watch out for in Plenaries*

- The aim of the plenary is not to write the exhaustive history of the group and its feelings, nor to find the perfect formulation of it. What is posted on the history line is only a support, a reminder of the story. What is essential is what is alive within the group. It is the quality of the exchanges that binds the group as a whole and helps it to become more truly a free subject of its own history.

- It is essential to be truly present to the person speaking and the group listening. The tone of voice, facial expression and silences may reveal more than the words. Respectful (or 'cardiac') listening will be the most important fruit of these time-consuming exercises.
- Tactful accompaniment will allow each person to dare to express what is most sensitive for them. This is not past history, but a set of events whose emotional impact they feel today.
- Personal prayer and sharing, in small groups and in plenary, give the opportunity for the feelings experienced to evolve in the course of the exercise. The disciples on the road to Emmaus, in conversation with the Risen One, moved from despair to experiencing 'burning hearts' (Lk 24:21, 32). Accompaniment should take care to identify this development, because it is the work of the Spirit. Pointing it out to the group provides a source of confidence to the faint-hearted to dare to go all the way in sharing about events that have caused suffering.
- The painful events should not be dwelt upon too long, lest some people develop a victim status. *The Spirit acts to heal here and now.*
- The expression of the unspoken will be encouraged. Ignatius notes that 'the enemy of human nature would like to remain secret' (*Spiritual Exercises*, 326). To dare to say what we think, and sometimes even to dare to think it, requires boldness. The gap between our deepest desires and our concrete achievements is frightening. We are not proud of this, and as a result this gap may not emerge in the group's consciousness but remain unspoken. This can cause subterranean discomfort, resentment, aggression and malaise, without anyone being able to name its source.
- When a negative remark is uttered, it should be delicately rephrased in words that do not condemn anyone, i.e. in terms of unfulfilled life desires. Examples of such desires are respect, freedom, cooperation, justice, dignity (see p. 68).
- At the end of the plenary or within it, a body exercise, or even a dance step, can enable tensions to be released in ways other than words.

It is important for the facilitators to continue with the History Line exercises if it seems that not everything has yet been said. Else what has not been expressed may not emerge later, or may do so in inappropriate ways. Offering time for further exchange will allow the pressure to be released little by little.

### Acknowledging the graces well received and those resisted

Starting from the History Line as it has been experienced up to now and which should be kept in view, the group can become aware of the graces that have been offered to them by the Lord: on the one hand, those that they have welcomed, and on the other, those that they have neglected or resisted.

The group can first name the graces they have received.

➤ *Prayer Sheet 11: The graces embraced in our history* can be used.

It is important to devote enough time to this exercise (for example, one hour for personal prayer, one hour for group sharing, and finally one hour in plenary). This exercise is essential because enables the members to realise that God was never absent in the history of the group, but was on the contrary very present, even in its difficult moments. This stage leads to thanksgiving to the Lord, gives the group more confidence and helps it to be better guided in the future. During this plenary, the graces embraced by the group are listed on a large sheet of paper or a board visible to all.

When the group has become aware that the Lord is walking with them and taking care of them, they are no longer afraid to face up to the resistance they have mounted against the divine action. This is very important because if the group does not become aware of these resistances, they are likely to resurface later on. For example, an Esdac team facilitated a group that distributed to its members a sheet of paper on which they kept a record of their resistance, in order to help them overcome it through a regular review exercise.

➤ With the History Line always in view, the group can now name the graces they have resisted.
➤ *Prayer Sheet 12: The graces resisted in our history* can be used.

In the plenary, the graces resisted will be collated on a large sheet of paper or on a board visible to all. The facilitators will be alert to check that everything has been said, not hesitating to ask if there are still things to be said by someone: then comes a time of silent reflection on them, and lastly a Spirit-led conversation.

This work can lead to a rich discovery, namely how the Lord acts in a very particular way with this group. Indeed, the Lord acts with each person and with each group both in a personalised way and also with constant graces. *Grace comes tailor-made*! For example, one group was able to see, when faced with the History Line, that every moment of serious difficulty was followed by a moment when the Lord gave himself to the group in a new way; this group became experientially aware that the passage from 'death' to 'resurrection' was not a mere idea but was a real movement in its experience.

If it seems appropriate and time allows,

➢ *Prayer Sheet 13: Evil is at work in our broken world* can be suggested.

This exercise brings the participants face to face with the collective and universal reality of evil at work in the world. This corresponds to the Spiritual Exercises, where St Ignatius proposes a meditation on sin as a reality operating in the world, even before we are part of that world (*Spiritual Exercises*, 45–54). Then he asks us to look at our own history and our personal resistance to grace (*Spiritual Exercises*, 55–61).

## Celebration of mercy

How can the facilitators sense that the time has come to introduce the community celebration of mercy?

At the end of the plenaries on the graces received and those resisted, each person could take a personal time of prayer in front of the History Line, asking themselves if they feel a perceptible sense of relief or of completion within the group. This relief must be experienced as a grace received from God and not as an opportunity to avoid the suffering of piercing a painful abscess.

It will also be possible to discern whether

- the 'old stories', the accumulated resentments, have been brought to light and placed in the hands of the Lord;
- the members are ready to forgive each other for their mistakes;

- The group recognises that it is wanted by God, that it has been pardoned, forgiven, freed from its shackles, and called to move towards more life and to enable that life to shine through;
- There is a more refined knowledge of the limits and vulnerable points of each person and of the group as such;
- The group experiences joy and gratitude in welcoming life for itself and the unconditional love of God and others.

➤ If possible, start with a time of personal prayer using *Prayer Sheet 14: I am complicit in the failures of my group.*

In the text of this Sheet, the prodigal son says to his father: 'I have sinned against heaven and against you' (Lk 15:21). With some groups, it may be useful to clarify that 'heaven' refers to God, and to clarify the notion of sin by distinguishing it from moral fault. 'Misguided love' may be more acceptable than the term 'sin'.

The awareness of sin implies faith in God and in God's gracious forgiveness.

The marvelous Ignatian cry of wonder can help here.

'This is a cry of wonder accompanied by surging emotion as I pass in review all creatures. How is it that they have permitted me to live, and have sustained me in life! Why have the angels, though they are the swords of God's justice, tolerated me, guarded me and prayed for me! Why have the saints interceded for me and asked favours for me! And the heavens, sun, moon, stars, and the elements; the fruits, birds, fishes, and other animals – why have they all been at my service! ... I will conclude with a colloquy (a Spirit-led conversation), extolling the mercy of God, pouring out my thoughts to him, and giving thanks to him that up to this moment he has granted me life. I will resolve with his grace to amend for the future' (*Spiritual Exercises*, 60; *Ivens*).

## *The celebration of mercy*

There will be no small groupings on the day. The atmosphere in the house should remain quiet during the preparation of the celebration of mercy, which may take up to half a day.

A variety of gestures may be chosen, such as the following:

- Identify or construct a symbolic object, allowing a word or song to rise in one's heart;
- Invent a gesture which in the celebration will help to express, even without words, the paralysis from which the Lord frees us;
- Go and find a person with whom you are in conflict and be reconciled with them. 'Leave your offering and go and be reconciled first' (Mt 5:24);
- Write a letter to send to a person with whom you wish to be reconciled;
- Take time for prayer for the others;
- Receive the Sacrament of Reconciliation, or a counselling session.

For the communal celebration of mercy and reconciliation, the facilitators will be creative in finding signs, symbols, and a process that will speak for itself. The primary goal here is not to receive the sacrament of forgiveness personally but *to welcome God who regenerates the bonds within the group.*

The facilitators might say: 'We will celebrate the path we have travelled, which is a gift from God. We must remain simple, humble and realistic. There is no such thing as perfect reconciliation, so we cannot simply decide that on such and such a day everyone will be reconciled. The rhythm is not the same for everyone. Mercy offers a path, a state of mind that is constantly being taken up. Even in the best retreat not everything is said, not everything is erased. The demons are not completely removed, the weaknesses of each person remain. Above all else then, we celebrate the goodness of God who walks with us and entrusts us with a common mission without expecting us to be perfect.'[59]

---

59 In terms of the Spiritual Exercises, this brings the First Week to a close.

- *Reviewing the History Line can motivate us as it did for the Hebrews*
- *When starting, name events without interpreting them. 'We closed a great parish!'*
- *The feelings in a past event – as in the Emmaus story – can colour the present*
- *The Spirit will be working to heal past hurts in the here and now*
- *We are 'wayward beloveds', with our history of grace received and resisted*
- *Be merciful as God is*
- *Work through disharmony: let nothing fester. God will be close at hand to help*

# Fostering Consensus on What We Are Called to Do

The question 'What are we called to?' reflects the Second Week of the Exercises. It can be asked at different times, such as:

- When a group, during or after Spirit-led conversations, asks, 'What consequences are demanded from what we have just shared? Do our exchanges change the way we conceive or formulate our identity and the way we embody it?
- When a group systematically goes through the Energy Cycle, and after evaluating its past action, arrives at recommendations for the future;
- When a group has done the History Line exercise, has celebrated mercy and feels urged onto a path of conversion, of rebirth;
- When a group has clarified its name of grace and seeks to better embody it.

Here are four responses of groups that have asked themselves the question: **'What are we called to'?** (Details are in App. 4)

- **The Founding Jesuits 1539:** When the small group around Ignatius asked itself, 'To what are we called?' it did not take long for their discernment to conclude with the answer: 'We are called to be an apostolic body that lasts in time'.

    This answer helped them to clearly formulate a second question which required another level of consensus and a much longer period of discernment, prayer, reflection and exchange: '**HOW** can we become a body? Is it by becoming a religious order, i.e. by obeying a member of the group, or by some other way?'
- **A Global Congregation:** A religious congregation with some 500 members in 10 different countries realised that they no longer had

sufficient sisters to take on the demands of Leadership. Further, given their demographic situation and their geographical locations, their traditional division into Provinces and Regions could even lead to a fragmentation that would be detrimental to their unity. To the question '**To WHAT are we called?**', they answered '*To move from the "I" to the "We"*', that is, to practise Spirit-led conversation in all their exchanges, both within the congregation and in their outside relations. To make this transition, deliberations in the General Chapter were necessary at the level of the '**HOW**', i.e. at the level of the structures of governance and the concrete means by which each sister could become more co-responsible for the internal life of the congregation as well as for its mission outside.

- **Rwandan Sisters:** After the Rwandan massacre and within the non-threatening framework of a spiritual retreat, a group of Sisters learned to practise Spirit-led conversation among themselves and engaged in the History Line. They then felt called to share with others the benefits of *'speaking truthfully, in Christ'*. This became their 'name of grace'.
- **Jesuits Today 2019–2029:** As noted above, the Jesuits recently carried out a broad discernment, engaging all members, in order to specify the Society's *'Universal Apostolic Preferences'*. They are

  - *To show the way to God through the Spiritual Exercises and discernment;*
  - *To walk with the poor, the outcasts of the world, those whose dignity has been violated, in a mission of reconciliation and justice;*
  - *To accompany young people in the creation of a hope-filled future;*
  - *To collaborate in the care of our Common Home.*

These guidelines describe **WHAT** the Society is called to do until 2029, but do not specify **HOW** to respond to this call. In confirming these apostolic preferences Pope Francis notes that the preference for the Spiritual Exercises and discernment 'is fundamental, since it presupposes the Jesuit's relationship with the Lord in a life of prayer, and in personal and community discernment'.

The following four exercises are intended to help a group to discern little by little **WHAT** the Lord is calling them to.

*Christ's call to the world and to each individual*
➢ Prayer Sheet 16: *Christ's call to the world and to each individual* can be used

This exercise aims to make the group available to what Ignatius names as the Lord's call 'to the whole world and to each individual' (*Spiritual Exercises*, 95).

Whatever the particularities of a group, it is called to follow Jesus 'for better or for worse', by the path that he first traced – the offering of his life in humble service to his sisters and brothers (Jn 13:1–17).

The consensus desired and requested by the members of the group is 'not to be deaf to the Lord's call, but to be prompt and diligent in carrying out his most holy will' (*Spiritual Exercises*, 91). No matter **WHAT** the Lord is specifically calling the group to do, it needs the grace to respond unconditionally.

*The Incarnation*
➢ Prayer Sheet 17: *The Incarnation* can be used.

This exercise prepares the incarnation of the group's name of grace in the concreteness of human history. The word 'incarnation' is appropriate: it reminds us that the eternal plan of love of the divine Persons (Eph 1:3–14) took shape at a decisive moment in human history; when 'the fullness of time had come' (Gal 4:4) the Son took on human flesh.

Contemplation of the Incarnation reveals **WHAT** the Son was called to – poverty and humility – and **HOW** the same Son of God became incarnate in history, in the choice to become a tiny, fragile, vulnerable baby.

Thus, Incarnation is not the act of an all-powerful God who comes to bring his solid identity and strength to the world: it is the risk that a vulnerable God takes to allow himself to be changed by the world. He enters into its chaos because he loves it; he enters the world without dominating or eliminating but transforming that chaos. He allows himself to be affected by it, even up to and including the Cross.

To be incarnated ourselves is therefore, in our turn, to be converted to others out of love. Intimacy with the other opens up new spaces in us. We open ourselves to the truth that comes to us and to a world where

God is active and busily at work. We inhabit a graced world already. We can only bring something to it if we allow it to bring us much.

Jesus is a man born of a woman and of the love of the Father for us all. He chose to come into the womb of a woman and to live fully the human condition; that is, his love became concrete in the body, hands and head of a human being. God's love now needs human hands and hearts in order to manifest itself in the chaos of our times. In the same way, the renewal of an organisation evokes a rebirth, something that is often painful.

If time permits it will be good to devote more time to this stage of discernment by proposing other contemplations of the hidden life of the Lord: the visitation, the nativity, the coming of the shepherds ... as presented in the Spiritual Exercises.

### *The external and internal context of the group (SWOT analysis)*
➤ *Prayer Sheet 18: Internal Strengths and Weaknesses / External Opportunities and Threats* can be used.

The decision on the Incarnation is made by the divine Persons when they look at the surface of the world, filled with human beings, and see them descending into that place of non-life and non-love which is the hell of hatred and meaninglessness (*Spiritual Exercises*, 102). In light of this, the group in turn is called to look at today's reality and to become incarnated in it in order to collaborate, with divine grace, in liberating the divine life and love hidden in the world.

This requires two types of analysis:

- **An external analysis** that examines the reality *within which* the group finds itself in the twenty-first century: the signs of the times, the needs of the world, the state of the Church, emerging trends, the body to which the group belongs, networks, partnerships, controversial issues...
- **An internal analysis** which looks at the reality *within* the group itself: the general mood, action reports, evaluations, statistics on the number and age of members, the mode of governance, the state of the finances ...

For this exercise, in addition to prayer sheets for meditation, reflection and Spirit-led conversation, participants must have access to all essential data, which should be provided while ensuring both transparency and discretion.

> ➤ *Prayer Sheet 18: Internal Strengths and Weaknesses / External Opportunities and Threats* enables the external reality check to be done.

The value of this process is that it relates the internal life of the group to the cries of the poor and of our wounded creation.

When everyone has filled out the chart, the small groups meet to share, after which they are invited to share in plenary the two or three most important points from each of the four boxes on the sheet.

## *The Lord's call to our group*
> ➤ *Prayer Sheet 19: The Lord's call to our group* can be used.

The word 'call' deserves attention. For example, when a person says that they feel 'called' to help migrants, they are indicating that something is urging them from within to take on this kind of commitment, as responding to one or more of their deepest human aspirations, such as a passion for justice or a thirst to collaborate for the well-being of others.

As we saw, our deepest human aspirations and longings mobilise our most vital energies and reflect the desires that the Holy Spirit imprints on our hearts. Often there is little or no awareness of this in the mind of those who feel 'called' to engage in mercy work. And yet, when they take time out to put themselves in silent relationship with their Lord in prayer, they often realise that it is he, the Lord of the universe, who is calling them in the depths of their soul, and calling them by the name that is proper to them: their name of grace.

In the discerning group, all are now invited, in silent prayer, to look for **WHAT** the Lord is calling the group to. In the small group sharing, it will become apparent that people may feel different personal calls. Some of these calls coincide, others do not. Some are concrete and detailed, others are more general. It can also happen that what has been felt as a call may be discerned as resulting from an attachment that restricts inner freedom. Spirit-led conversation in small groups and in plenary, informed by distinguishing the spirits at work, is about identifying true calls, then those which are more important and, of these, which is the most important.

When the group has difficulty discerning what the Lord really wants from them, they can be invited to imagine Jesus coming into the plenary room and, after listening to each person, affirm, '**This is what I want from you.**' This makes the Lord's call powerful and dynamic: 'I am calling you to … and/or sending you …' In many cases, this call is so compelling that the group chooses to recall it regularly. For example, one international congregation printed this call on a leaflet so that each sister could have it in front of her and use it for her personal and community re-reading.

When the members have discerned **WHAT** the Lord is calling them to, they are often full of vitality and want to move on quickly to discern **HOW** to respond to the call. However such a rapid move risks depriving the group of a time of gratitude, celebration and deepening of the consolation received. Instead, what has been given should be tasted and savoured, so that the soul is satisfied (*Spiritual Exercises*, 2). Planning an outing together, a break, a vigil, is beneficial and avoids losing the climate of consolation which, at this stage of discernment, is necessary, because the work that remains to be done requires considerable energy and sacrifice. The temptation to consider that the essential work has already been done is not from the good spirit. It is also the case that if the group does not take the time to set specific objectives and an implementation/action plan it will remain in a state of inertia.

### *Three good moments to make a decision*

Ignatius distinguishes three moments within which it is possible to make a good decision. The first time is immediate; the other two are long-term. Here we focus on group decisions.

- FIRST MOMENT (*Spiritual Exercises*, 175). It could be that the Lord's call is so clear and obvious to all that the decision falls like a ripe fruit, without anyone questioning its correctness. For Matthew and Paul, there was no hesitation; likewise the apostolic group at Pentecost, without consulting each other, addressed the crowd immediately (Acts 2:1–5).

Some commentators say that this First Moment, where God's will for the group is revealed immediately, is less rare than we usually think.

- SECOND MOMENT (*Spiritual Exercises*, 176). Following personal prayer times and exchanges in small groups and in plenary, the call to the group becomes sufficiently clear through the alternation of consolations and desolations and through the awareness of thoughts that promote or thwart the vital energy (élan vital) of the group. This happened to the two disciples on their way to Emmaus; after an experience during which their hearts had time to change from sadness to joy, they decided to return to Jerusalem (Lk 24:17–32).

  This is an eventful time, where the progressive awareness of different feelings allows a group to make its way forward in discovering the Lord's call.

  In the Second Moment, as in the first, it is again the breath of the Holy Spirit that guides each person and the group as a whole. The Spirit's action is recognised through the consolations and desolations experienced.

- THIRD MOMENT (*Spiritual Exercises*, 177–188). Perhaps no consensus emerges after a certain period of time; the hearts of the members are very quiet, without the alternations of the consolation/desolation which characterises the second stage, or without these alternations providing sufficient indications to reach a consensus. It is then advisable to systematically weigh together the elements that tip the balance to one side rather than the other. The first Jesuits were faced with a dilemma: 'In order to respond to the Lord's call, is it better for our group to adopt a structure recognised by the Church, or not?' The process is to work together prayerfully to become free regarding both options, so that only the touch of the Spirit will tip the balance and not illusory attractions (*Spiritual Exercises*, 15 and 179). In 1540, when the pope – after much debate – approved the founding Jesuits, he said, 'The finger of God is here!'

## *For and against*

A simple strategy for a divided group to come to consensus is to get everyone, including the diehards, to collaborate in writing up all the arguments they can imagine in favour of the proposed decision. They do the same with the arguments against it. Then everyone takes time to pray, in the group or otherwise, while trying to notice how they are being drawn.

The strategy of engaging everyone in the same task reduces the risk of two opposing camps: instead all are *searching together* for the arguments for the option and then Against. In one Workshop of twelve people, there were numerous arguments Against and only a handful. But after private prayer the vote was taken and showed 11/1 in favour. As one surprised member said: 'The arguments Against were strong – but they were dead'! The twelfth person admitted: 'I voted with my left brain, not my heart: I'm changing my vote!' And so unanimity was achieved.

Using a more complex strategy the group can reflect and share on the basis of a four-column table, as follows:

> *Prayer Sheet 20: Advantages & benefits / disadvantages & dangers of a proposed decision* can be used.

They then list 'advantages, benefits' and 'disadvantages, dangers' of one of the Options:

| Within a structure recognised by the Church | | Without a structure recognised by the Church | |
|---|---|---|---|
| Advantages and benefits | Disadvantages and dangers | Advantages and benefits | Disadvantages and dangers |
| - ............... | - ............... | - ............... | - ............... |
| - ............... | - ............... | - ............... | - ............... |
| - ............... | - ............... | - ............... | - ............... |

Members are asked to reflect, first personally and then together, on the *advantages and benefits* of the Option: 'Adopt a structure recognised by the Church'.

Then they reflect (first personally and then together) on the *disadvantages and dangers* of the Option.

A similar procedure is used to fill in the Option: 'Do not adopt a structure recognised by the Church'.[60]

---

60 It can sometimes be fruitful even to use a 6-column table. Add a column next to the 2nd and another next to the 4th column above to indicate 'Remedies'. This is because you will have to choose a solution that will have drawbacks and dangers anyway. One element to consider

As in the First and Second Moments, in the Third Moment it is still the Holy Spirit who enlightens intelligence and purifies affections and wills, but now through the reasonings exchanged.[61]

> - *Implementation of a graced decision is demanded by group authenticity*
> - *We are sent to work with God*
> - *We must relate our inner lives to the cries of the poor and the planet*
> - *Some decisions may come quickly, others through weighing consolation and desolation, or through reasoning*
> - *The last is 'the time of ordinary grace'*
> - *Decision brings reflection to an end, not the other way round!*

in making a good choice is therefore to discern the possible *remedies* to these disadvantages and dangers. A significant example of the process is provided in the experience of the first ten Jesuits.

61 When a group is looking for 'WHAT God is calling them to', the decision is often made in the First or Second Moment. However, when the group is exploring 'HOW to respond to the call', it will be more usual to use the procedure described above for the Third Moment. However, the facilitator should be careful not to use the Third Moment when the decision can be clearly made in the First or Second Moment. In the case of a very important decision, however, a decision taken in the Second Moment may be confirmed by a Third Moment exercise.

# Fostering Consensus on How to Respond to the Call

When at last the communal decision has been made, and the group has discerned **WHAT** the Lord is calling them to, a temptation to be identified is the feeling that the main work is done and that what remains is a mopping up operation.

But it is now necessary to seek **HOW** to respond to this call concretely and in an orderly way. This is a demanding task: the decision will bite into our hearts and meet resistance because as humans we are reluctant to change our habits.

It can help to distinguish between the *specific objectives* to be pursued and the *action plan*, as we shall show. The following exercises can help.[62]

### Identifying Specific objectives
➤ *Prayer Sheet 22: Goals and objectives* can be used.

In order to implement the call, it is first necessary to identify the different objectives that the group will have to pursue. So the group is invited to brainstorm. This liberates creativity rather than censoring it. The Holy Spirit can surprise us and put ideas into our minds that no one had previously thought of, as scripture abundantly testifies. Who for example could have predicted the Annunciation?

In a second step, after brainstorming, we specify the *most important objectives*. For these objectives to be effective and followed through in action, it is often necessary to make them 'SMART'. The five elements are:

---

[62] Note that in a small group the discernment of the specific objectives and the action plan, while distinct, can be done in one step.

- *Specific:* well defined, clear and unambiguous.
- *Measurable:* with criteria that measure progress towards their achievement.
- *Appropriate:* relevant to the group's mission, with a real response to the divine call.
- *Realistic*: achievable, within the reach of the group and the resources available to it.
- *Time-bound:* with a clear timeline, including a start date and a deadline; the idea is to create a sense of urgency.

**The action plan**
➤ *Prayer Sheet 23: The action plan* can be used.

Now it is time to plan in detail the implementation of each unit of the specific objectives. Taking advantage of the group's momentum to see the decision through to the end, the aim is to come up with a coherent, precise, and costed action plan so that everyone knows what has to be done and who will do it.

An action plan will specify:

- the persons responsible and other members involved through delegation and collaboration;
- the agenda for subsequent meetings, deadlines, milestones, times;
- necessary materials, premises, budget, means of financing;
- administrative structure, procedures;
- the date for dialogue with the mandated authority to confirm the decision;
- how to communicate decisions;
- the dates on which evaluations of the implementation process will be made;
- the inevitable consequences of decisions taken and the foreseeable difficulties to be faced ...

Care should be taken to maintain during this exercise a climate of prayer, interiority and discernment. The prospect of returning to the concrete aspects of life carries the risk of losing this atmosphere, especially as the work required may now put some people off.

After personal prayer on the Prayer Sheet, small groups might work on different objectives to define the action plan. All depends on the number of objectives, the time available and the group's willingness to trust the small groups. In plenary, each objective is then discussed in the light of the small group reports. Then the overall action plan is authorised by consensus.

### *Encouragement*
During the exchanges around 'HOW to respond to the call', tensions may arise. The envisaged decision will demand that the group members make some renunciations – of time, priorities, positions, perks, locations ... Such are some of the inevitable consequences of the common decision.

It also happens that the details involved in the decision bring up pre-existing tensions. 'The devil is in the details' and the old demons are already coming out!

The facilitator's task is to encourage the members who experience desolation (*Spiritual Exercises*, 7): the fact that there are tensions is a good sign that the participants are truly engaging with Jesus in his struggle against the dynamics of evil (*Spiritual Exercises*, 139).[63] The group is now experiencing itself as being inserted into the Paschal Mystery.

### *Passion and Death*
➤ *Prayer Sheet 21: Jesus and the tempter* can be used.

Humiliations will occur in acting for a just cause, but rather than dreading them, it is possible to rejoice in them (Mt 5:11), as the apostles did: '*They rejoiced that they were deemed worthy to suffer humiliation for the name of Jesus*' (Acts 5:41).

Ignatius goes further. He invites the retreatant to ask for the grace to be placed with Jesus in enduring humiliations and injustices provided that there is 'no sin on anyone's part and no displeasure on the part of the divine Majesty' (*Spiritual Exercises*, 147).

---

63 Ignatius would show concern if a retreatant were experiencing no turbulence or agitation, and would check on the person's level of engagement with the process (*Spiritual Exercises*, 6).

The facilitators will remind the group that their decision was made under the guidance of the Holy Spirit who therefore unites it to Jesus and his labor (*Spiritual Exercises*, 236) so that his people might have real and eternal life, better than they ever dreamed of (see Jn 10:10).

The group receives the grace of being united to the suffering that Jesus experiences in each of the least of the brethren (Mt 25:40; Acts 9:5; 1 Cor 12:26). Jesus promised to give us the necessary strength to follow him (Mt 11:28–30 and *Spiritual Exercises*, 320).

If it seems necessary to continue in this direction, a Prayer Sheet based on the text of the Last Supper (*Spiritual Exercises*, 289) or the washing of the feet (Jn 13:1–30) could be proposed.

- *Prayer Sheet 24: Taking up your cross and following Jesus* can be used.

### Resurrection

When the time is right, *Prayer Sheet 25: Being resurrected with Jesus* (p. 212) can be offered.

It will be helpful also to recall the 'Life–Death–Resurrection Cycle', the 'Group Name of Grace', the 'Energy Cycle' and the 'Three Styles of Authority'. These teachings will mean more in the light of the group's experience at this stage.

What may be new for the participants is to realise that these texts shed light on precisely what they are currently experiencing: a **resurrection**. Facilitators also will become more aware that the word 'accompaniment' refers to their *walking* with the group as Jesus did on the Emmaus road, and *opening* their minds to the understanding of the Scriptures (Lk 24:27).

### Confirmation of the decision

If the Workshop is to bear lasting fruit, it will be necessary to plan when and how regular evaluations will be made, to ensure that the decisions are having the desired effect. If this is happening, thanks be to God: the momentum is being maintained. If not, the group must look at the level at which the questions arise: at the level of the concrete means used to respond to God's call (the HOW); or at a deeper level: 'WHAT are we called to?'. This may mean modifying some details of what had been decided before.

The decision that concludes a Workshop may fall directly within the competence of the group. If not, the group must decide to make a recommendation to the competent authority. Another aspect of confirmation includes the reception of the decision by those who will be affected by it, and its success when activated.[64]

We consider first the confirmation which the group experienced, which brings the discernment process to a conclusion. It verifies that the power of the Spirit is given to the participants to choose one option over another, to overcome the resistances and fears aroused by the decision, to commit themselves with full knowledge of the facts, and to take action.

### *True consolation?*

The consolation associated with consensus, when ongoing, is experienced as a confirmation.[65] But is the group in consolation? It is up to all the participants to decide. If anyone has any doubts about this, they should say so. The facilitators will help the group to make this discernment.

Without this consolation the decision cannot be confirmed. What should be done then? It will be necessary to discern whether, given the time available and the state of the group, it is reasonable to expect to reach confirmation during the current Workshop or whether it seems preferable to seek it later.

At that point we should start from the consensus discovered at the level of **WHAT**, i.e. at the level of the call received from the Lord. We specify, at the level of the **HOW**, the elements on which there is agreement, and the elements on which there is disagreement. Recall what was indicated earlier on whether we should seek for unanimity, consensus, or decision by majority vote'.

---

64 Discernment, however, is not based on the criterion of subsequent success/failure but on the belief that this or that is what the Lord wants done. In 1773 a number of Jesuits were missioned to serve in Latin America: during their voyage the Society was suppressed, and when the boat docked, they had to turn back without ever setting foot on Latin American soil. Was the discernment to mission them flawed?

65 *Spiritual Intimacy and Community*, p. 155.

- *After brainstorming, discern the most important objectives*
- *Objectives should measure up to SMART criteria*
- *The action plan follows: Who does What, When*
- *Tensions indicate the level of engagement of the members*
- *Encouragement needed*
- *Foreseen losses are seen within the lens of the Paschal Mystery, which overarches all*
- *Confirmation is linked to true consolation across the group*

# 'What Wind Blows My Boat Along?'

**Note**
While this chapter is important, parts of it may be beyond the reach of some participants, unless they have had prior training. Patience is required to catch on to the elusive world of our emotions, out of which our choices emerge. 'What's driving me in my choices?' is a critical question. The facilitators will judge how to present the essential content in a suitable way that helps the members to make good choices. Ignatius offers a starting point familiar to us all: he talks about *consolation* and *desolation*. He says that when you are faced Godward, no matter what outer difficulties you may have, you experience God's drawing like 'a drop of water penetrating a sponge': this is consolation. On the other hand when you find yourself facing away from God, you experience disturbance and upset, which may be compared to a drop of water falling on a stone: this is desolation (*Spiritual Exercises*, 335).

If I felt I should have got a bigger share in a will, what might be my attitudes towards the others? If I got news that the publishers had rejected this book, would I experience turmoil, and if so, how might I sort it out?

*'What's going on inside?'*
Discernment is necessary to recognise what's going on in ourselves. We have our moods, but sometimes we do not even notice them, or where they are coming from or leading us. What do I know of my own inner world with all its moods and tenses, its unconscious and sub-conscious motivations? How can I develop a healthy inner life? How can I recognise the voice of the Holy Spirit in the whirlwind of my day?

We will develop these questions briefly, looking first at the lives of individuals and then at the life of a discerning group.

We experience contrary energies in ourselves, impulses that either promote or sap our vitality (*élan vital*). Though most of us no longer believe in demons we do speak of the spirit that animates us; for example, we say: 'There's great spirit in that group!', or 'That was a mean-spirited remark!'. We speak of wholesome and unwholesome influences. When shocked by evil actions we ask; 'What *got into* those people to make them do that?' Through psycho-analysis we have come to recognise that those who manipulate and dominate others, or commit crimes against humanity, are often manipulated by forces of which they may or may not be conscious.

The more we become sensitive to our inner thoughts and feelings, the quicker we can get back on track, and allow our sails be filled by the wind of the Good Spirit (Jn 3:8; Acts 2:2). Imagine yourself as a sailor, enduring a cold and blustery wind, but your compass reading shows that by holding to it you will keep on course for the distant harbor. Alternately imagine a warm and seductive breeze, but it is sending you off course, into the doldrums or towards the rocks. What to do when something feels good but is pulling you in the wrong direction?

Examples:

- Albert is retired from management and finance but is still active. To keep himself occupied he plays a good deal of golf, and also enjoys Bridge. He gets angry at all the bad news on TV; he attends the funerals of old colleagues, but is glad to get away, and doesn't visit sick friends because he can't stand hospitals. He has a nodding relationship with a distant God. He's become dull: he's in the doldrums and has lost any real sense of purpose. He feels life has become empty. He might live another twenty years like this but finds excuses for not offering his services to needy causes: he is like those who do little harm but also little good (see Mt 25:31–46). Is there any outward-bound love hidden in his life?
- Joan is twenty-six: she graduated well but finds it hard to settle into her well-paid job. She has had a few boyfriends, and floats in and out of the drink and drugs scene. But she's a searcher, and hears of a firm that takes on cases dealing with structural injustice: this touches something deep in her heart, but then she's confused: is the new job worth the cut in salary and in her affluent lifestyle? Most importantly, will it alienate her friends?

### *Ignatius and his moods*

Ignatius 'played the scene' in his younger years. He was a warrior, a wastrel, a womaniser, a brawler: he craved the honour of the world and the hand of a beautiful lady. Then came his 'cannon-ball moment' which put a stop to his gallop. He began to read, though the only books to hand were pious ones. The rest is history, as told in his *Autobiography*.[66] Let's look briefly at what winds filled his sails, in order to identify those that fill our own.

While convalescing it took the young Ignatius a long time to notice that some of his thoughts brought him sadness, while others left him joyous. He tells us that the prospect of resuming his knightly mode of life gave him some pleasure, but afterwards he felt unhappy, deflated, unenthused. On the other hand, the prospect of imitating Jesus and the saints gave him joy, but what was remarkable to him was that this joy persisted after the daydream was over. He stopped to think, and began to ponder over the difference: gradually the insight grew in him that God, who wants to give us every blessing, desires us to live joyful lives, not only occasionally but continuously. Ignatius came to believe that sustained joy is a sign of closeness to God – it is the tug of God.

Ignatius decides to follow his joy, which crystallises as following Jesus: this, he judges, is the steady road to God and is accompanied by joy. He tells us elsewhere that he could not live without 'consolation' which he understood as the conviction that what he was doing was pleasing to God. He becomes a master at distinguishing between inner movements that draw him to God, who is Joy Itself, and others that draw the heart away from God. This he names as the 'discernment of spirits' by which he was able to help so many people to find God and to resist the forces that distract from God. He began to engage more and more in 'Spirit-led conversation, which became a basic ministry among the early Jesuits. In doing this, of course, he was taking his cue from Jesus, as revealed for example, in relation to the Samaritan woman at the well and the nocturnal chat with Nicodemus.

What revolutionised Ignatius' life, then, was the realisation that some projects gave him lasting joy, while others, though good in themselves,

---

66  Ignatius, *Personal Writings*, p. 13 and following.

left him unfulfilled. He interprets this as God-at-work, and this awareness of God's tugs at the affective level is the essential basis for his understanding of spiritual discernment. Whether or not one has religious beliefs the meaning hidden in sadness and joy can be unearthed by reflective living. Too frequently, to quote T. S. Eliot again, we have the experience but miss the meaning. But this need not be so.

Take a moment now to ponder the situation of Albert and Joan. How would you advise them?

A framework of meaning within which to help them is provided by Ignatius's Principle and Foundation: 'We are created to praise, reverence and serve God' (*Spiritual Exercises*, 23). Made in the image of God (Gn 1:27), Albert and Joan are infinitely loved and are destined to be the daughters and sons of God (Jn 1:12); they are to be as compassionate as God (Mt 5:48) and are challenged to imitate Jesus in their love for others (Jn 15:12). They are to use their talents to help others rather than bury them (1 Pt 4:10). And so on ... This is a theological background-sketch for Spirit-led conversation and for the interpretation of their consolation and desolation.

*Inner resonances*
In order to discern the path to God, I need to take into account not only my thoughts but my emotions, feelings and bodily sensations, because these resonances help to indicate to me whether or not the aspirations most deeply inscribed in my heart by God are being fulfilled.

There are four main families of emotions: joy, sadness, fear and anger, and within them are found a spectrum of feelings such as gratitude, wonder, anxiety, shame, guilt, distrust, discouragement, enthusiasm ...

Body sensations – tensions, knots and pains – are also precious indicators of what is going on within us. It is rightly said that 'the issues are in the tissues' – meaning that what goes on in our minds has bodily resonances, to which we do well to pay attention.

*Thoughts*
In the Exercises, before talking about emotions and feelings, Ignatius draws attention to my *thought processes* (*Spiritual Exercises*, 32; *Ivens*, 36).

He presupposes that there are three kinds of thoughts in me, the first of which is purely mine, born of my freedom and my will; the other two come from outside, one from the good spirit, the other from negative influences. Their effect is:

- either to *encourage* my creative energy, to dare to be truly myself, to encourage me to give myself generously to God and/or to others, and to fight against everything that opposes it ('You are on the right track, don't deviate, continue!'),
- or to *block* my life-giving impulses, by making me afraid of what others may think of me; or becoming discouraged; or by giving in to superficial pleasures that do not satisfy my heart ('Why bother?' 'What will people think?' 'If it feels good, do it!' 'Do your thing!').

We all engage in 'mood wars' or what used to be called 'spiritual warfare'. Ignatius speaks of conquering ourselves in the most difficult part of ourselves, 'the area where desires and opinions are formed'.[67]

Jesus is shown as being faced with opposing choices, not only in the Temptations and the Agony in the Garden, but throughout the gospels. When he asks his disciples 'Who am I?', Simon answers, 'You are the Christ, the Son of the living God'. And Jesus says to him, 'Blessed are you, Simon son of Jonah!' But when, immediately after this, Jesus foretells his passion, Simon Peter cries out: 'God forbid, Lord! this will not happen to you'. Jesus' response is shocking: 'Get behind me, Satan! You are a stumbling block to me, for you are setting your mind not on divine things but on human things' (Mt 16:15–23). Ponder on what thoughts and moods were at play here between Jesus and his 'friend' Peter.

➢ *Prayer Sheet 21: Jesus and the tempter* can be helpful here.

### *Joy and Sadness*
Jesus speaks of sadness and joy when he announces his forthcoming death to his disciples. 'You will be sad, but your sadness will be turned into joy' (Jn 16:20). This change from sadness to joy is beautifully described in the story, noted above, of the Emmaus-bound disciples.

---

[67] Ignatius, *Personal Writings*, p. 260.

Before being joined by Jesus they were sad, discouraged, sick of heart, but as he disappeared from the supper table they said: 'Were not our hearts burning within us as he spoke to us on the road and opened the Scriptures to us?' (Lk 24:32).

Again, Jesus emerges from his inner struggle against desolation in Gethsemane into what may be called 'wintry consolation' – he willingly goes to his passion, convinced that the Father was asking this of him in order to reveal the limitless love of God for humankind.

Ignatius uses the terms 'spiritual consolation' and 'spiritual desolation' to describe our response of sadness or joy in situations that affect us at the deep level of spirit. Some of his Letters end with the prayer, 'May the Lord change us from being weak and sad to being strong and joyful'. The core of consolation may be tough, as when a group may have to decide to terminate a worthwhile and cherished work. Consolation can be stripped down to a sober conviction that a certain course of action is the one to follow, because it is God's call to the group. When he commented that 'he could not live without consolation' Ignatius did not mean that he had to be always in 'top form' but that he could only do something if he was convinced that it was for the greater glory of God. This is what made him a man of steely determination: once God signaled, Ignatius followed, which is why he is described as being 'a person led by Another'.

## *Ignatius's definitions*

How can you tell when we are in consolation or desolation? Ignatius does his best to articulate in sixteenth-century terms what goes on in the human heart. Read his definitions with an eye on your own inner experiences: notice for instance what it is that keeps you reading this dense material, and also what threatens to draw you away to something more immediately satisfying, like watching TV! Keep your eye on what direction you are heading: are you outward-bound or self-referential, in a downward or an upward spiral?

> ***Spiritual consolation:*** *I call it consolation when an interior movement is aroused in the soul by which it is inflamed with love of its Creator and Lord, and as a consequence, can love no creature on the face of the earth for its own sake, but only in the Creator of them all.*

*It is likewise consolation when the soul sheds tears which bring it to the love of its Lord, whether it be because of sorrow for sins or because of the sufferings of Christ our Lord, or for any other reason that is immediately directed to the praise and service of God.*

*Finally, I call consolation every increase of hope, faith and love, and all interior joy that invites and attracts to what is heavenly and to the salvation of one's soul by filling it with peace and quiet in its Creator and Lord (Spiritual Exercises, 316).*

*It is characteristic of the good Spirit to give courage and strength, consolations, tears, inspirations, and peace. This the Spirit does by making all easy, by removing all obstacles so that the soul goes forward in doing good (Spiritual Exercises, 315).*

**Spiritual desolation:** *I call desolation darkness of soul, turmoil of spirit, inclination to what is low and earthly, restlessness rising from many disturbances and temptations, which lead to want of faith, want of hope, want of love. The soul is wholly slothful, tepid, sad, and separated, as it were, from its Creator and Lord (Spiritual Exercises, 317).*[68]

## *Signs of group joy*

Does spiritual consolation occur in groups? Yes! We take two examples from the first Christians.

- The apostles as a group were consoled on the evening of the resurrection. *'Jesus said to them, 'Peace be with you!' He showed them his hands and his side. The disciples were filled with joy when they saw the Lord'* (Jn 20:19–20). It seems that, despite what Jesus had promised them earlier, none of them had expected him to rise. But now, against all hope they experience joy at the Lord's presence. It *filled them with joy*

---

[68] Down-to-earth descriptions of consolation include: 'I feel right about this decision. It's authentic. I can tell my wife about it and not feel ashamed.' 'This won't be a cake-walk, it'll be costly, but we must go ahead, and God will be with us. This must be what it means to be Christian …' Descriptions of desolation may be formulated as the opposite. 'Of course I sympathise with refugees, but we have to look after our own jobs first!' 'This is an awful mess we've got into. C'mon out and we'll drown our sorrows'.

*as a group* and gave them the energy needed for their mission. Note how it is the Holy Spirit who gets the Christian Energy Cycle under way, as the Acts of the Apostles abundantly illustrate.
- On the day of Pentecost those gathered in the Upper Room again felt a common consolation. They were waiting for Jesus' promise to be fulfilled: *'You will receive power when the Holy Spirit comes upon you'* (Acts 1:8) so *'with one heart they were diligent in prayer, with women, with Mary the mother of Jesus, and with his brothers'* (Acts 1:14). Suddenly all were filled with the Holy Spirit and became the carriers to the world of the Good News of the risen Jesus.

Today, in a conversation where each person, after having prayed personally, tries to listen attentively to the other, both become receptive to what the Holy Spirit is trying to communicate, and this helps them to find the right words to express what is moving their hearts. This sense of harmony is a source of common consolation because both are listening to the Holy Spirit.

Likewise with groups: the signs of group consolation are given by the quality of the Spirit-led conversation: each listens carefully to the others: they check whether they have understood each other correctly by expressing in their own words what they have heard. In the second round of sharing, some can say what has touched them in the words of the others, what attracts them, what challenges them or poses questions. There is a decentering of oneself, a common movement towards true life, towards spiritual poverty, humility and the union of hearts and minds. The words exchanged are calm and lead to thanksgiving.

Mutual support and respect for the well-being of others are signs of group consolation. On the contrary, lack of attention to others and the formation of cliques are warning signals that another spirit is insinuating itself.

A collective spiritual consolation is confirmed when, during a 'weather round', it appears that the members personally experience joy in connection with the life of the group. Their spiritual life is being nourished by what the group is experiencing at the moment—a strong sense of belonging and shared meaning. This helps to underline what was noted above, that interactions within a group transform its members from an aggregate of individuals to a team or a body. 'If one member suffers, all suffer with it; if one member is honoured, all rejoice together with it. Now you are the body of Christ and individually members of it' (1 Cor 12:26–27). The whole body rejoices.

It is appropriate to give thanks humbly for consolation: it is a gift to enjoy, and the memory of it can keep us going in desolation (*Spiritual Exercises*, 324). This is Mary's attitude at the Annunciation: she recognises that the Lord is doing great things in her, and she gives thanks in her Magnificat (Lk 1:47–48). Later the sword will pierce her heart, but she remains steadfast (Lk 2:35).

### *True joy*

There are challenges in life that are off-putting, but we sense that they will contribute to the well-being of others – think of the demands of parental life or the decision to join an NGO and work in a devastated region. We say to ourselves: 'I freely choose to do this unpleasant thing because I hope it will bring some joy to those I'll serve'. This is the work of the Holy Spirit who joins our spirit and gives us the strength to do what is demanding for human nature. To die for humankind shows the uttermost limits of love, yet Jesus is tempted to desolation. He says: 'My soul is sorrowful to the point of death' (Mt 26:38). His sweat became like blood (Lk 22:44). On Calvary he prays Psalm 22: 'My God, my God, why have you forsaken me' (Mt 27:46). Bonhoeffer warns us that grace can be costly, not cheap, but costly grace is still consolation: when I am broken-hearted at the death of a loved one, or I feel in the dumps, this is not to be simply equated with desolation: what matters is *the direction to which I am turned*. Jesus was fighting desolation, the temptation to abandon his mission, but he stayed steadily fixed on God and adhered with all his will to the eternal 'consensus' of the Trinity, that the extravagant love of God must be revealed to humankind, whatever the cost. This is what Karl Rahner calls 'wintry consolation' which is radical but carries little or no emotional attachment.

It is the power of the Holy Spirit that gives Jesus this capacity for agreement. His sensitivity is tested to the point of losing his sense of union with God, but the core of his being stands firm and is victorious, something the apostles will understand only later, which is why in the Garden 'all of them deserted him and fled' (Mk 14:50). They will, however, later be 'clothed with power from on high' and the Holy Spirit will give them a share in Jesus' victory. They will become alive again and be reborn to faith, hope and charity. They will no longer act out of fear but will have the courage to leave all and go to the ends of the earth to witness to this victory of Jesus over death: they will go right into the heart of the Roman Empire.

- What wind is blowing the group's boat along right now, and to where
- Sensitivity to our inner world helps restore equilibrium in stormy conditions
- 'Peace!' This is a gift of the risen Lord to our group
- Group joy leads to great energy for what is good
- Jesus speaks of sadness and joy from personal experience
- His was 'wintry consolation' in the Passion, but he held firm to his belief in his Father
- He did the wisest and most loving thing: 'O loving wisdom of our God ...' – Newman

# Group Sadness or Desolation

*'Is something out of tune?'*
When groups are beginning to build a relationship of trust through their Spirit-led conversations, the facilitators will point out that *it is much easier to share on consolation* than on personal desolation or on dryness in prayer. The members may not be aware of this, or they may feel that speaking of desolation will let the group down. Blaming the process or the facilitator or sharing only at the level of ideas is much easier than stopping to examine one's uncomfortable inner movements and what may be causing them.

The issue can come to a head in the plenary. Both participants and facilitators may feel deflated by something that has just been shared in the circle. But what does the change of mood mean? Someone may suggest: 'We need to take a break' which may be true, but before or after the break they need to name what they are feeling. They need to detect when the inner change of mood and conviction occurred – perhaps following a particular intervention or comment. When and why did silence or heaviness take over? They must learn inner freedom here, believing that by remaining close to Jesus they will come to know the truth, and that the truth will make them free (Jn 8:31–32).

The facilitators will guide the members to the personal and group review mentioned earlier, which will help to focus awareness of the differing movements each has felt and may facilitate a return to the previous time of consolation. The facilitators will also engage in this task.

Discernment is an arena where the stakes are often high: it can be the place of intense spiritual struggle. For instance, it is so hard for zealous people to think of letting go the people and works to which they have committed their lives. 'How could God be asking this – that we abandon all these needy people?' Each person should therefore devote time to reviewing their day, in order to thank the Lord for graces received, to welcome God's mercy and to ask for divine help in living out the next day.

*Ingredients of group desolation*
Group desolation often originates in a lack of inner freedom or of generosity towards the Lord (*Spiritual Exercises*, 5). These shortcomings can be expressed in very down-to-earth ways.

Here is a list of some ingredients for group desolation. Like a disruptive strategist, a bad spirit enters the group through its weakest points. The facilitators have to point this out with tact and humor, while noting that God works creatively even in what is chaotic, as in the story of creation (Gn chapter 1).

*(1) Failure to follow the guidelines for Spirit-led conversation*
- The time for prayer is used for reading e-mails or in talking to others.
- Someone is monopolising the time and the others don't dare to point this out.
- Not everyone gets a fair chance to speak.
- Some people arrive late.
- People cut others off and don't really listen.
- Someone persists in being silent.
- The differences between the three rounds of sharing are not respected.

*(2) The absence of a spirit of community*
- Some people do not seek community within the group.
- Others blame, accuse, suspect and condemn.
- One or more try to prove that they are right.
- A spirit of division is at work.

*(3) Avoiding suffering*
- Elements of the past are left in the wardrobe. There are whole sections of reality that we prefer not to see or talk about.
- We are imprisoned in past wounds.
- We turn the page on suffering but it continues to influence us unconsciously.
- Without realising it, we have put someone on a pedestal.

*(4) Confidentiality issues*
- What should have been kept confidential was shared outside the group (p. 58).

- What was shared in pairs after a plenary, and is important for the group's process, was not brought back into the common conversation in the next plenary.

(5) *Head eclipses heart*
- Ideas are discussed without expressing emotions, feelings, sensations, wishes, aspirations, needs, longings.
- I-statements are missing, so experience is ignored.

(6) *Different forms of fear dominate*
- Fear of being despised by others, which prevents us from speaking out.
- Fear of hurting others.
- Fear of being excluded from the group if one disagrees.
- Fear of being invaded by others.
- Fear of loneliness.
- Fear of change.
- Fear of the future.
- Fear of God whom we falsely imagine to be sadistic and condemnatory.

(7) *Discouragement and negativity*
- 'It's no use, it's always the same in this group, it will never change.'
- Regret around an unhappy past situation that has not yet been brought into the world of purifying grace.

(8) *The desire for glory and success*
- 'We are the elite of the Church'.
- Clericalism: authoritarianism; clinging to power and using the weapon of domination.
- Rigidity and intolerance.
- Comfort-seeking and consumerism.

*False consolation*

False consolation occurs when a group abdicates responsibility, and allows itself to be led by one or more of its members (especially by a leader who takes advantage of their status to rule without sharing), or by a fashion, an ideology, an authority external to the group. The right questions are not asked, and the little voices that would urge caution are stifled.

The remedy consists in remembering that the Holy Spirit is offered to each person and that it is up to each to show discernment and courage, to dare to think, speak and act in conscience, even if this goes against the majority and puts one's own life at risk (Lk 12:5).[69] The events of the Lord's Passion should be kept in mind. When Pilate asked what evil Jesus had done, the crowd abdicated reason and allowed itself to be manipulated by the religious authorities. So they replied: 'Let him be crucified' (Mt 27:20–23). Paul calls on us to speak out boldly as befits the sons and daughters of God.

False consolation also occurs when the whole group gets over-excited about an idealistic project that may not be inspired by God. When the question 'To **What** are we called?' arises, it gives permission to dream, and to imagine goals and objectives that are exciting but perhaps unrealistic. A reality-check is needed, through giving more time to the arguments against the project.

But when a group is enthused about a project *that has much merit* but at first glance might seem too ambitious, such as setting up a foundation abroad, one of the best things to do is to move on to the next question: '**How** do we answer the call expressed in this new project?' We should remember that even with our limited means, God achieves great things in us. *'The kingdom of heaven is like a mustard seed that a man took and sowed in his field. It is the smallest of all the seeds, but when it has grown, it surpasses the other vegetable plants and becomes a tree, so that the birds make their nests in its branches'* (Mt 13:31–32).

## *A note on abuse*

The contemporary issue of abuse is linked with false consolation. Having had an intense experience of consolation that is genuinely given by the Holy Spirit, a spiritual guide concludes that he is free to engage sexually with a person he is accompanying. He justifies his action by saying to himself – and perhaps to his victim also – that the (authentic)

---

69 The Greek term for open speech is *parrhesia*, as in 2 Corinthians 3:12–4:2. Pope Francis invites us to exercise this gift as synodal people. It infers open speech as between equals, without concealment or ambiguity; it requires that we do not yield to shame or fear. Jesus is its exemplar throughout his life and in his passion. Our prayer to God should also be open, unafraid, trusting.

mystical experience he has enjoyed places him above the common person. This is erroneous: his sexual behaviour will be mired in false consolation. How can a thought that puts him 'above the common person' come from the Lord, who tells us to serve others and to take the last place?

The person being accompanied should be careful *not to stifle* the discomfort they may feel when seemingly innocent sexual proposals are made: they need to find ways to disentangle themselves from the trap of another's illusions. While it is true that we should have a favorable attitude towards our neighbour (*Spiritual Exercises*, 22), yet it is imprudent to put anyone on a pedestal, no matter what aura that person may enjoy in the Church or in society. Some proposals and actions are objectively bad, even if they come from someone who is revered. The 'man of God' remains only a man and can be the victim of illusions. It is God who must be obeyed; God, who speaks to our hearts in personal conscience.[70]

### Detecting false joy

How can we detect those deceptive consolations that are caused not by the Holy Spirit, but by an evil influence (*Spiritual Exercises*, 328–336)? Ignatius would say: 'Watch the outcome of your choice'. If the course of our thoughts finally leads us to something bad, or leaves us worried or troubled, it is a sign that this 'consolation' does not come from God (*Spiritual Exercises*, 333).

The facilitators take a period for personal reflection:

- What do I feel? What spirit is at work *in me*?
- What's happening *in the group*? What spirit is at work?
- When were we still clearly in consolation? What has happened since? What thoughts have been expressed?
- Through which weak point did the spirit of discouragement enter?

The facilitators enlist the resources within the group:

---

[70] *Gaudium et Spes*, 16.

- Give the floor to people who are experiencing disturbance and invite the group to listen carefully. Then ask if anyone sees things differently than they had earlier.
- Be very vigilant: if even one person in a group is desolate, this can de-stabilise the whole group.
- In this case, the desolate person should be briefly questioned to check whether their desolation is linked to the group, or is a personal problem (physical discomfort, reawakening of a poorly resolved conflict, etc.). In the latter case, the facilitator can say: 'Thank you for sharing your difficulty. If you wish, you can talk about it privately with a member of the group or with someone competent outside the group'.
- If the member is in a state of desolation such that it prevents the group from pursuing its objectives, either that person should take a break from the group, however briefly, or, if they remain, the group must make a conscious decision to change its objectives or the way in which it achieves them.
- Build on the people who are perceived to have remained in consolation, or temporarily end the session and resume it later when consolation returns.
- When there is unanimity, it is important to check whether the group is really in consolation or whether they feel content to have escaped a difficult issue. To this end, it is good for the group to review its process, examine the nature of its satisfaction and describe the state of contentment it is experiencing.
- Consolation is a gift from the Lord to the group. It is therefore appropriate for the group to give thanks for it, for example in the third round of sharing, and not to behave as if they were the source of the consolation (*Spiritual Exercises*, 322, 324).
- If the situation is tense or touches on very sensitive points, propose a time of personal prayer and reflection, followed by a time of small groups.

In times of desolation, Ignatius advises:

a) Don't change a decision made in consolation (*Spiritual Exercises*, 318),

b) Do the exact opposite of what the 'enemy' suggests (*Spiritual Exercises*, 325) in order to maintain your freedom; e.g. eat/spend less when tempted to eat/spend more,
c) Stay faithful to the times for prayer and reflection that you had decided on (*Spiritual Exercises*, 319). Say 'I choose to do this: it is right to do it, even though I don't feel like it now.'
d) Realise that you have sufficient grace to resist temptation (*Spiritual Exercises*, 320).

> - *Within the group are some denying personal dryness or desolation?*
> - *Are some demands of the process being ignored? Are fears dominating?*
> - *In false consolation the group abdicates responsibility and allows itself to be led astray*
> - *To get back on track, notice the desolate ones and build on those who have remained in consolation*
> - *Put no one on a pedestal! Keep conscience clear. Don't be led along by others*

# Part Four: Facilitation

## Facilitation of Groups

*The Emmaus Story*

'Accompanying' consists in going along in the company of another. As we have seen, this is one of the meanings of the word 'synodality' (see p. 20). We look again at how Jesus accompanied two disciples on the road to Emmaus (Lk 24:13–35). He is the facilitator par excellence!

First, he invites himself into their conversation, notes their crestfallen mood, gets them to tell their story. He pays attention to their concerns, their emotions, their unfulfilled desires, their interpretation of events, especially of the passion and bloody death of their leader. He notices their hearts' desire that things might have been different. *They want him back!* This is the beginning of Easter faith. If there were no desire in them there would have been no Emmaus event. They have a basic level of openness, so Jesus can reveal himself to them.

He links their experiences to the promises of scripture; this opens their hearts to a revised appreciation of what is upsetting them—the death of the one in whom they had placed all their hope. He says to them 'Why can't you see that all these things had to happen to the Messiah: *only then* could he enter into his glory?' (see Lk 24:26). He shows them that the real story is only beginning, and so a new flame of hope is lit in their hearts.

When they arrive at their destination, Jesus pretends to go further, as if he does not want to impose his presence any longer and wishes rather to leave his fellow-travellers free. During the meal that follows he allows himself to be recognised in the gesture of the breaking of bread. They pick up this delicate hint as to who this stranger is, and this changes their lives, even though he disappears from their sight.[71]

Like Jesus, facilitators start from the experience of the group and listen with great respect to what is entrusted to them. They link this experience to Scripture texts that will help the group to cross a threshold and enter into deeper faith, hope and charity, thus enabling them to experience consolation on a deeper level than before. A facilitator helps, not by imposing, but rather by encouraging the group's freedom, leaving it free to decide what to do next.

### *Facilitators are missioned*

Like Jesus (Lk 4:43) and like the apostles (Lk 10:1), facilitators are sent, they do not act on their own initiative. Rather Jesus goes ahead and they follow: the Holy Spirit has already 'renewed the face of the earth' for them: they are told, 'Be not afraid'. They enter into what is already sacred space. Theirs is not the main role; their role instead is humbly to prepare the way of the Lord (*Spiritual Exercises*, 15).

This parallels the role assigned to John the Baptist. John made his message clear to the crowds who came to him, but he did not overstep his role. He constantly referred to the one who would come after him, underlining his own unworthiness (Jn 1:19, 27). In the same way, the facilitators are not afraid to play their role to the full, while taking a back seat to Jesus.

Observed from the outside, the accompaniment could appear to be a relationship between the group and the facilitators. But in fact it is a triangular relationship *in which the Lord plays the central role*: both the group and the facilitators constantly refer to him (Mt 18:20; *Spiritual Exercises*, 236). What is at stake is the relationship between the group and God. Facilitators are at the service of this relationship, and seek to foster it; their greatest joy is to *contemplate* what is happening between God and the group.

'Contemplatives in action' was the term applied to the early Jesuits. Ignatius did not lay down rules for his followers regarding length of prayer, but instead required them to be always contemplative: each

---

71 The scene at the Emmaus inn is excellently portrayed by Velasquez; and Denise Levertov, having seen the painting, wrote a poem about it: 'The Servant Girl at Emmaus'.

should 'keep God *always* before his eyes'.[72] This provides the prayerful background which leads on to graced action through discernment. The facilitators model this approach, such that the group becomes contemplative, focused on God and trying to discern what God wants done. Jesus acted thus, and it enabled him to assert in Jn 8:29, 'I always do what pleases him (the Father)'. Further help along this line of thought, so easy to miss, is Judith Roemer's *The Group Meeting as a Contemplative Experience.*

## *The Spirit goes ahead*

Jesus instructs the disciples to undertake their mission with very little: no bread, no bag, no coins in their belts, no spare tunic, but only what they need for the journey: a staff and sandals (Mk 6:7–11).

By not taking anything with them, facilitators choose to make themselves dependent on the group who will welcome them. There is giving and receiving; the facilitators offer the good news of Jesus, and the group as host offers food and shelter.

Facilitators, as we said, are preceded by the Holy Spirit who has already established a bond between them and their host-group, as was done between Peter and Cornelius (Acts 10). In this way, mutual dignity and interdependence are experienced, and the spirit of community within the group itself and with the facilitators flourishes.

## *Sent in pairs*

Jesus sends his disciples out two by two (Lk 10:1). He does not say why! Perhaps the reason lies in his promise: *'If two of you on earth agree to ask for anything, they will receive it from my Father in heaven. For when two or three are gathered together in my name, I am there among them'* (Mt 18:19–20).

Similarly, the Esdac companions go as facilitators in pairs, woman and man if possible. To fulfil their mission, they have to practise the quality of Spirit-led conversation that they will recommend to the group. Their complementarity makes each of them better able to listen to the Holy Spirit. This collaboration between companions begins when the first contacts are made with the requesting group: it continues

---

72  *Formula of the Institute*, 1.

through the drafting of a Workshop program, and through the evaluation of each session.

If there are two facilitators, each must be free enough during review time to dare to tell the other what they feel about the way they work together. They should also pray for one another, welcoming, as best they can, the other's way of doing things: together they seek to serve the Lord and the group better. The quality of their relationship has a great impact on the climate of the sessions. Experience shows that working in pairs helps both members

- to work together to deal with the unexpected,
- to help each other to deal with emotions,
- to support each other and avoid drifting,
- to deepen their self-knowledge. 'Did you notice you were using sexist language?' or 'That was a really helpful intervention you made!' or 'Were you ignoring X when she wanted to speak?' or 'Does Y irritate you?' or 'You sounded tired' …

### *Introducing the Prayer Sheets*

Preparing the Workshop involves for the facilitators the personalising of the Prayer Sheets which introduce each exercise, at least the first ones. All the sheets can be modified to take account of the group's progress. Agreement between the facilitators on the words used and their meaning is essential to make sure that the members understand each other and to help them move towards an agreement among themselves.

The facilitators must respect, as best possible, the different psychological types of participants: rational, emotional, intuitive, etc. and when calling on experience, mention as much as possible the different experiences that have already come up since the beginning of the Workshop.

A key word, possibly taken from the text reproduced at the beginning of the Prayer Sheet, should run through it and its various parts in order to emphasise the unity of the process.

When the grace has been clarified, the facilitator will ask: 'What text should we choose to ask for around this grace?' In Ignatius' experience, the Gospel has a special place. It was from reading it, in relation to the lives of the saints and his own experience, that he was converted. The stories of the founding events of salvation history are also suitable, as are texts from the liturgy of the day or of the time of year. This is especially appropriate if the group has to join a parish or other assembly to participate in the Eucharist: it opens up the group to experience a wider dimension than itself.

A founding text of the group, a spiritual or secular text, a photo or a short video clip may be appropriate. If possible, let the group decide – it needs to be able to reach consensus on small as well as weighty issues!

When presenting a scripture text, it may be necessary to offer a brief commentary, which will reveal the relevance of the text for today and for the needs of the group.

In choosing these texts,

- Beware of personal preferences: it is not because a text has spoken to a facilitator that it will speak to the group. We can take texts that have already spoken to the group and that still say something about what it is called to. Hence the importance of knowing the group well.
- Reject texts that suggest a ready-made solution. It is up to the group, listening to the Spirit, to discover for itself the appropriate solution.
- Avoid texts that 'lock up' and do not give sufficient perspective. Remember that the aim of facilitation is to set the group and its individual members *free*.

In the plenary, the facilitators will introduce the personal time of prayer and reflection that will follow. They will point out the importance of this time of personal prayer for the good outcome of the Workshop, and that it is normal to experience contrasting feelings during prayer: resistance, anxiety, discouragement or, on the contrary, enthusiasm, liking, encouragement ... Awareness of these contrasting feelings and states of mind throws light on the discernment of spirits.

For groups accustomed to praying the Word of God, it will be sufficient to comment briefly on the Prayer Sheets; they follow a progression as indicated earlier. The facilitators will formulate the progress expected from each exercise, indicate how important this step is, and stimulate the desire to take it. They should make explicit the grace requested, and check whether this grace is well understood. Participants can be invited to reformulate it in their own words.

The participants should not go directly to the Prayer Sheets but rather take the time to immerse themselves in the text and let it act on their hearts. Often, while learning the art of Spirit-led conversation, newcomers reassure themselves by first looking at the Prayer Sheets, for fear of having nothing to share in the small group,

## Brief explanation

Ignatius recommends that a retreat guide be content to give short and summary explanations so that the retreatants may find, on their own and with the light received from the Spirit, something that illuminates the story to be contemplated (*Spiritual Exercises*, 2). Many people today have not received a consistent religious and biblical education or have rejected it. It will be good, therefore, to ensure that the commentary on the text, while remaining brief, clarifies what might be misunderstood. Then the facilitators will step aside to let 'the Creator act without intermediary with the creature, and the creature with his Creator and Lord' (*Spiritual Exercises*, 15). Note the surprising nature of this statement: it carries the radical imagery of intimate friendship between the Lord and ourselves. This got Ignatius into a lot of hot water: he was accused of bypassing the authority of the Church over its members. But he survived!

Participants should be free from excessive fidelity to the Prayer Sheets: these are intended simply as a help, a path, not a straitjacket. They will be invited to reflect on their own and to *feel and taste* personally what is given to them. For some the prayer will be nourished by following a single hint, or the simple statement of the grace desired may suffice.

## Places to pray in

Participants choose a place to pray in that helps them to enter into themselves and into the Mystery of God: a chapel, their room, the garden, the plenary room ...

Having several people in the same place – for example in the chapel or in the plenary room – can sometimes support the effort of personal prayer. The facilitators can decide whether it is appropriate to join the participants in this time of personal prayer. The latter are always helped by knowing that the facilitators take quality time to intercede for them.

*For beginners in prayer*
There are several possibilities.

(a) **Begin in plenary**
The personal prayer may be initiated by a facilitator in a plenary session, before distributing the Prayer Sheet, with the following elements:

- A reminder of God's presence (*Spiritual Exercises*, 46), 'I will consider how God our Lord beholds me' (*Spiritual Exercises*, 75),
- The reading or proclamation of the Prayer Sheet text.
- Brief commentary.
- The request for the grace specific to this Prayer Sheet may then be made aloud, addressing God, and replacing the 'I' with a 'we': 'Lord, give *us* the grace of …'
- Distribute the Prayer Sheet only at this point.
- Comment on the Prayer Sheet to show that its purpose is to help make the link between the text and the members' personal experience.
- Remind the group that conversation with the Lord invites them to move from personal reflection to talk to him and to listen to what he says. Prayer is a chat between good friends (*Spiritual Exercises*, 54).
- Invite them to go to their place of choice to continue the prayer individually.[73]

(b) **Gospel sharing**
Alternately it can sometimes be fruitful, before giving the Prayer Sheet, to share the Gospel in plenary, for example for half an hour. A small sheet carrying the Bible text alone may be distributed, or not. This encourages a common appropriation of the text and makes it possible to experience that the Holy Spirit can speak to everyone. It also avoids the temptation to go immediately to the prayer hints without having taken the time to be personally touched by the Word of God. The full Prayer Sheet is then distributed, and the prayer continues individually.

---

73 Note that in the early monasteries, when books were few and readers perhaps still fewer, a monk read a scripture passage to the community in chapel. After a pause, during which a monk could exit quietly, the text was read again. Again there was a pause for more monks to exit, after which the text was read yet again until all were 'caught' by the message of the text. See John Veltri SJ, *Orientations 1* (Guelph: 1979), p. 25.

If putting words in Jesus' mouth seems too subjective, invite a person to whisper the actual words of Jesus to themselves: 'What do you want?' 'Come and see!' 'Put down your net!' 'Go and sin no more!' 'Do not be afraid' 'If you have faith …' 'Go and tell …' etc.

### (c) Bibliodrama

For a group that is not yet very open to faith, it may help to suggest acting out a biblical story or doing a role-play. In this case, the most important instruction is to ban the condemnation of any figure represented in the role-play! Respecting this instruction makes it possible to experience the central message of the Gospel: 'God sent his Son into the world, not to judge the world, but that through him *everyone* might be saved' (Jn 3:17).

The facilitator begins by inviting volunteers to play the role of the characters in a Bible text. This is called Bibliodrama, and offers a good introduction to contemplation – seeing the characters, hearing what they say, watching what they do (*Spiritual Exercises,* 106–108, 121–125). Bibliodrama can help a person to leave the realm of ideas and enter the world of feelings.

To begin, the volunteers choose from the story a character whose experience they want to explore. They are then asked to explain why they have chosen this role. Examples: the prodigal; the woman taken in adultery; the Last Supper; Jesus in the Garden, Emmaus, etc.

During the drama, the volunteers act out the scene, using their imagination. They recreate the context, enter the story as actors, and get into the skin of their character. From there on they let their heart take over rather than follow a script.

After the action, time is set aside for a review of what has happened. Once again, it is the preparation of, and then the re-reading of the exercise that gives it its transformative power.

### (d) Guided prayer

This prayer brings the whole group together in one place. It is guided, step by step, by brief indications punctuated by times of silence. It is important to consider whether this kind of guidance and the way it is offered will help the group and not be perceived as pressure on them.

**(e) Games and Symbols**
There are times when it is good to invite the group members to move around to allow the body and not only the mind to participate in the life received and given. The facilitator will propose a group task, which some may call 'a game' because of its playful nature. Some instructions will be given (rules, time limit …). The 'game' frees the body and the soul, and melts the reserve created when we limit ourselves to exchanging words.

Examples of 'games':

- Build a statue expressing the emotional state of the small group at a given moment.
- In the garden, pass a ball from one to the other without dropping it.
- Try to untie a knot in a rope together …

Participants are invited to enter into the exercise while keeping not only their outer eyes but their inner eyes open.

The review of the experience will take place after a period of silence, and according to the three rounds of Spirit-led conversation (p. 43). It is the sharing of personal reflections that transforms the experience into real learning.

Cooperative games are often proposed during three-day retreats for young adults who have little or no faith. Some such games can be played as a family. Even in a serious adult retreat, it can help to access our inner child through a 'game'. It is not just relaxation; it is another way of accessing our inner being. We should remember that Wisdom has always *played* alongside the Lord (Prov 8: 31, and see 2 Sam 6:21, where David plays before the Lord).

The Esdac process will tend to privilege words and conversation. However, everything is language: a body attitude, a gesture, a mimic, a look, a silence, the place one occupies. It is therefore important to make wide use of symbolic expression. Even the simplest of things, such as a stone, can 'speak'. A symbol is a reservoir capable of releasing powerful psychic and spiritual energy: it gives voice to the unconscious: it creates new relationships between things, ideas and feelings. An image unifies what is perceived by the intellect, the emotions, the intuition and the five senses. Here are some examples:

- Rublev's icon of the Trinity can illustrate the Spirit-led conversation between the divine Persons and humans. Similarly, a representation of the Annunciation by Fra Angelico will allow us to taste the respect and interiority of this scene. Many other works of art, such as Sieger Koder's, have the capacity to support the effort to encounter God.
- Wherever possible, the Prayer Sheet given to participants should begin with a story, rather than an abstract text, to set the imagination in motion. Then suggest seeing the characters, hearing what they say, watching what they do (*Spiritual Exercises*, 106–108).
- A celebration, a liturgy, a vigil are moments when it is judged important that the creativity of the group be released. After a conflict, a hand extended to another will not be forgotten. A group dance, song or music express communion, which can also be experienced in a completely different way, for example during silent Eucharistic adoration.
- Games help us to recover the simplicity of the child hidden within us and to discover areas of ourselves of which we are hardly aware in our working or thinking hours. Cooperative games teach communication and consultation, especially when the review puts into words what was played out between the protagonists. Many people are competitive and enjoy a challenging game.
- Asking the group to draw a picture of the state of the group at a given moment, and then to comment on this work, can help to free up thoughts that are difficult to externalise. Symbols can also help.
- The dynamic can be shifted by inviting the group to prepare a simple meal, go for a walk, visit a place of interest or make a short pilgrimage.

It is good to start by asking: *'What is our goal now? What exactly do we expect from the next plenary? What grace, then, should we ask the Lord in order to achieve this goal?'*

## Facilitation of Groups

- *Learn the art of facilitation from Jesus, written across the gospel pages*
- *Facilitators are SENT, to link the group with the Spiri.*
- *They contemplate the group, and so the meeting becomes a contemplative experience*
- *They are sent in pairs, to support and be honest with one another*
- *Don't write personal preferences into your Prayer Sheets: pray for inspiration*
- *Notice where beginners are at and adjust accordingly*
- *Stress the goal of prayer, lest its energy gets dissipated*

# Team Aspects of Facilitation

*a) Teamwork*
When there are two facilitators, one is 'at the front', attentive to the **content** of the exchanges: the other remains a little behind, attentive to how the **process** is unfolding. They may consult each other during breaks, or even during a plenary session. It may happen that during a plenary session, unforeseen circumstances arise and it is appropriate to suspend the session so that the facilitators can briefly consult each other. There is no dishonour in showing the group that the facilitators do not have a ready-made solution to a certain question and that a joint reflection is necessary. On the contrary, experience has shown that the groups perceive the seriousness with which the facilitators are trying to help them, and they learn for themselves how to deal with tensions and problems. Unexpected events are not to be lamented as catastrophes, but as learning opportunities. Grace is always at work!

*b) Mutual help re emotions*
During a session, facilitators may find themselves emotionally affected by situations raised by the participants. This capacity for empathy with the group is good: it indicates that they are staying close to the members and focused on what they are revealing about themselves. However a facilitator may on occasion find a strange similarity between what is evoked by a participant and fragments of their own life. The coincidence can resonate to the point where emotional confusion may appear. Is the facilitator still listening or have they already slipped into their own world and become unavailable to what is happening in the here and now?

It is not uncommon that the experience of another can be superimposed on one's own; one's past is revived and its associated emotions invade the present. When this happens it is necessary to take distance as soon as possible in order to be able to return to the *present* situation of being psychically available and listening. The facilitator in question needs to talk with their companion: talking enables appropriate distancing from the entanglement.

It can also happen that facilitators are surprised, even de-stabilised, by becoming the perhaps unconscious target of certain participants. These movements, frequent in any group dynamic, are called 'transfers'. They need to be identified, as well as the facilitator's reactions to them, which are called 'counter-transfers'. It is important that the facilitators become aware of these phenomena and integrate them so as to remain capable of framing and protecting the group even in its unconscious movements.

It is also possible that a facilitator experiences strong feelings of attraction or rejection towards a particular person in the group. Here again, it is essential to distance oneself from this situation, to analyse it and to see how it can be integrated into the task of accompaniment.

Hence the importance of living the mission of facilitation well by praying constantly. One asks to be a good servant, to welcome the group as it is, to consider it as a sacred land which one approaches with respect. The mission of accompaniment is one which we never finish exploring, but it is helped firstly and above all by exchanging with another facilitator, or with someone else who can offer a listening ear.

This awareness-raising, this re-reading of a situation and sharing may be necessary not only *after* the session as part of its evaluation, but also *during* it, to keep the accompaniment on track.

### c) Challenging each other

Paired facilitation is a valuable self-correcting process for dealing with the many temptations that facilitation raises. Temptations occur such as the following:

- Using one's authority as a counsellor to one's advantage, in one way or another. One must be aware of the risks of taking control of the group, of trying to impose one's ideas, of changing the group according to one's wishes. It is important to flush out the traps of omnipotence which often arise without our realising it.
- False humility and anxiety: 'Who am I to hope to help this group in its difficulties?' The facilitators should remember that they are only an instrument of God, like Mary, who humbles herself and gives

thanks for having been chosen as the Lord's servant (*Spiritual Exercises*, 108).
- Too much flexibility and suppleness and continuous adaptation, under the pretext of offering greater freedom, can originate in personal unsureness and end up causing confusion.
- Too much rigidity to the point of holding the group hostage to Prayer Sheets, to the three times of an exercise, the schedule ... Such leads to irritation and a sense of being dominated.
- Trying to get the group to feel good about themselves, about how they do things.
- Giving more credit to certain people such as leaders or people with whom one feels more affinity ... Often the self-effacing one who is ignored could offer an enlightening intuition.
- Wanting to control the process in order 'to help the group', or trying to give it 'my solution'.

What facilitator has not had an intuition that seemed to respond to the group's problems? Shouldn't this be shared with the group to avoid long and perhaps fruitless trial and error? But prudence requires asking the following question: 'Am I putting myself in the place of the Spirit instead of the Spirit's service?' 'Am I running ahead of the Spirit because I need to feel wise?'

Experience shows that the group can feel manipulated by a facilitator who gives it a ready-made solution: trust can then be broken. If, after a dialogue between the facilitators, the intuition of one of them is judged to be useful to the group, they do better *by asking questions* that may put the group on the right track. They will not insist if no attention is paid to the intuition, but will keep it in mind and ask God to set up an opportunity for it to come to light.

The language, pace or styles of the facilitators can be very different, and one of them may feel compelled to intervene and complement or clarify the words of the other to 'maximise the learning of the group'. But one needs inner assurance that such an intervention will do more good than harm and will not damage the understanding within the pair.

It is necessary to share about the temptations I am aware of in myself: the mere fact of talking about them often dispels them (*Spiritual*

*Exercises*, 326). However, it is also important to discuss, with delicacy and goodwill, the risk that I can see in the other's attitude. The way companions function with each other and deal with their own difficulties requires mutual 'taming' and has a pedagogical effect on the group. As mentioned earlier, communal discernment is a scouring process for all involved, and this includes facilitators; but at the same time it can foster inner growth and self-knowledge.

### d) *Protecting the group*

The group that seeks accompaniment may not yet know that it is carrying the seed of rebirth (Jn 3:3–4). The facilitators work to ensure that the conditions for renewal are met, so that their own confidence is gradually transmitted to the group that calls on them.

The participants will agree to become personally involved in the group process only if they are convinced that it is a safe place for them, a sanctuary. It is up to the facilitators to put in place the framework and style of conducting the meetings that will ensure the protection of all, so that members allow themselves to become untied and to confide to the group what is personal and otherwise unspeakable. The Bavarian devotion to Our Lady, Untier/Undoer of Knots, so dear to Pope Francis, can be mentioned.

This protective framework will allow the members of the group to dare to speak out, honestly and frankly. This atmosphere allows a certain distance to be established from one's emotional world, and avoids the expression of affect in violent words or actions.

For this reason, at the beginning of the session, the facilitators should clearly specify to the participants the instructions to be observed so that a conversation is truly Spirit-led.

### *Instructions*
- Ensure that all instructions are understood and followed in practice.
- Support the speaker.
- Listen, paying attention not only to the words spoken, but also to postures, faces, everything that the body can express. Often, the way the facilitator listens 'rubs off' on the group. Attentive and respectful listening on the part of the facilitator facilitates such listening by the group members among themselves, especially as participants

sometimes tend to address the facilitator and watch for their reactions.
- Offer the floor to the shy members: encourage them so that they can act against the inner whispers that tell them: 'I am not competent', 'I have nothing to say', 'I would like to speak, but I have had too many negative experiences with this group to say what I think'. We spoke above about thoughts that thwart the flow of creativity.
- Help the group to observe itself 'from above', to understand the dynamics at play and to take control of them rather than becoming unwary victims.
- With tact and delicacy, point out incongruities and inconsistencies: 'Yesterday you said blue, today you say yellow. Can you please clarify what you now wish to propose?'
- Keep in mind that the person whose attitude is disturbing and annoying is not necessarily the *cause* of a group dysfunction, but the *indicator*.
- Take stock of the group well before the end of an emotionally charged plenary, especially at the close of the day, so that no one is left alone to deal with a difficult emotional situation. The point is not to deal with the issue, but to allow it to be formulated, expressed, heard, and noted, so as to enable a peaceful night's rest for all. It is better to allow too much time for this emotional assessment rather than too little.

### e) Interpersonal conflict

When a participant mentions interpersonal conflicts, the facilitator can say: 'I can hear the difficulties you are experiencing in your relationship with this person. This is your personal experience. Our assembly is not the place to talk about it, but if you want, please talk about it to someone you trust. Or a member of the facilitation team may be able to help you later to see how to move forward and work on this.'

Genuine listening encourages people to express themselves freely. But sometimes there are things that are difficult to share. The art of accompaniment is then to allow these things to be said. This has to do with the general atmosphere of the session, hence the importance of taking care of it. It also depends on the empathy that the facilitators have for the group.

But this is not always enough, for example, when old unspoken words are still festering: when a situation of control hinders or prevents speaking, when a person in the group is questioned.

There is no general solution to be implemented in such a case. One has to look for ways to help the group, taking into account the situation and the circumstances. This may be by taking up a particular intervention and asking for it to be developed; or by tactfully introducing an unplanned Prayer Sheet so that, before the Lord, people can see how to move forward using non-accusatory words. Non-verbal expression can also be used, for example by asking small groups to do a mime, or to express themselves through a picture, or to put a cross on a board in front of what seems to be the most important issue, or to draw a picture.

Emotions, gestures, symbols, have an important power of expression but can also provoke resistance. Non-verbal expression also involves projections and externalises a part of personal experience that is perhaps less conscious but none the less operative. Alternating verbal and non-verbal expression sometimes helps to ensure that exchanges do not become too rigid.

### f) *Abuse issues*

Esdac was not created to intervene in situations of abuse of conscience or power, sexual or otherwise. These situations have to be dealt with on several levels (legal, psychological, spiritual …), with primary care for the victims.

However Esdac has accompanied groups in which abuse had taken place. Such a group was wounded and their trust was damaged: they were asking for help to look forward. The fact of re-reading together their common history; by naming the facts; by putting words on the numerous, diverse and often violent emotions aroused; by seeking together to understand what happened in order to learn from it – such exercises enabled their sharing to flow again, and began to restore confidence and trust.

It has also happened that Esdac facilitators unexpectedly found themselves in a situation of proven abuse. After discerning among themselves and consulting a third person (for example a supervisor), they decided to talk about it with the group leader. But when they were not listened to, they denounced the situation to a higher authority, thus taking on the role of whistleblowers.

### g) One-to-one accompaniment
A facilitator may be asked by a member to accompany them personally throughout the Workshop. What to do?

Remember that the mission of the team of facilitators is to be at the service of the group, at the service of 'us' and not of each individual. Moreover, a short session does not lend itself to personal accompaniment. Furthermore, if there are requests from several people in the group, accompanying them can be problematic if interpersonal relationships are at stake.

In most cases, therefore, a request for personal accompaniment should not be accepted, with an explanation of why. If, however, the request for a personal interview has a specific purpose in relation to the Workshop, this interview may help the person to deal with a particular difficulty and may therefore be accepted, making it clear that it is a one-off. In this case, it may be useful to give the results of this interview to the large group, provided that this is done with tact and in consultation with the person who requested the interview, so as not to create suspicions of asides or coalitions, which would be harmful to the dynamics of the group.

The Workshop may have revealed a problem and the need for further work. It is a good idea for the facilitators to talk to the leader about this at the end of the Workshop, or shortly afterwards.

### h) After the Workshop, is there a need for follow-up?
A facilitator may wonder what happens to the group after a Workshop: 'Is what we were able to initiate bearing fruit? Is the sense of community still there? Has the group fallen back into its usual rut? Is it staying with the decision it made?' It is good to ask oneself: 'Why these questions? Is it a matter of curiosity to reassure ourselves about the validity of the Workshop we have accompanied? Do we need a 'Thank You' from the group?!'

Shouldn't we leave this to the Lord? After all, it is God's business and that of the group. Why should we be concerned for the group? The parable of the sower shows a sower who leaves the seed where it fell, without worrying about the stones or thorns (Lk 8:5–8). The facilitator is not responsible for what happens between the group and its Creator. Like John the Baptist, one can say regarding relationship with the group: *'He (Jesus) must grow, and I must shrink'* (Jn 3:30).

Experience shows that it is seldom good to contact the group or some of its members after the Workshop. It is better to leave them free. Not offering your services avoids any suspicion of curiosity. If a group wishes to be accompanied again, it is up to them freely to decide this, and a fresh accompaniment may be better done by another team. Yet it is healthy, as we have said, to review the Workshop with whatever help is to hand.

*i) Inner attitudes – selfless service and gratitude*

Facilitators are at the service of the Lord who works in the group. *'Unless the Lord builds the house, the masons labour in vain'* (Ps 126:1).

They must be careful not to seek gratification other than that of honestly doing their part of the work and being able to contemplate the fruits of God's action in the group. It is important that they do not attribute to themselves what belongs to divine grace, nor make the group the occasion of their own self-importance by instrumentalising it.

In this respect, facilitators do everything within their reach to prepare and encourage the conditions for the group's encounter with the Lord. But they must be aware that everything depends on God, who alone has the initiative.

All accompaniment is lived intensely by those who facilitate and is happily the occasion of ongoing personal conversion on their part. The Lord uses their gifts, their weaknesses and their poverty: they can only give thanks for this. For both the group and the facilitators, moments of pain and death become places of resurrection and mission, because they have been meeting the risen Lord.

- *Work as a team, one of you for content, the other for process*
- *Help one another to grow in self-awareness*
- *Make the group a safe place for all, including the shy, to participate as fully as they would wish*
- *Be cautious about one-to-one accompaniment*
- *Be grateful to be called to serve the group and their God*
- *Notice self-transformation: 'I see things better, I'm more full of the mystery of how God works"*

# Recognising the Spirit's Signature

Evaluation of the Workshop both by the facilitators and the group is important: it is a rich experience of how the Spirit writes straight on crooked lines, and in a quiet way deepens experience of the Mystery of God. St Paul found this to be so as he concluded his reflections on the history of our salvation: 'O the depth of the riches and wisdom and knowledge of God!' (Rom 11:33).

*The facilitators*
Facilitators can evaluate their completed work, first by each privately, and then in an exchange between them.

It is first of all a moment for the team to realise how the Lord has intervened in the group, despite the imperfection of his servants. *'The Spirit comes to the rescue of our weakness'* (Rom 8:26).

Even before that, it is good to see that it was the Spirit who inspired the requesting group to come together ... and inspired Esdac to exist ... Esdac, as noted above, is the fruit of one man's seeding-experience during an assembly in Canada in 1992. Jean Charlier had observed that the procedure used by some North American Jesuits was more apt than others to open a group to the action of the Holy Spirit.

It is also a time to notice, with gratitude, how the team has allowed itself to be led by the Spirit. For Ignatius, ingratitude would be a serious failure.

Shortcomings and mistakes are occasions of grace. This provides an opportunity to learn from them and to see what further training might be needed.

Finally, such an evaluation, written down, is useful for all Esdac members: it can inform them of an innovation, of how a difficulty was overcome, and of the need for training on a particular point.

## Supervision

In order to avoid slipping into a process of control over a group, despite good intentions, it is highly desirable that facilitators find a safe and competent place to review their work and to examine with an independent party how they positioned themselves in relation to the group.

The Workshop itself can become a place which evokes very intimate dimensions in the participants; some may feel pressurised and in great difficulty, and this can easily lead them to put themselves at the mercy of someone whom they treat as an authority figure.

Since this can happen unconsciously, the labour of putting into words what has been experienced is the only way of distancing oneself from that dynamic, and therefore of protecting oneself from the trap of controlling the group.

Similarly, it may happen that a facilitator had difficulties that could not be resolved in dialogue with the other facilitator. Such may happen to an inexperienced coach in a training session. It may also happen that both facilitators find themselves at a loss when faced with a situation such as negative reactions from the group leaders. In both these cases, it is good to be able to step back and offer the possibility to talk with a supervisor. This consultation can be done on an *ad hoc* basis, by telephone consultation, or by internet, or on a more permanent basis.

## We share what we have received

Giving and receiving are the terms that, for Ignatius, define love: 'Love consists in mutual communication. That is to say, the one who loves gives and communicates to the beloved his good or a part of his good or his power; likewise, in return, the beloved gives to the one who loves' (*Spiritual Exercises*, 231). Thus in the *Spiritual Exercises* he does not use the terms 'facilitator' and 'retreatant', but 'the one who *gives* the Exercises' and 'the one who *receives* them' (*Spiritual Exercises*, 21). We can therefore consider that Ignatius considers the Exercises as a gift, a jewel, that he has received from God, and that it is up to him to share it in turn with others. The Esdac companions view things similarly: they see the Esdac journey as a treasure that they have received, which holds them together and which they are eager to share with the Church and the world.

## *What made it possible?*
At the end of a workshop, facilitators can ask: 'What made it possible for the Holy Spirit to be experienced?' Mostly the answer is: 'The trust that prevailed, the kindness, the listening …'

The next question is: 'What are the factors that have favored the growth of that trust, goodwill and listening?'

As we have seen, these factors are very concrete and they converge on the experience of listening. For example:

- *dividing a large group into small groups,*
- *arranging the circle,*
- *ensuring that everyone is given equal time to speak,*
- *listening to each person in turn,*
- *looking for what, in this listening, sheds light, what touches the heart, etc.*
- *searching together for consensus.*

In other words, the deepest values flourish better where the conditions for their growth are respected. By humbly accepting the use of a proven method – Esdac – the group has trusted us and we have trusted them.

At the heart of the Esdac process is the celebration of mercy. As the members of a group review their chaotic history, they end up marveling at the fact that they are still alive (*Spiritual Exercises*, 61) and have stayed together. They then realise that this is because the Divine Majesty, the Lord of History, has been watching over them.

## *The Spirit likes groups!*
The Church (and this is true of every follower of Jesus) will always be tempted to show the world a wrinkle-free face, a flawless system. And yet, humbly acknowledging the chaos in our 'living together' opens us up to the Spirit's creative work. Those who exercise authority (that is, all of us, in one way or another) can do so in a healthy way only by being alert to the temptations to abuse from which the Holy Spirit saves them.

The Holy Spirit satisfies our deepest thirst: to love and be loved. As the hymn, *Come, Holy Spirit* says, the Spirit transforms hearts of stone into hearts of flesh, rekindles the flames that were about to be extinguished, straightens what is twisted, softens what is stiff, and warms what had frozen. The Spirit turns mourning into joy (Jer 31:13). 'Enemies at last speak to each other, adversaries reach out to each other' (Eucharistic Prayer 2 for Reconciliation).

This book proclaims our conviction that *the Holy Spirit is offered to all*. It concludes with the testimony that *the Holy Spirit is indeed received by many*.

Everyone receives the grace of the Spirit for the good of the whole body, including the poorest, the least appreciated. Recognising that the Lord is present and active in the midst of the group is a source of deep joy and community and makes it cry out like Jacob: *'Truly, the Lord is in this place! And I did not know it'* (Gen 28:16).

Groups, large and small, are privileged places where the Holy Spirit is offered, received and transmitted, a little like the flame at the Easter vigil which is shared from candle to candle. The Spirit renews people, restores the link between them, and makes them fit to be one body for a common mission. And the Spirit does this even with people who might say, as the first disciples in Ephesus said to St Paul: *'We have not even heard that there is a Holy Spirit'* (Acts 19:2).

Often, Spirit-led conversation is the treasure par excellence that groups retain from a Workshop, because it gives equal voice to all members, makes them attentive to each other, and opens them to the spirit of communion and truth working in each of them and between them. It makes them move from 'I' to 'we' and from 'we' to 'I'.

### Shared governance

The Church of today, led by Pope Francis, is calling for shared governance or synodality. This shows a beautiful spirit of openness. Do Christians realise the richness they can receive from the methods of the 'managerial' world? And, in return, do they compute the immeasurable 'plus' that their faith can confer on the world of business? 'When a community welcomes the proclamation of salvation, the Holy Spirit fertilises its culture with the transforming power of the Gospel. On the other hand, the Church herself lives a journey of reception that enriches her with what the Spirit has already mysteriously sown in that culture.'[74]

If in our dioceses and parishes, in our couples, in our gatherings and meetings, Jesus sees us desolate, will we let him take part in our conversations? Will we accept that he asks us, as he did the Twelve and the disciples on the road to Emmaus, *'What are you discussing?'* And are we ready to hear him say to us: *'O, how foolish you are! Was it not necessary that the Messiah should suffer these things and then enter into his glory?'* (Lk 24:25).

Generously entered into, a discernment in common is both a grace-filled and a demanding process. Only as we go along do we learn just what is being demanded of us: that the precious ideas, principles, preferences, that have held our lives together may have to go. Think of a group of clergy who recognise to their horror that through their style of living, clericalism has been rampant among them, and that it had kept them safe, on their pedestals. They come to see that they are only servants of the Great Mystery; that power is indeed given, but that it is for sharing, that synodality with all its levelling out of differences is God's desire for them. This awareness is grace-filled; emerging into a new mode of relating to the People of God is indeed demanding.

A process of communal discernment may – God willing – result in documents with 'specific objectives' and a 'plan of action', but this is not its essential fruit. The very process of participation encourages the slow germination of community between all: community for which Jesus offered his life, community that will finally blossom as the ultimate community of love.

### *The Group evaluation*

Because God can be found in all things, it is important and life-giving for the group itself to review the Workshop both personally and together. They will realise that

---

74  Pope Francis, *Querida Amazonia*, 68.

- the Holy Spirit has not been lacking, for it is the Spirit who arouses the desire to take action and stimulates the energy necessary for commitment;
- the group may at times have been blind to what was happening;
- the inevitable consequences of the group decision require everyone's commitment.

The group must also clarify what helped and what did not help the Workshop to run smoothly.

➤ *Prayer Sheet 26: Evaluation of the session & conclusion of the Workshop* can be used.

### *Closure and thanksgiving*

Communal discernment mobilises many emotions in participants. What is at stake is intimate, often even radical. Certain emotions resurface, without the members necessarily being aware of them or having the tools to contain them. What some people have been able to reveal from their inner world during the sessions, they need to close in the right conditions.

It is therefore necessary, before the Workshop ends, for the facilitators to allow a reasonable amount of time to take a weather report in plenary, in order to check that no one lacks the means required to live out the communal decision in peace, with dynamism, and with a satisfied heart.

We conclude by recalling that the Lord has been present throughout the Workshop, and we give thanks for his help and faithfulness.

### *Post-script*

The words of St Irenaeus (AD 130–202) still ring true today and express the heart of the Esdac project: 'The glory of God is the human person fully alive'. In every detail, Esdac tries to help individuals become more alive, more themselves, more open to the world's needs and to the dreams of God.

The God behind this project is active in drawing people together to build a better world: all are invited to participate, including those of differing belief systems, theists and non-theists alike. Inspired by the ultimate values of truth, justice and love, and with the Spirit's unobtrusive leading they labour together to make the best decision in any given circumstance, whether it be in the making of a will, in international or local conflicts, in hearing the cry of the poor and of the planet.

> **FALLING IN LOVE WITH GOD**
> *'Nothing is more practical than finding God,*
> *that is, than falling in love in an absolute, final way.*
> *What you are in love with,*
> *what seizes your imagination,*
> *will affect everything.*
> *It will decide what will get you out of bed in the mornings,*
> *what you will do with your evenings,*
> *how you spend your weekends,*
> *what you read, who you know, what breaks your heart,*
> *and what amazes you with love and gratitude.*
> *Fall in love, stay in love, and it will decide everything!'*
>
> (Attributed to Pedro Arrupe SJ, this reflection was in fact written by his contemporary, Joseph Whelan SJ, 1932–1994)

# Appendices

## Appendix 1: Negotiating and Planning a Workshop

*Agreement between the requesting group and the team of facilitators*
By 'requesting group', we mean: a parish, a cluster of parishes, a religious community, an association, a school, a club, a business, a team of couples, a couple, a family, etc. In order to agree to accompany a requesting group, several issues must be clarified.

This clarification between the leader(s) of the requesting group and the team of facilitators is important: the details that emerge from this contact can be clues as to how the future meetings will be organised. For example, the team may be able to detect how authority is experienced within the group and whether this needs review. The clarification may result in declining the request because the necessary conditions for the Workshop are not met. What is agreed may be formalised in a written document exchanged between the requesting group and the facilitators.

Next the leader of the requesting group can bring together a few future participants to prepare the discernment programme with the team of facilitators. A full day would allow many issues to be addressed and enable mutual trust and freedom to be established within the requesting group and with the facilitators. Such a day could be introduced by a Prayer Sheet, followed by a personal time of prayer and reflection, so that intending participants can experience how the sessions will run.

## The purpose of the request

Often, the explicit formulation of the purpose of the request requires real work. It may happen that the initial formulation hides something else. For example, the leader may believe that the dysfunction to be remedied is caused by poor organisational structure, but in conversation with the facilitating team it emerges that the style of the leader is problematic, or that members of the requesting group do not take time to talk openly with each other.

What are the possible purposes of a request? The list below mentions only the most common ones.

- *Better listening:* To 'free up the floor' in the requesting group so that its members listen better to each other.
- *Spirit-led conversation:* To make progress in the practice of Spirit-led conversation, by opening up more to the Holy Spirit in exchanges and by challenging whatever hinders the Spirit. The result will be more freedom, flexibility, creativity and mutual esteem. The process may generate a celebration of mercy and a question: 'What consequences follow on what we have just shared?'
- *Community:* To form a 'body', a community.
- *Sharing values:* To get to know each other better by sharing our experiences, our deepest aspirations, our way of seeing our life together; to formulate what unites us.
- *Evaluation:* To evaluate the life of the group. What is a source of vitality and what raises difficulties? To review an event that has destabilised the group; to draw up recommendations for improving procedures.
- *Reconciliation:* To work towards group reconciliation. This requires exercises in Spirit-led conversation, and re-reading, if possible, the initial History Line, followed by a celebration of mercy.
- *Emerging calls:* To discern contemporary calls and seek ways to respond to them. Since the world keeps changing, the group, like any living organism, is called to change while remaining faithful to its fundamental identity. For example: 'Given the changes in religious practice caused by the recent health crisis, what can our diocese do to stimulate emerging shoots of new life?'

Examples of questions for the applicant group which clarify the request:

- What prompted the request for facilitation?
- Why is it being done now?
- What situation is causing the problem?
- Who is suffering from this situation?
- What has already been tried to remedy it? With what success?
- Who will benefit from the solution?
- Who benefits from the *status quo*?
- What is the expected outcome of the process?
- Are there any conflicts? If so, on what issues?
- Have there already been experiences of joint discernment? Were they good/bad?
- Were decisions made that have not been implemented?
- In what terms can the purpose of the discernment be formulated?

*The identity and mission of the group*
It is important for the team of facilitators to find out about the group, its purpose, identity and mission, as expressed in the applicants' words. Does the presented formulation correspond to the statutes/documents submitted?

Getting to know the group enables the development of a pathway that is in line with this identity and mission. The facilitators are called upon to broaden their own understandings in order to serve the reality of this new group; they must accompany *the group* on its journey, without relying on their own personal but limited categories. 'In my day …' will not do!

An 'inner' knowledge of the group allows for better shaping of the conditions going forward. This knowledge also helps to nourish the prayer of the facilitators: they present the group to the Lord, and ask his help in accompanying it.

Examples of questions for the facilitators:

- What brings the members together? What is the purpose of the group? What is its mission?
- How is it organised? What are its structures?
- What is its history? What has happened recently?

*Appendices*

### *Who is the ultimate authority?*
A key question is: 'Who has the ultimate statutory power of decision in this group?'

If the power of decision does not lie with the group, is the group aware of this? To what extent is the person in charge of the group committed to the conclusions of the discernment? There is nothing more destructive for a group than to have made a discernment and then to find that it will not be followed.

### *The place of the leader of the requesting group*
We have seen in 'The Authority in the group' that during the Workshop, the facilitators will have authority over the group.

Questions to ask:

- Is it appropriate for the group leader to attend the Workshop? If so, what can be done to encourage its freedom of speech? Is it preferable for the leader not to participate in the session, and if so, what can be done to inform him or her of the outcomes of the Workshop?
- If the request is for reconciliation between group members, is the leader of the group aware that he or she may be the main focus of the negativity that will be expressed? Is the leader strong enough to withstand this ordeal?
- Would it be appropriate to hold a mini-session with the group leader and board prior to the proposed Workshop, on the themes of authority, power and participation?

### *The participants*
The requesting group will need to consider who should participate in the Workshop and ensure that no one is left out who should be present. Depending on the situation, the options are:

- Where possible, all members of the group would attend so that no one feels left out and so that the 'little ones' can contribute;
- Or choose only those who have the capacity to grasp the facts and information required;

- Or restrict choice to those who are statutorily designated as the group delegates, such as members of a council, a chapter, a synod, etc.
- Ensure that at least one representative of each of the affected groups participates in the discernment. Thus, in a parish, the catechists, the visitors to the sick, the weekend faithful, the parents of catechumens, the members of the clergy and the choir, etc., should have a voice, without forgetting the secretaries, the treasurer, the helpers...

In communal discernment, there should always be representatives of those whom we risk forgetting: children dying of hunger; women who have no voice; the ecologically threatened ... Systematically taking into account those whom we tend to omit would defuse certain anxieties. Recall again the story in the Introduction, 'Who speaks for Wolf?'
Questions to ask:

- How and on what basis will participants be chosen?
- Will they feel free, or constrained by a vow of obedience or an employment contract?
- Can we assume that they will come willingly or with leaden feet? Will they attend out of curiosity?
- Regarding the structure of the Spirit-led conversation which will have been outlined – personal, small group sharing, plenary – do they accept this procedure or fear it?
- Is there anything foreseen that might disrupt the goal of communion within the group, and if so, what?
- If the group is composed of Religious, what will be the common daily liturgical celebration? Might the Office of the Hours be lightened, or even omitted? This would allow for a tranquil entry into personal prayer, small group sharing, plenary meetings etc, since these are integral moments of encounter with the Lord in communal discernment
- Is it desirable that there be other times of silence in addition to those required for personal prayer and reflection?
- Should there be substantial rest time, to respect the stamina of each?
- Is it appropriate to meet in the evening?

The facilitators will ensure that the following information will be made known to those invited:

- That a request for facilitation has been made with a view to a communal discernment.
- That the topic for discernment will be …
- That the title of the Workshop will be … For example: 'Go out into the deep', or 'If you knew the gift of God …' Specifying the title can make the participants feel more comfortable.
- That the process includes personal time for prayer and reflection, sharings in small groups, plenary.
- That the ultimate power of decision will rest with …
- That the group leader will or will not be present, or may be present in part as follows …
- That no individual accompaniments will be organised; but that this does not preclude a person in difficulty from benefiting from the once-off help of a facilitator or of some other suitable person present.

### *Nuts'n'Bolts : duration, location, cost, setting*

The number of hours or days planned for the Workshop should be calculated accurately if its agreed aim is to be achieved. If the group does not have the time to experience everything in a single session, it should be made clear from the start that there will be more; the subsequent session(s) should not be too far apart in time, so that the group can keep up its momentum, even if this requires group assistance between sessions.

If the group has difficulty in accepting the length of time required to meet its expectations, the facilitators should try to bring agreement, but if this fails, it should not hesitate to say that it cannot follow up the request until this is settled.

Clarity is also needed as to whether the group should remain in its usual living space, or move out to allow full commitment to the Workshop without the interruptions of its regular occupations.

A budget will be needed to pay for the location if the group moves out, and also to compensate the facilitators.

*Setting:* The way in which a group is seated is already a form of language. Ideally the size of the plenary room should allow people to sit in a circle so that they can all see each other. No stage is arranged for the facilitators. Mobile seating allows the room to be easily rearranged to allow everyone, for example, to look at the History Line.

*The circle:* The inner space of the circle will symbolically manifest what is going on. Without a table in front of the seats, without decoration, this space could be initially left empty, to signify the expectation of words. In the center, only a pen or a feather or a crucifix, with a microphone. A candle, an icon or a Bible will remind us of the presence of the Lord. As the Workshop moves along, flowers, baskets of fruit, dead wood, footprints etc can represent what the group is experiencing.

*Loving details:* The climate of the Workshop will be positively influenced by an array of small attentions: spacious and luminous places, comfortable seats, hearing aids such as loops, a sufficient number of small group rooms close to the plenary room, a room for the facilitators, badges for the participants, drinks for the breaks, panels or walls for displaying the group's productions, a board where the timetable will be written ... All such deepen the 'incarnational' process: God incarnates divine love in concrete gestures.

A few days before the Workshop, the necessary materials will be assembled: computer, printer and/or photocopier, if possible a video projector, pad of paper, felt pens, post-it notes, a large roll of paper for the History Line, allocation of rooms and small group rooms, signposting of the various places ...

## *Developing the Workshop journey*

If agreement is reached between the requesting group and the facilitators, the latter will draw up the plan of the Workshop.

The facilitator(s) don't reproduce what may have been done elsewhere. Each request has its own particularities; every group has its own personality, its unique charisma and history that have brought it together. The Holy Spirit acts *here and now* and does not 'copy and paste'. While there are constants that guide the facilitation, each time we must ask ourselves anew about the path that will best help *this group* to be attentive to the Spirit and to discern their call. Graced decisions must be 'tailor-made'.

The facilitators address the group's points of view; they try to see what underlies their respective thoughts and, in so doing, they build a pathway adapted to the group. The danger is to start a discussion: instead the exchange should be conducted in the mode of a Spirit-led conversation: first the facilitators pray personally; they look with the eyes of God at the group entrusted to them, reflect on what could best help it, and then talk about it together, always keeping a favorable attitude towards the ideas of others.

Even if we cannot predict how a group will behave, it is important not to proceed haphazardly but to design a schedule and present it beforehand, even if it must be modified along the way. The aim is to answer the question: *'What will enable the group, as we know it now, to listen to the Spirit, to discern on the point that is the subject of the request?'* But it is not the facilitator's job to solve the problems of the group, nor to provide the answers to its questions. It is the Lord who must guide and lead the group. In a situation where the group does not see a way forward it is the Lord who 'opens a way' (Ps 30:9b. See also Jn 21:1–13 where the Lord directs the fishing crew so that they make a good catch!).

The job of the facilitators is to organise the necessary steps, to plan their duration in a realistic way, all within the timeframe set, in order to achieve the objective, while allowing for the unexpected. Indeed, the further along the journey, the more it may be necessary to change what was planned.

### *Follow-up?*
'How will the Workshop be followed up?' Sometimes a Workshop ends with the making of important decisions, but without any indication of how these will be implemented and by whom, or when the evaluation(s) will be made. It is the task of the facilitator to help the group to organise its follow-up before the Workshop terminates.

- *Why this request?*
- *Clarify the identity of the group*
- *Clarify the role of the group leader*
- *Choose and brief participants carefully*
- *Take time over nuts'n'bolts*
- *Let the Spirit generate creativity in the group and in your own approach*
- *Focus the group on Implementation and Follow-up*

# Appendix 2: A Sample Workshop Schedule and Timetable

This is the schedule of a Workshop to evaluate the internal life of a group which had never taken the needed time to formulate its raison d'être or to review its history.

## Day 0
From 15:00 onwards: Arrivals.
19:00 Meal.
20:15 Plenary: presentations.

## Following days

| Day 1<br>Desires /<br>Experiences. | Day 2<br>History Line | Day 3<br>History Line | Day 4<br>Reconciliation |
|---|---|---|---|
| « My deepest desires and dreams »<br>Instructions for spirit-led conversation<br>Small groups<br>Plenary | « The history of our group – the events »<br>Small groups<br>Plenary | « Graces received in our history »<br>Small groups<br>Plenary | Personal Prayer : « I am complicit »<br>Preparation of communal celebration of mercy<br>Silence |
| 13.00 Meal ||||

*Appendix 2: A Sample Workshop Schedule and Timetable*

| « My deepest experiences of God » Small group Plenary Eucharist | « The history of our group – Feelings » Small groups Plenary Eucharist | « Graces not (or badly) received in our history » Small groups Plenary Eucharist | Communal celebration of mercy Free time Eucharist |
|---|---|---|---|
| \multicolumn{4}{c}{19.00 Meal} |
| Free time Personal review | Free time Personal review | Free time Personal review | Free time Personal review |

| Day 5 | Day 6 | Day 7 | Day 8 |
|---|---|---|---|
| Name of grace | Call and response | Confirmation | Evaluation |
| « Personal name of grace » | « What are we called to? » | Confirmation « Take the cross and follow Jesus » | Last clarifications Evaluation of the Workshop Eucharist |
| \multicolumn{4}{c}{13.00 Meal} |
| « Name of grace of the group » Eucharist | « How to answer the call ? » Eucharist | « Resurrecting with Jesus » Eucharist | Departure |
| \multicolumn{4}{c}{19.00 Meal} |
| Free time Personal review | Free time Personal review | Feast Personal review | |

### Schedule for the first day
9:00: Plenary. Singing. Clarity about our goal/desire / Request for grace.
9.15: Presentation of the first Prayer Sheet.
9:25: Personal prayer.
10:25: Break.

10:40: Plenary: Instructions for Spirit-led conversation
11:00: Small groups.
12:00: Plenary.
13:00: Lunch.
15:00: Plenary: presentation of the second Prayer Sheet.
15:10: Personal prayer.
16:10: Break.
16:25 Small groups.
17:25 Plenary session.
18:15: Eucharist.
19:00: Meal.
20.00: Free time with 15 minutes of personal reflection.

# Appendix 3: Prayer Sheets

## Note

As emphasised above, the term 'Prayer Sheet' should not be understood as being exclusively relevant to believers. The words and events of Jesus' life can be read by non-Christians as coming from one of the world's greatest teachers of wisdom, and can be used for self-reflection and pondering by anyone of goodwill.

When presenting Jesus on the cross, Ignatius writes: 'I shall *reflect* upon myself ... and I shall *ponder* upon what presents itself to my mind' (*Spiritual Exercises*, 53). Reflection, consideration, pondering etc are directives used by Ignatius to engage the reader in the subject matter. He would hint that what is presented to my mind, with its accompanying feelings and emotions, may well be coming from the good Spirit.

The following Prayer Sheets provide inspiration, but facilitators may need to design new ones, depending on how the group is progressing. See page 148 for how to write a prayer sheet.

### *Prayer Sheet 1: Listening to one another in Spirit-led conversation*

**Text**
Jesus, tired out by his journey, was sitting by Jacob's well. It was about noon. A Samaritan woman came to draw water, and Jesus said to her, 'Give me a drink'. The Samaritan woman said to him, 'How is it that you, a Jew, ask a drink of me, a woman of Samaria?' Jesus answered her, 'If you knew the gift of God, and who it is that is saying to you, 'Give me a drink', you would have asked him, and he would have given you living water' (Jn 4: 6–10).

**Grace to pray for**
'Lord, help me to become a better listener.'

*Appendices*

### Helps for reflection and prayer
- In the text I see the characters, I hear what they say and their tone. And I watch what they do.
- What emotions and desires are at play in them? What does this scene awaken in me?
- I link into my experience by recalling some life-giving encounter I have had: what happened when I felt heard? What emotions and desires were awakened in me?

### Conversation with the Lord
I imagine myself sitting next to Jesus, perhaps aware of my own tiredness. Jesus speaks to me as he did to the Samaritan woman. What does he say to me? I listen and talk to him, heart to heart.

### Harvesting
A few minutes before the prayer time ends I review it:

- *What helped me? (my prayer place, body posture ...)*
- *What gave me joy, sadness, peace, anxiety ...?*

I make a brief note of what touched me most and what I want to share with my small group.

### *Prayer Sheet 2: Talking in front of others*
**Text**

Jesus returned from the region of Tyre and went towards the Sea of Galilee. They brought to him a deaf man who also had a speech impediment; and they begged him to lay his hand on him. He took him aside, away from the crowd, put his fingers into his ears, and spat and touched his tongue. Then looking up to heaven, he sighed and said to him, 'Ephphatha', that is, 'Be opened.' And immediately his ears were opened, his tongue was released, and he spoke plainly. Then Jesus ordered them to tell no one; but the more he ordered them, the more zealously they proclaimed it. They were astounded beyond measure, saying, 'He has done everything well; he even makes the deaf to hear and the mute to speak' (Mk 7: 31–37).

Peter said to the cripple, 'I have no silver or gold, but what I have I give you; in the name of Jesus Christ of Nazareth, stand up and walk' (Acts 3: 6).

**Grace to pray for**
'Give me, Lord, the grace to know better what to say and how to say it.'

**Helps for Reflection and Prayer**
- I imagine Jesus with the deaf and dumb man. He takes him aside, touches his tongue and says 'Open up'. The man's tongue is loosened ...
- In what circumstances have I experienced difficulty in speaking in front of others? What is my difficulty? ('What I have to say is not interesting, I have difficulty finding the right words, I repeat the same things over and over again' ...)
- I identify with the cured man. Jesus, who makes the mute speak, touches my tongue and says 'Open up!' What does this mean for me?
- As I listen to Peter speak to the cripple, what does this teach me about my way of speaking?

**Conversation with the Lord**
I ask Jesus to speak to me; I tell him my difficulty, in all confidence. How does he reply? I listen to him.

**Harvesting**
I briefly note what touched me most and what I want to share with my small group, believing that the Lord has loosened my tongue.

*Prayer Sheet 3: Respecting what others say*
**Texts**
Jesus set out and went away to the region of Tyre. He entered a house and did not want anyone to know he was there. Yet he could not escape notice, but a woman whose little daughter had an unclean spirit immediately heard about him, and she came and bowed down at his feet. Now the woman was a Gentile, of Syrophoenician origin. She

begged him to cast the demon out of her daughter. He said to her, 'Let the children be fed first, for it is not fair to take the children's food and throw it to the dogs.' But she answered him, 'Sir, even the dogs under the table eat the children's crumbs.' Then he said to her, 'For saying that you may go – the demon has left your daughter.' So she went home, found the child lying on the bed, and the demon gone. (Mk 7: 24–30).

It should be presupposed that every good Christian should be readier to justify rather than to condemn a neighbour's statement. If no justification can be found, one should ask the other in what sense the statement is to be taken, and if that sense is wrong the other should be corrected with love. Should this not be sufficient, let every appropriate means be sought whereby to have the statement interpreted in a good sense and so to justify it (*Spiritual Exercises*, 22).

### Grace to pray for
'Lord, grant me the grace to be more inclined to accept the words of others than to condemn them.'

### Helps for reflection and prayer
- I re-read the above Gospel text. I see Jesus and the Syro-Phoenician woman. I hear what they say and the tone in which they say it. I watch what they do. I reflect and draw fruit from what I see, hear and watch.
- I re-read the presupposition of Ignatius (*Spiritual Exercises*, 22) and draw fruit from it.
- I ask the Lord to remind me of one or two conversations where I have condemned another. I ask myself what appropriate means I could have used to salvage their words: where I could discern the Holy Spirit at work in the other person. What were the signs, what were the fruits?

### Conversation with the Lord
I speak freely with Jesus, giving him 'the feather' and then taking it back, in turn.

**Harvesting**
I note down what touched me most and what I wish to share with others.

*Prayer Sheet 4: Serving others but not being used by them*
**Text**
Jesus was teaching his disciples, saying to them, 'The Son of Man is to be betrayed into human hands, and they will kill him, and three days after being killed, he will rise again.' But they did not understand what he was saying and were afraid to ask him. Then they came to Capernaum; and when he was in the house he asked them, 'What were you arguing about on the way?' But they were silent, for on the way they had argued with one another about who was the greatest. He sat down, called the twelve, and said to them, 'Whoever wants to be first must be last of all and servant of all' (Mk 9: 31–35).

**Grace to pray for**
'Lord, grant that I may become more of a servant in my interactions.'

**Helps for reflection and prayer**
I read this Gospel text again. I see and hear the dialogue between Jesus and his disciples.

I ask the Lord to remind me of a moment or an encounter when

- I wanted to take the lead,
- I wanted to take the first place,
- I did not dare to express what I thought was important,
- I dared to say what I thought,
- I took my rightful place, and was both responsible and serving.

**Conversation with the Lord**
I offer to the Lord what I have experienced in prayer and all the graces I have received. I listen and dialogue with him about what springs up in my heart.

## Harvesting

I note down what touched me most and what I wish to share with my small group.

### *Prayer Sheet 5: My attitude to the exercise of authority*
**Text**
I recall

- the cycle of energy and power (p. 69)
- the three styles of exercising authority (p. 81)

### Grace to pray for
'Help me, Lord, to have a well-adjusted attitude to the exercise of authority.'

### Helps for reflection and prayer
Visualise, in the form of a picture – perhaps even a caricature – my usual attitude to the exercise of authority. Which animal would best symbolise this attitude?

What style of authority do I spontaneously prefer: directive, consultative, participative?

- when I exercise authority?
- when someone else exercises authority?

When I exercise authority:

- what is easiest for me is ...
- what is most difficult for me is ...

In the way others exercise authority :

- I appreciate in others ...
- I fear in others ...

Am I able to change my style of authority according to the circumstances, the state of the group, the issues to be dealt with?

Can I delegate by giving confidence to the person accepting the delegation?

Do the members of the group give me confidence in my abilities as a leader?

## Conversation with the Lord
Dialogue freely with Jesus, who, after washing the disciples' feet, calls himself 'Teacher and Lord' (Jn 13:13).

## Harvesting
Prepare for the small group: in the first round, share as usual the fruits of your prayer. In the second round, exchange suggestions to help each other with the difficulties mentioned.

## *Prayer Sheet 6: My deepest desires and dreams*
### Text
As Jesus and his disciples and a large crowd were leaving Jericho, Bartimaeus, a blind beggar, was sitting by the roadside. When he heard that it was Jesus of Nazareth, he began to shout out and say, 'Jesus, Son of David, have mercy on me!' Many sternly ordered him to be quiet, but he cried out even more loudly, 'Son of David, have mercy on me!' Jesus stood still and said, 'Call him here.' And they called the blind man, saying to him, 'Take heart; get up, he is calling you.' So throwing off his cloak, he sprang up and came to Jesus. Then Jesus said to him, 'What do you want me to do for you?' The blind man said to him, 'My teacher, let me see again.' Jesus said to him, 'Go; your faith has made you well.' Immediately he regained his sight and followed him on the way (Mk 10: 46–52).

### Grace to pray for
'Lord, make me aware of my deepest aspirations, desires and dreams.'

### Helps for reflection and prayer
- I take time to be touched by the above text; to see the characters, hear what they say, watch what they do and draw fruit for my own life.
- I ask myself what are my deepest aspirations both for myself and for humankind today? What desire burns in my heart?

- I imagine that I am at the point of death: what would I like to have achieved in my life? (*Spiritual Exercises*, 186).

**Conversation with the Lord**
I imagine what Jesus might say to me. I listen to him, and speak with him, heart to heart, as one friend with another.

**Harvesting**
A few minutes before the end of the prayer time, I review my prayer time:

- What helped me? (Where I chose to pray; bodily posture …).
- What gave me joy, sadness, peace, anxiety …?

I make a brief note of what touched me most and what I want to share with the small group.

*Prayer Sheet 7: My deep experiences of God*
**Text**
In those days John the Baptist appeared in the wilderness of Judea, proclaiming, 'Repent, for the kingdom of heaven has come near.' Then the people of Jerusalem and all Judea were going out to him, and all the region along the Jordan, and they were baptised by him in the river Jordan, confessing their sins. Then Jesus came from Galilee to be baptiszed by him. John would have prevented him, saying, 'I need to be baptised by you, and do you come to me?' But Jesus answered him, 'Let it be so now; for it is proper for us in this way to fulfil all righteousness.' Then he consented. And just as Jesus came up from the water, suddenly the heavens were opened to him, and he saw the Spirit of God descending like a dove and alighting on him. And a voice from heaven said, 'This is my Son, the Beloved, with whom I am well pleased' (Mt 3: 1–2.5–6.13–17).

**Grace to pray for**
'Lord, help me to remember some of the profound experiences I have had of your presence, your action, your love.'

**Helps for reflection and prayer**
- I contemplate the Gospel scene and see the characters, hear what they say and observe what they do.
- I ask myself how this Gospel scene illuminates my life.
- I re-read my life
- I let the key experiences that have marked my relationship with God, with others and with myself come to mind (I review the places, the moments, the people …).

**Conversation with the Lord**
I imagine what he might say to me. I listen to him, and I speak to him, heart to heart, like a friend with his friend.

**Harvesting**
A few minutes before the end of the prayer time, I make a brief note of what touched me most and what I want to share.

*Prayer Sheet 8: My name of grace*
**Text**
Jesus said to the disciples, 'But who do you say that I am?' Simon Peter answered, 'You are the Messiah, the Son of the living God.' And Jesus answered him, 'Blessed are you, Simon, son of Jonah! For flesh and blood has not revealed this to you, but my Father in heaven. And I tell you, you are Peter, and on this rock I will build my church, and the gates of Hades will not prevail against it'. (Mt 16:15–18).

'Do not rejoice that the spirits submit to you, but rejoice that your names are written in heaven' (Lk 10:20).

**Grace to pray for**
'Give me, Lord, the grace to discover or deepen my name of grace, my identity, my vocation, my mission.'

**Helps for reflection and prayer**
(*Choose what speaks to your heart*)

- In exercise 6, 'My deepest desires', what emerged?
- In exercise 7, 'My deepest experiences of God', what emerged?

*Appendices*

- At least once in my life have I felt spontaneously close to God?
- What makes me more alive? (See the re-reading exercise)
- When I re-read my history (my family, events, encounters ...), what very personal, unique meaning has God given it?
- What very special gifts has God given me?
- How would I formulate, in a single expression, my identity, my vocation, my mission in this world?
- What would those close to me say about this?
- When have I given my best, been useful, fruitful?
- When have I been able to say, 'This is really me'?
- When have I felt joy, peace, confidence, hope, love, strength, energy?
- When have I felt most in tune with myself, with others, with God?
- What words or passages of Scripture speak to me most?
- In the evening of my life, at my death, what would I like to have been?

**Conversation with the Lord**
I thank the Lord for calling me by my name, which is unique to me.

**Harvesting**
I note down what touched me most and what I want to share with the small group

*Prayer Sheet 9: The story of our group: its events*
**Texts**
As Jesus passed along the Sea of Galilee, he saw Simon and his brother Andrew casting a net into the sea – for they were fishermen. And Jesus said to them, 'Follow me and I will make you fish for peopl'. And immediately they left their nets and followed him (Mk 1:16–18).

And he said, 'I have told you that no one can come to me unless it is granted by the Father.' Because of this many of his disciples turned back and no longer went about with him. So Jesus asked the twelve, 'Do you also wish to go away?' Simon Peter answered him, 'Lord, to whom can we go? You have the words of eternal life' (Jn 6:65–68).

'You did not choose me, I chose you' (Jn 15:16).

## Grace to pray for
'Give me, Lord, the ability to discern the more significant events in our group's history.'

## Helps for reflection and prayer
I taste and savour the biblical texts above.

I recall, as simple facts, the events that I think are the more significant in the history of our group:

- happy or difficult moments,
- moments of communion or of distance and conflict,
- moments of fruitfulness or discouragement, etc.

## Conversation with the Lord
I thank the Lord for his unseen but very real presence throughout our history.

## Harvesting
I note down the events that I wish to share with the group.

*(At this point, it is important to try to formulate an event without interpretation. This requires work, because if the event is considered important, it will have left a strong emotional trace in your memory. The repercussion that these events have in the affectivity will be the matter of the prayer and sharing that will follow).*

## *Prayer Sheet 10: The story of our group: the feelings*
### Texts
The seventy returned with joy, saying, 'Lord, in your name even the demons submit to us!' At that same hour Jesus rejoiced in the Holy Spirit and said, 'I thank you, Father, Lord of heaven and earth, because you have hidden these things from the wise and the intelligent and have revealed them to infants; yes, Father, for such was your gracious will' (Lk 10:17.21).

As Jesus came near and saw the city, he wept over it, saying, 'If you, even you, had only recognised on this day the things that make for peace! But now they are hidden from your eyes. Indeed, the days will come upon you, when your enemies will set up ramparts around you and surround you and hem you in on every side. They will crush you to the ground, you and your children within you, and they will not leave within you one stone upon another; because you did not recognise the time of your visitation from God' (Lk 19:41–44).

**Grace to pray for**
'Give me, Lord, in the light of our History Line, the grace to let the feelings (emotions, sentiments, sensations) that I have now rise up in me.'

**Helps for reflection and prayer**
In the texts above, I contemplate Jesus as he lets his feelings rise up in him.

- In the first text, he expresses his joy at the satisfaction of one of his deepest desires.
- In the second text, his tears signal a vital unfulfilled desire.

Recalling the major events of our History Line and our exchanges about them, what are my feelings (emotions, sentiments, sensations)?
Can I identify, in relation to a particular feeling, which vital desire was or was not satisfied in me?

**Conversation with the Lord**
I dialogue with the Lord about what I am experiencing.

**Harvesting**
I note down what touched me most and which I decide to share.

*Prayer Sheet 11: The graces embraced in our history*
**Text**
Again Jesus began to teach beside the sea. Such a very large crowd gathered around him that he got into a boat on the sea and sat there, while the whole crowd was beside the sea on the land. He began to teach them many things in parables, and in his teaching he said to them: 'Listen! A sower went out to sow. And as he sowed, some seed

fell on the path, and the birds came and ate it up. Other seed fell on rocky ground, and it sprang up quickly, since it had no depth of soil. And when the sun rose, it was scorched; and since it had no root, it withered away. Other seed fell among thorns, and the thorns grew up and choked it, and it yielded no grain. Other seed fell into good soil and brought forth grain, growing up and increasing and yielding thirty and sixty and a hundredfold. And he said, 'Let anyone with ears to hear listen!' (Mk 4:1–9).

### Grace to pray for
'Give me, Lord, the grace to see the good seed that is growing in our group.

### Helps for reflection and prayer
I listen to Jesus teaching us in this parable.

- I re-read our group experience.
- What gives us wings? What are the areas where our group freedom is greater?
- What opens us more to the Holy Spirit? What ways of being and doing, what attitudes, what habits, what activities …?
- I see and feel how much this gives us life and nourishes our communion.
- How do I see that the Holy Spirit has such and such a way with our group?

### Conversation with the Lord
I tell the Lord my gratitude for the good seed that he is sowing in our life together. I ask for his help so that we can continue to be more open to his grace. I listen to him.

### Harvesting
I note down and share two or three main graces that we received and that help us as a group to grow towards what we are truly and deeply called to be. I note also the way in which the Holy Spirit tends to act with us.

## *Prayer Sheet 12: The graces resisted in our history*
### Text
Again Jesus began to teach beside the sea. Such a very large crowd gathered around him that he got into a boat on the sea and sat there, while the whole crowd was beside the sea on the land. He began to teach them many things in parables, and in his teaching he said to them: 'Listen! A sower went out to sow. And as he sowed, some seed fell on the path, and the birds came and ate it up. Other seed fell on rocky ground, and it sprang up quickly, since it had no depth of soil. And when the sun rose, it was scorched; and since it had no root, it withered away. Other seed fell among thorns, and the thorns grew up and choked it, and it yielded no grain. Other seed fell into good soil and brought forth grain, growing up and increasing and yielding thirty and sixty and a hundredfold. And he said, 'Let anyone with ears to hear listen!' (Mk 4:1–9).

### Grace to pray for
'Grant me, Lord, the grace to become aware of the evil that is at work within us. Give us the grace to feel pain from it so that we may be motivated to change.'

### Helps for reflection and prayer
- Again I listen to Jesus teaching us in this parable.
- I re-read our group experience.
- What holds us back, hinders us, shackles us? What are the areas where our lack of freedom is most obvious?
- What prevents us from being more open to the Holy Spirit: our habits, fears, assumptions, criticisms, grudges…?
- I try to see and feel how much this distorts and spoils our relationships.

### Conversation with the Lord
I tell the Lord my shame and my desire for change. I ask him to help us and thank him because he works constantly to enable the good grain to grow.

### Harvesting
I note for sharing two or three black spots in which our group can get stuck.

*Prayer Sheet 13: Evil is at work in our broken world*
**Texts**
The light shines in the darkness, and the darkness did not overcome it. The true light, which enlightens everyone, was coming into the world. He was in the world, and the world came into being through him; yet the world did not know him. He came to what was his own and his own people did not accept him. (Jn 1:5.9–11)

'The disturbances which so frequently occur in the social order result in part from the natural tensions of economic, political and social forms. But at a deeper level they flow from human pride and selfishness, which contaminate even the social sphere. As a result, all of human life, whether individual or collective, shows itself to be a dramatic struggle between good and evil, between light and darkness'.[75]

**Grace to pray for**
'Give me, Lord, a deep awareness of the disorder and evil that affect planet earth – our common home – and give me a wounded heart.'

**Helps for reflection and prayer**
In imagination I contemplate the map of the world and the places where people and Christ himself are on the cross today.
 I meditate on the above texts.

- What situations of evil and suffering have I seen, heard and experienced recently in my immediate environment?
- I see and feel how the power of darkness is at work in all such disorders, tensions and conflicts.
- I contemplate the fact that God is heartbroken.

**Conversation with the Lord**
Imagining Christ our Lord before us, placed on the cross, I ask him how he, the eternal Son, came to become man and thus to die for our sins (*Spiritual Exercises*, 53). And I, and you, and we, what do we do to help those who suffer most? I talk with him about this.

---

75  *Gaudium et Spes*, 13:2, 25:3.

# Appendices

**Harvesting**
I note what touched me most and which I wish to share with the group.

## *Prayer Sheet 14: I am complicit in the failures of my group*
**Texts**
Jesus said, 'There was a man who had two sons. The younger said to his father, "Father, give me the share of the property that will belong to me." So he divided his property between them. A few days later the younger son gathered all he had and travelled to a distant country, and there he squandered his property in dissolute living. Then a severe famine took place throughout that country, and he began to be in need. But when he came to himself he said, "Here I am dying of hunger! I will get up and go to my father, and I will say to him, 'Father, I have sinned against heaven and before you; I am no longer worthy to be called your son; treat me like one of your hired hands.'" So he set off and went to his father. But while he was still far off, his father saw him and was filled with compassion; he ran and put his arms around him and kissed him. Then the son said to him, "Father, I have sinned against heaven and before you; I am no longer worthy to be called your son." But the father said to his slaves, "Quickly, bring out a robe – the best one – and put it on him; put a ring on his finger and sandals on his feet. And get the fatted calf and kill it, and let us eat and celebrate; for this son of mine was dead and is alive again; he was lost and is found!" And they began to celebrate.

'Now his elder son was in the field and heard music and dancing. He called one of the slaves and asked what was going on. He replied, "Your brother has come, and your father has killed the fatted calf, because he has got him back safe and sound." Then he became angry and refused to go in. His father came out and began to plead with him. But he answered his father, "Listen! For all these years I have been working like a slave for you, and I have never disobeyed your command; yet you have never given me even a young goat so that I might celebrate with my friends. But when this son of yours came back, who has devoured your property with prostitutes, you killed the fatted calf for him!" Then the father said to him, "Son, you are always with me, and all that is mine is yours. But we had to celebrate and rejoice, because this brother of yours was dead and has come to life; he was lost and has been found."' (Luke 15:11–32).

### Grace to pray for
'Give me, Lord, the grace to see more clearly my personal responsibility for the wounds my group suffers.'

### Helps for reflection and prayer
- I let the story of the younger son sink in. Identify with him.
- I weigh up all that has been shared in the recent plenary, about the wanderings of my group.
- I acknowledge and feel that I am part of these mistakes.
- What is the most painful, the most difficult to acknowledge?
- I prepare to participate in the celebration of communal reconciliation by choosing an object that symbolises my desire for conversion.

### Conversation with the Lord
I talk with the Lord, telling him that my heart is heavy. I listen to him speak to me like a father whose love is unconditional, undeserved and free. Then I shout with joy and rejoice that I am still alive (*Spiritual Exercises*, 60). I had lost my way but Jesus has found me. I let gratitude flood my heart.

### Harvesting
I note what has touched me most and which I wish to share with the group.

## *Prayer Sheet 15: The name of grace of the group*
### Texts
Jesus said, 'I thank you, Father, Lord of heaven and earth, because you have hidden these things from the wise and the intelligent and have revealed them to infants; yes, Father, for such was your gracious will. All things have been handed over to me by my Father; and no one knows the Son except the Father, and no one knows the Father except the Son and anyone to whom the Son chooses to reveal him' (Mt 11:25–27).

'You are the light of the world. A city built on a hill cannot be hid. In the same way, let your light shine before others, so that they may see your good works and give glory to your Father in heaven' (Mt 5:14, 16).

**Grace to pray for**
'Help me, Lord, to discover or deepen the name of grace of our group.'

**Helps for reflection and prayer**
I recall the graces received by our group, listed on the history line.
  I recall all the grace that we have experienced since the beginning of our discernment journey: personal prayer, group sharing, plenaries, relaxation, meals, atmosphere …

- Where and when did I feel that our group was experiencing more joy, peace, trust, hope, love, strength, energy?
- What do these experiences reveal about the identity, vocation and mission of our group?
- What do the people who are aware of our group say about it? What gifts do they recognise in it?
- Through what experiences have I felt that our group is contributing something to the world, and to the surrounding society? Where do I feel that our group could be a sign for others?

**Conversation with the Lord**
I entrust to God what I have understood better about the group, and listen to what God wants to tell me about it.

**Harvesting**
I write down what I wish to share with the group about the fruit of my prayer.

### *Prayer Sheet 16: Christ's call to the world and to each individual*
**Text**
He called the crowd with his disciples, and said to them, 'If any want to become my followers, let them deny themselves and take up their cross and follow me. For those who want to save their life will lose it, and those

who lose their life for my sake, and for the sake of the gospel, will save it. For what will it profit them to gain the whole world and forfeit their life? Indeed, what can they give in return for their life?' (Mk 8:34–37).

I imagine a great cause – ecological, health, educational ... – which responds to the deepest human aspirations and which demands a personal response. I consider how cowardly it would be not to respond to such a cause (see *Spiritual Exercises*, 91–94).

I realise how the cause of Jesus Christ is infinitely superior to any worldly cause because it aims at the complete eradication from human behaviour of everything that is hostile to the action of the Holy Spirit. Jesus calls the whole world, and each person in particular, to unite intimately with him in this work, so that having shared his pain and suffering, all share with him the joy of victory (see *Spiritual Exercises*, 95–98).

### Grace to pray for
'Give me, Lord, the grace not to remain deaf to your call.'

### Helps for reflection and prayer
Consider how reasonable it is to offer one's whole person to the cause of Christ.

Those who want to love their Lord more and to distinguish themselves in his total service will go against the attraction of the senses, the love of comfort and the search for consideration; they will offer him their lives' (see *Spiritual Exercises*, 97).

### Conversation with the Lord
My offering:

'Lord Jesus, trusting in your help, I offer myself entirely to you, in the presence of Mary your mother, and of all the saints. I want and desire to follow you, enduring injustice and adversity, and every form of poverty, both actual and spiritual, if you want to choose me and receive me into your company' (see 98).

### Harvesting
I write down what I wish to share with the group about the fruit of my prayer.

*Appendices*

## Prayer Sheet 17: The Incarnation
### Texts
The three divine Persons look down upon the face and circuit of the world, filled with people, and on seeing that all were going down into hell, they decree in their eternity that the Second Person would become human to save the human race. Thus, when 'the fullness of time' came, they sent the Angel Gabriel to Our Lady (see *Spiritual Exercises*, 102).

And he came to her and said, 'Greetings, favoured one! The Lord is with you.' But she was much perplexed by his words and pondered what sort of greeting this might be. The angel said to her, 'Do not be afraid, Mary, for you have found favour with God. And now, you will conceive in your womb and bear a son, and you will name him Jesus. He will be great and will be called the Son of the Most High, and the Lord God will give to him the throne of his ancestor David. He will reign over the house of Jacob forever, and of his kingdom there will be no end'. Mary said to the angel, 'How can this be, since I am a virgin?' The angel said to her, 'The Holy Spirit will come upon you, and the power of the Most High will overshadow you; therefore the child to be born will be holy; he will be called Son of God. And now, your relative Elizabeth in her old age has also conceived a son; and this is the sixth month for her who was said to be barren. For nothing will be impossible with God'. Then Mary said, 'Here am I, the servant of the Lord; let it be with me according to your word.' Then the angel departed from her (Lk 1:28–38).

### Grace to pray for
'Grant me, Lord, to know you intimately, so that I may love you more.'

### Helps for reflection and prayer
I gaze on the divine Persons, and the people in the world, the angel Gabriel, and Mary. I listen to what they say. I look at what they do. I reflect and profit from what I see, hear, contemplate.

To realise their infinitely great project, the divine Persons choose the incarnation of the Son in what is infinitely small – Mary, the baby in the womb …

## Conversation with the Lord
With Mary, I offer myself to the Lord.

## Harvesting
I note what touched me and what I wish to share with the group.

## Prayer Sheet 18: *Internal Strengths and Weaknesses / External Opportunities and Threats*

### Texts
Neither is new wine put into old wineskins; otherwise, the skins burst, and the wine is spilled, and the skins are destroyed; but new wine is put into fresh wineskins, and so both are preserved (Mt 9:17).

And Jesus said to them, 'Follow me and I will make you fish for people' (Mk 1:17).

'Very truly, I tell you, unless a grain of wheat falls into the earth and dies, it remains just a single grain; but if it dies, it bears much fruit' (Jn 12: 24).

### Grace to pray for
'Give me your light, Lord, so that I may understand in depth our situation inside and outside the group.'

### Helps for reflection and prayer
- I recall our name of grace and the Lord's call to follow him in humility and poverty.
- I identify the strengths and weaknesses within our group, as well as the opportunities and threats outside.
- I determine which of these factors are most important.
- I consider this table and become aware of the feelings it arouses in me:

| Internal factors | External factors |
|---|---|
| Strengths | Opportunities |
|  |  |
|  |  |
| Weaknesses | Threats |
|  |  |
|  |  |

**Conversation with the Lord**
I listen to what he would like to say to me, and talk to him, heart to heart.

**Harvesting**
I note what touches me most and what I wish to share with the group.

*Prayer Sheet 19: The Lord's call to our group*
**Texts**
'I came that they may have life and have it abundantly' (Jn 10:10).

'That they may all be one. As you, Father, are in me and I am in you, may they also be in us, so that the world may believe that you have sent me' (Jn 17:21).

So Jesus asked the twelve, 'Do you also wish to go away?' Simon Peter answered him, 'Lord, to whom can we go? You have the words of eternal life. We have come to believe and know that you are the Holy One of God'. (Jn 6:67–69).

**Grace to pray for**
'Give me your help, Lord, to discern which call you are addressing to our group.'

**Helps for reflection and prayer**
- I recall our 'name of grace' or the specific grace received during these days as written up on a board: 'Graces received in our history'.
- I recall the dreams and desires shared during the first morning of the workshop – also written on a board – as well as the suggestions heard during these days, suggestions which are 'calls' among which we establish priorities.
- From this review, I compare these calls with our name of grace or with the specific grace received during these days.
- Among the different calls, I look for the one that seems to me to be the priority call, that is, the most important of all.
- Without yet looking for 'how to respond' to this call, I write: 'In my view, the Lord is currently calling us to …'.

**Conversation with the Lord**
I ask the Lord to confirm or adjust my formulation of the priority call.

## Harvesting
I gather what I wish to share with the group from my reflection and prayer.

## Prayer Sheet 20: *Advantages & benefits / disadvantages & dangers of a proposed decision*

### Text
I need to be indifferent and free from any disordered attachment, so that I am not more inclined or attracted to accepting the thing before me than to refusing it, nor to refusing it rather than to accepting it. Rather, I should be as though in the centre of a pair of scales, or as a balance at equilibrium, ready to follow the direction I perceive to be more to the glory and praise of God our Lord and the salvation of my soul. (see *Spiritual Exercises*, 179).

### Grace to pray for
'Give me, Lord, the inner freedom I need to choose what pleases you.'

### Helps for reflection and prayer
- Through reflection, I discover what advantages and benefits there are for us in saying Yes to the option under consideration. I note them down. Conversely, I note the disadvantages and dangers of saying Yes.
- Then I do the same on the other side: I see the advantages and benefits of saying No to the option under consideration and note them. Then I note the disadvantages and dangers of saying No (see *Spiritual Exercises*, 181).
- I imagine an unknown group that wants to make the decision in our situation that will please the Lord more. What would I advise them to do? (see *Spiritual Exercises*, 185).

### Conversation with the Lord
I ask the Virgin Mary to obtain for me from her Son the grace to be placed with him as one who serves and not as one who is served (see Mk 10:45).

I ask the same of the Son so that he may obtain this grace for me from the Father.

I ask the same of the Father, that he may grant this grace to me (see *Spiritual Exercises*, 147).

# Appendices

**Harvesting**
I note what touched me most and what I will share.

## *Prayer Sheet 21: Jesus and the Tempter*
**Text**
When Jesus had been baptised, just as he came up from the water, suddenly the heavens were opened to him, and he saw the Spirit of God descending like a dove and alighting on him. And a voice from heaven said, 'This is my Son, the Beloved, with whom I am well pleased. Then Jesus was led up by the Spirit into the wilderness to be tempted by the devil. He fasted forty days and forty nights, and afterwards he was famished.

The tempter came and said to him, 'If you are the Son of God, command these stones to become loaves of bread.' But he answered, 'It is written, "One does not live by bread alone but by every word that comes from the mouth of God."' Then the devil took him to the holy city and placed him on the pinnacle of the temple, saying to him, 'If you are the Son of God, throw yourself down; for it is written, "He will command his angels concerning you", and "On their hands they will bear you up, so that you will not dash your foot against a stone."' Jesus said to him, 'Again it is written, "Do not put the Lord your God to the test."' Again, the devil took him to a very high mountain and showed him all the kingdoms of the world and their splendour; and he said to him, 'All these I will give you, if you will fall down and worship me.' Jesus said to him, 'Away with you, Satan! for it is written, "Worship the Lord your God, and serve only him."' Then the devil left him, and suddenly angels came and waited on him (Mt 3:16–4:11).

**Grace to pray for**
'Lord, help me to detect the deceptions of the Evil One, so that I may guard against them and discern the true life you teach. So may I imitate you' (*Spiritual Exercises*, 139).

**Helps for reflection and prayer**
- We are in a struggle. On the one hand, Jesus teaches the true life and draws us in. On the other hand, the Tempter sets his traps for us; he is a liar and a mortal enemy of our human nature (see Jn 8:44).

- Recall from Scripture how Christ came to rescue and liberate humankind: he chose simplicity, poverty, humility, obedience ...
- When have we experienced, personally and as a group, that the means proposed by Christ are life-giving?
- When have I and my group, like Jesus, been attracted to turn away from God, even under good pretences? I try to name two or three such illusions.

**Conversation with the Lord**
I ask the Father to be put with his Son Jesus, poor and humble, and to keep me there.

**Harvesting**
I write down what touched me most and what I want to share with the group.

*Prayer Sheet 22: Goals and objectives*
**Text**
When the disciples were increasing in number, the Hellenists complained against the Hebrews because their widows were being neglected in the daily distribution of food. And the twelve called together the whole community of the disciples and said, 'It is not right that we should neglect the word of God in order to wait on tables. Therefore, friends, select from among yourselves seven men of good standing, full of the Spirit and of wisdom, whom we may appoint to this task, while we, for our part, will devote ourselves to prayer and to serving the Word' (Acts 6:1–4).
 The Lord's call to our group today has been formulated as follows: ...

**Grace to pray for**
'Help me, Lord, to identify what goals we need to pursue in order to respond to your call.'

**Helps for reflection and prayer**
- I immerse myself in this Gospel text: the apostles differentiated the objectives they were pursuing.
- I hear in my heart the call that the Lord is addressing to us today.

- What would be, in my eyes, the objectives that we should pursue in order to respond adequately to our call from the Lord?

### Conversation with the Lord
I present the result of my reflections to the Lord and ask him to make me open to the proposals of the other members of the group.

### Harvesting
I note down the objectives I intend to propose.

### *Prayer Sheet 23: The action plan*
### Text
'Which of you, intending to build a tower, does not first sit down and estimate the cost, to see whether he has enough to complete it? Otherwise, when he has laid a foundation and is not able to finish, all who see it will begin to ridicule him, saying, "This fellow began to build and was not able to finish."

'Or what king, going out to wage war against another king, will not sit down first and consider whether he is able with ten thousand to oppose the one who comes against him with twenty thousand? If he cannot, then, while the other is still far away, he sends a delegation and asks for the terms of peace. So therefore, none of you can become my disciple if you do not give up all your possessions' (Lk 14:28–33).

Love ought to find its expression in deeds rather than in words (*Spiritual Exercises*, 230).

The specific objectives that the group considered essential to respond to the call are as follows: ...

### Grace to pray for
'Help us, Lord, to develop a concrete plan of action to implement the goals that respond to your call.'

### Helps for reflection and prayer
- After I have made the Gospel text my own, I look at the objective(s) that are necessary to respond to the Lord's call to us today.
- What would be, in my eyes, the concrete, realistic and daring means to implement this (these) objective(s)? (personnel, finances,

structures, responsibilities, delegations, collaborations, steps, dates, places ...)
- Am I ready to commit myself personally to this implementation? How can I do this?

**Conversation with the Lord**
I present the result of my reflections to the Lord and ask him to make me open to the proposals of the other members of the group.

**Harvesting**
I note down this proposed action plan which I will tentatively share.

*Prayer Sheet 24: Taking up your cross and following Jesus*
**Text**
As they led Jesus away, they seized a man, Simon of Cyrene, who was coming from the country, and they laid the cross on him, and made him carry it behind Jesus. The leaders scoffed at him, saying, 'He saved others; let him save himself if he is the Messiah of God, his chosen one!'

Then Jesus, crying with a loud voice, said, 'Father, into your hands I commend my spirit' (Lk 23:26.35.46).

Jesus said, 'It is finished.' Then he bowed his head and gave up his spirit (Jn 19:30).

'For this reason the Father loves me, because I lay down my life in order to take it up again. No one takes it from me, but I lay it down of my own accord' (Jn 10:17–18).

**Grace to pray for**
'Lord, confirm our provisional decision, so that we may be ready, with you and at whatever cost, to accomplish what you have given us to desire and to decide.'

**Helps for reflection and prayer**
- I contemplate Jesus freely giving his life so that we may live fully.
- I try to foresee and measure the resistance, obstacles, fears, misunderstandings, rejections, humiliations to be faced ... as well as the inevitable consequences of our decision – for the group, for each of

its members and for the dialogue with those in authority. Am I ready to take on these struggles to the end, like Jesus, and with him?
- Does our decision bring us closer to those who suffer most in the world?

**Conversation with the Lord**
I present our decision to the Lord for confirmation.

**Harvesting**
I write down what touched me most and what I will share with the group.

*Prayer Sheet 25: Being resurrected with Jesus*
**Text**
Two of them were going to a village called Emmaus, about seven miles from Jerusalem, and talking with each other about all these things that had happened. While they were talking and discussing, Jesus himself came near and went with them, but their eyes were kept from recognising him. And he said to them, 'What are you discussing with each other while you walk along?' They stood still, looking sad. Then he said to them, 'Oh, how foolish you are, and how slow of heart to believe all that the prophets have declared! Was it not necessary that the Messiah should suffer these things and then enter into his glory?' Then their eyes were opened, and they recognised him; and he vanished from their sight. They said to each other, 'Were not our hearts burning within us while he was talking to us on the road, while he was opening the scriptures to us?' (Lk 24:13–17; 25–26; 31–32).

'Take, Lord, and receive all my liberty, my memory, my understanding, and my entire will – all that I have and possess. You gave it all to me; to you, Lord, I give it all back. All is yours, dispose of it entirely according to your will. Give me the grace to love you, for that is enough for me.' (*Spiritual Exercises*, 234).[76]

**Grace to pray for**
'Lord, come and confirm our decision. Grant us the joy and gladness of being raised with you.'

---

76 See also, Ignatius, *Personal Writings*, p. 329.

### Helps for reflection and prayer
I contemplate the Gospel scene: I see the characters, hear what they say, watch what they do, enter into their feelings and aspirations.

Bearing in mind our provisional decision, I observe Jesus who casts out sadness, dries tears, removes fear, restores confidence, makes hearts burn with love, is victorious over the forces that paralyze us and take away life.

### Conversation with the Lord
I make my own Ignatius' prayer:

'Take, Lord, and receive all my liberty, my memory, my understanding, and my entire will – all that I have and possess. You gave it all to me; to you, Lord, I give it all back. All is yours, dispose of it entirely according to your will. Give me the grace to love you, for that is enough for me.' (*Spiritual Exercises*, 234).[77]

### Harvesting
I write down what touched me most and what I will share.

## *Prayer Sheet 26: Evaluation of the session & conclusion of the Workshop*
### Texts
I am confident of this, that the one who began a good work among you will bring it to completion by the day of Jesus Christ. And this is my prayer, that your love may overflow more and more with knowledge and full insight to help you to determine what is best. (Phil 1:6, 9–10).

For this reason I bow my knees before the Father, from whom every family in heaven and on earth takes its name. I pray that, according to the riches of his glory, he may grant that you may be strengthened in your inner being with power through his Spirit, and that Christ may dwell in your hearts through faith, as you are being rooted and grounded in love. I pray that you may have the power to comprehend, with all the saints, what is the breadth and length and height and depth, and to know the love of Christ that surpasses knowledge, so that you may be filled with all the fullness of God (Eph 3:14–19).

---

77  See also, Ignatius, *Personal Writings,* p. 329.

## Grace to pray for
'Make me aware, Lord, of how you have worked during this session through the various means you have used.'

## Helps for reflection and prayer
- How did I recognise God's action in the group? In what ways can I say that the group has made progress? What has become clear to them?
- What is the main fruit of this journey for me? What has become clearer for me? What are the inevitable consequences for me of what has emerged for the group? What commitment does this require from me?
- What did I find helpful (rhythm, schedule, ways of doing things, prayer times, prayer sheets, sharing, relaxation, places etc.)?
- What did I find less helpful?
- What improvements would be desirable for a similar type of workshop?
- Would a follow-up be desirable? In what form?

## Conversation with the Lord
I give thanks to the Lord in the words of Mary's Magnificat.

# Appendix 4: Discernment Journeys of Diverse Groups

Esdac is sometimes approached by Christian-inspired groups of which several people are invited members or coopted because of their financial, administrative or legal skills, rather than because of a Christian commitment. This may be the case, for example, of a hospital board of directors, a school parents' committee, or a social service leadership team. These people have responded to an invitation either out of sympathy for the person who contacted them, or to defend the interests of the beneficiaries of these institutions and the values they promote. Is it possible to use the Esdac approach with such groups?

*Common ground*
The answer is unequivocally 'yes', because if, in any group, its members take the time to explain to each other what, deep down, motivates them, they will inevitably find convergences to which they can commit themselves.

There are more and more groups in the world that share the conviction that if we sit in a circle around an empty space, if we let go of all our certainties, if we allow silence to invade us, if we then listen to each other and allow ourselves to be inwardly touched, something completely new will emerge on which we can base our action.

As M. Scott Peck says:

> Genuine community of sorts can usually be established in a few hours when the group is instructed from the outset to refrain from generalisations, to speak personally, to be vulnerable, to avoid attempting to heal or convert, to empty itself, to listen wholeheartedly, and to embrace the painful as well as the pleasant.[78]

---

78  M. Scott Peck, *The Different Drum: Community-Making and Peace*, p. 128.

'Practising Esdac' means creating the conditions in which it makes sense to speak, to listen and to welcome what is said by any person, because deep down in each there is common ground with all the others, a ground on which we rely and which allows us to overcome our fears of conflict and find a way to join in. We must encourage ourselves and everyone to dare to assert ourselves in truth. The necessary trust will not be present in the group from the outset, but it will be built up little by little through honest conversation.

## *Inclusive vocabulary*

The requesting group will know that the Esdac facilitators are motivated by religious convictions. And, for their part, the members of the facilitating team will make sure to have moments when they can share their faith with each other, for example by praying for the group.

When facilitating the group, care should be taken to use a vocabulary that everyone can understand. For example:

- Instead of saying that 'The Holy Spirit is available to all', we can say, 'Every person is important', or 'Every person is important because we regularly experience in our activities that the Holy Spirit can speak through every person'.
- The term 'Spirit-led conversation' should not be used, but, for example, 'truthful, real conversation'.
- Instead of asking, 'What is the Lord calling us to?', we will say, 'What are we called to?'

These are important adaptations, but the essence is deeper. The facilitators will show their appreciation of the commitment in a Christian institution of people considered to have little or no faith. They deserve admiration, respect and recognition. Without these commitments, which are often voluntary or poorly paid, the institution might not survive.

## *Life*

The facilitators will try to show that one of the deepest desires of human beings is to give and receive life, to live in joy, to be united, to forgive enemies and to donate oneself for one's friends. The vocabulary chosen should put non-Christians at their ease and dust off and correct distorted images of God, and thus contribute to communion between all. This is the vocabulary out of which Jesus speaks: *'May they have **life**'* (Jn 10:10); *'May your joy be complete'* (Jn 15:11); *'May they all be **one**'* (Jn 17:21); *'No one has greater love than this, to* **lay down** *one's life for one's friends'* (Jn 15:13).

If the climate of the group lends itself to it, it may be possible to articulate the Christian belief that the desire to give life has its source in the Father. But sometimes we must be silent, leaving it to the Holy Spirit to touch hearts in God's own time.

The stories which follow below show how by using the various Esdac exercises, different groups gained a new or increased awareness of **being one body**. For Christian groups the time spent personally and together under God's loving and creative gaze enabled them to speak frankly, to listen to each other with respect, to dare to express their desires and fears openly, to articulate the unspoken as required by Jesus (see Mt 10:26–27), and to let go of what binds them, as Jesus frees the entombed Lazarus (Jn 11:44) and open themselves to the life Jesus came to bring (Jn 10:10). They gradually moved from an isolated 'I' to a united 'we'.

Those who are not religiously affiliated but work together have a passion for justice and truth which is sometimes more impressive than is found in lukewarm Christians. The limitless resources of Christian faith lie dormant in many of the 2.4 billion Christians in today's world. But God is God of all, and, like the wind which cannot be tamed, the Spirit works *incognito* across the cosmos. Pope Francis recognises this in *Laudato Si'*: 'I wish to address *every person* living on this planet ... and to enter into dialogue with *all people* about our common home'.[79]

The Spirit is offered to all, and it is essential to listen for us to people outside our usual circles if we are to hear the divine voice fully, else the Good News will never spread. Jesus conversed with non-Jews: with a Samaritan woman (Jn 4:5–42) and a distraught Syro-Phoenician mother (Mk 7:24–29). Peter crossed the threshold of a non-Jew and became aware that the Gospel was for the Gentiles as well as the Jews (Acts 10). Pope Francis speaks of going to the peripheries. 'We do not

---

79  Pope Francis, *Laudato Si'*, 3.

have to go to society to bring it the Gospel, but we have to open ourselves to society to challenge our own views of the Gospel.' Tomáš Halík in *The Afternooon of Christianity: The Courage to Change*, (2024) offers a perceptive analysis of the Church's need to transcend its own boundaries. It must begin to dialogue with the anonymous multitude who are searching for universal fraternity as sketched out in Pope Francis' encyclical *Fratelli Tutti*, 2020. In such dialogue each contributes to the search for truth and diversity is fully respected.

### *Grace is inter-active*

When we make ourselves truly and warmly present to another person, something new happens in the two of us: the current of grace flows. And for this to happen, as we saw earlier, it is sufficient that at least one of the interlocutors has experienced in their life the action of the spirit of communion and truth and has learned how to help others to open up to it. The disciples of Jesus were formed to be 'missionary disciples', that is, people who know that this spirit of communion and truth is the Holy Spirit, and who are willing to transmit its ardour and love to the world.

Good-willed people can be invited to *experience* the Spirit's enriching action through sincere relationships, as Saint Francis explains to Brother Léon in this dialogue imagined by Éloi Leclerc:

*'The Lord has sent us to evangelise. But have you ever thought about what it means to evangelise people? To evangelise a person, you see, is to tell him: "You too are loved by God in the Lord Jesus". And not just tell him, but really think it. And not only to mean it, but to behave in such a way that he feels and discovers that there is something saved in him, something greater and nobler than he thought, so that he thus awakens to a new self-awareness. This is what it means to tell him the good news. You can only do this by offering him your friendship. A real, selfless friendship, without condescension, made of deep trust and esteem.'*

Journeys of the groups included here reveal a level of goodwill and openness such that the participants can share, listen, reflect, search their hearts, notice what brings them either joy or disquiet, and commit themselves to implement what they judge in conscience to be wise and good, even at personal cost.

*The journeys are arranged as follows:*
1. The Founding of the Society of Jesus (p. 219)
2. The Monks of Tibhirine (p. 223)
3. The Evolution of a Religious Congregation (p. 225)
4. Finding God after Genocide (p. 229)
5. A CLC World Assembly (p. 234)
6. The Birth of a Lay Association (p. 237)
7. Accompaniment in a Student Residence (p. 240)
8. A Religious Community Meeting (p. 241)
9. A Family Prayer (p. 243)
10. Classroom Retreats (p. 244)
11. Brief Communal Discernment (p. 245)

*1: The Founding of the Society of Jesus*
**It was a discernment made without the help of external facilitators**
The decision to found the religious order of the Society of Jesus was taken by a group of ten men, and then ratified by the Pope, following a common discernment carried out without the help of external guides. This is important to note, because often discernments in common are carried out without the help of facilitators. It is instructive to examine how these ten proceeded.

It strengthens our trust in communal discernment to note that so convinced was Ignatius that it was God who had inspired the decision to found the Society of Jesus, that Ignatius affirms that 'the Society was not instituted by human means... but through the grace and omnipotent hand of Christ, Our Lord and God'.[80] Ideally our human decisions can be thought to carry the same divine stamp of approval.

In November 1538, Ignatius and his nine companions had decided to place themselves at the disposal of the Pope, to be sent by him on mission as the apostles were by Jesus (Mt 10:5). This would lead to their dispersion throughout the world. So the question that arose was formulated as follows: 'Does the Lord call us to remain united in an apostolic body or to disperse?'

Until then there had been no leader among them; what united them was friendship. Of course Ignatius had the primary influence on the

---

80 *Constitutions*, 812.

group, but decisions were taken together, enabled by the common experience lived by each one during the Spiritual Exercises.

They gradually worked out together, in the light of circumstances, the procedure to follow for this discernment in common, so their first – unanimous – decision was to take time together to reflect and pray. For this purpose, they met in Rome from March to later June, 1539.

**Consensus to continue as a body emerged easily**
*'Since the Lord, we thought, had deigned in his mercy and clemency to bring us together, poor men from different countries with so many different customs, to unite us closely, we were not to break up the union of this grouping wrought by God, but rather to continue to strengthen and stabilise it by becoming one body. Mutual care and full understanding of one another would ensure more abundant fruit for souls: forces that unite have more strength and energy to carry out great and difficult undertakings than when they divide and scatter.'*[81]

So far, so good: but by deciding the WHAT – that they were called to remain united as an apostolic body – next the question of HOW arose: 'How do we respond to this call? By obeying one of us, i.e. by becoming a religious order, or by finding another strategy?'

In the methodology proper to the Spiritual Exercises, this first discernment was carried out according to 'the second stage of making a sound and good choice' (*Spiritual Exercises*, 176), that is, by receiving 'sufficient light and knowledge through the experience of consolations and desolations' (*Spiritual Exercises*, 316–336) and 'through the experience of discerning the spirits' (*Spiritual Exercises*, 314–315). By keeping in mind the consolation experienced together regarding the decision to remain united the companions had the energy to face the difficulties related to the issue of promising obedience to one of themselves.

**Consensus on HOW to be one body came slowly**
*'Once the first problem was settled and resolved, we came to a more difficult one. We had all taken the vow of perpetual chastity and the vow of*

---

81 *Deliberation of our First Fathers*, 3.

*poverty. Was it necessary to take the third (vow), that of obedience to one of ourselves?'*[82]

*'As we had spent many days praying earnestly and thinking about this question without anything satisfactory presenting itself to our minds, we put our hope in the Lord and began to discuss among ourselves some means of resolving our doubt more happily.'*[83]

Together they agreed on a procedure for answering this question.[84]

*'First, would it not be expedient for us all to retire to a hermitage and remain there for thirty or forty days? Or should not three or four, on behalf of all, go there for the same purpose? Or if no one were to go to this hermitage, we could, remaining in Rome, devote half the day solely to our task; meditation, reflection and prayer would be more convenient and more extensive. The rest of the day we would use for our usual ministries of preaching and confessions. Finally we decided that we would all stay in Rome.'*[85]

## They worked hard to make themselves interiorly free or 'indifferent'

*'[It was proposed] that each and every one of us should make the following three arrangements in our hearts.*

*'The first would be that each one would prepare and apply himself so well to prayer, to the holy sacrifice and meditation, that all his efforts would be directed towards finding joy and peace in the Holy Spirit on the subject of obedience, working as much as he could to incline his will more to obey than to command, if there were to follow an equal glory of God and an equal praise of His Majesty. The second inner disposition would be that no companion would speak of the matter to another or ask him his reasons; thus no one would be influenced by the opinion of another. The third would be that each one would consider himself personally as a stranger to our group and as if he were never to be received in it.'*[86]

---

82  *Deliberation of our First Fathers*, 4.
83  *Deliberation of our First Fathers*, 5.
84  Consensus about the final outcome of the overall discernment is thus enabled by the intermediate consensus about the procedures to be used.
85  *Deliberation of our First Fathers*, 6.
86  *Deliberation of our First Fathers*, 6.

### They examined the advantages and benefits, the disadvantages and dangers of obedience (*Spiritual Exercises, 181*)

'It was with these prior inner dispositions that we decided to meet, all prepared, on the following day, to express each of us **the objections** that could be made against obedience. One said, for example, "The name 'obedience' does not have the good name among the Christian people that it should have". Another said: "If we want to live under obedience, we will perhaps be forced by the Sovereign Pontiff to live under another rule which already exists."

'Very soon afterwards, on another day, we would discuss the opposite point of view, proposing all the **advantages and benefits** of obedience. For example, someone would say: "Supposing that our group is entrusted with an apostolic enterprise without the yoke of obedience, no one will really be responsible, each one will put the burden on the other, as we have experienced several times." Similarly: "Suppose there is no authority, the group will not last or maintain itself for long." Another said: "The Supreme Pontiff will not be able to deal with the innumerable particulars of our daily life: hence we need obedience to our own leader."'[87]

A comment: This second discernment was carried out according to the 'third stage of making a sound and good election' (*Spiritual Exercises*, 177–188). Through reflection all looked together for the disadvantages and dangers of obedience, and then, at other times, all looked together for the advantages and benefits of obeying one of them. This way of proceeding avoided conflict between supporters and opponents of a solution. Everyone worked on the same task. The type of listening involved was not only listening with the intellect but also with the heart and the will – the latter being understood as 'an inclination to love'.[88] Time was spent on getting into the right frame of mind so that no-one would dominate or be dominated by the others.

### Unanimity was reached over three months, not without much prayer and labour

'And so after many days of thinking through the many pros and cons and examining the more serious and weighty arguments, and while carrying

---

[87] *Deliberation of our First Fathers*, 7.
[88] The term 'cardiac listening' can be helpful in describing what went on.

*out our usual exercises of prayer, meditation and reflection, at last, with the help of the Lord, we arrived at our conclusion, not just by a majority, but without even one dissenting.'*[89]

*Retaining the same method of discussion and procedure in all remaining questions, always proposing both sides, we continued in these and other deliberations for nearly three months from the middle of Lent through the feast of John the Baptist. On this day everything was concluded joyfully and in complete concord of spirit – not without having previously engaged in many vigils and prayers and labours of mind and body before we had deliberated and made our decisions.*[90]

## Confirmation

Their discernment was approved and confirmed by Pope Paul III in 1540. Without his seal the Society could not have come into being. This sheds light on a crucial point concerning discernment in common. Most of the time, it consists of preparing decisions together, which are then taken by the legitimate authority, in this case the pope.

There are also circumstances in which discernment in common consists not only in preparing decisions together but also in taking them together. This was the case when the first companions chose, by vote, their first Superior General: Ignatius.[91]

### 2: *The Monks of Tibhirine*

The Trappists of Tibhirine were not accompanied by an Esdac team: the following account simply throws light on the personal name of grace of the Prior, the name of grace of the group, and the quality of the discernment that occasioned their deaths.

The book by Marie-Christine Ray: *Christian de Chergé, prieur de Tibhirine* begins with the event which was at the root of Christian de Chergé's personal vocation. In 1959, when he was 23 years old and in military service in the bloody conflict between France and the Algerian

---

89 *Deliberation of our First Fathers*, 8.
90 *Deliberation of our First Fathers*, 9.
91 For text and commentaries on the process see Jules J Toner SJ, 'The Deliberation that started the Jesuits', in *Studies in the Spirituality of Jesuits*, 6, June 1974. Also Futrell, *Making an Apostolic Community of Love*. The texts given above are adapted from the original.

people, he developed a deep friendship with an Algerian field guard, Mohamed, father of ten children, a man of faith and prayer.

Mohamed saved Christian's life but the next day was found murdered. Knowing that he was under threat, Mohamed had accepted that Christian pray for him: 'I know you will pray for me. But you see, Christians don't know how to pray!' Christian writes: 'I know that I can place his single commandment within my hope for the communion of all the chosen ones with Christ, this friend who lived until death for me. And each Eucharist makes him infinitely present to me, in the Body of Glory where the gift of his life has now taken on its full dimension for me and for the many. The Koran says: 'Those who save one person are considered as if they had saved all'.

From Marie-Christine Ray we learn the full story:

*From its foundation in 1938, the Cistercian community of Tibhirine in the Atlas mountains of Algeria was made up of 'agglomerates'. It lacked a common appreciation of the meaning of its presence in Algeria. Christian de Chergè was the only member of the community to have chosen Algeria to live in, as a spiritual presence in a Muslim environment: he wanted to become a prayerful person in the midst of other prayerful people.*

*On October 17, 1975 the monks received an order from the gendarmerie to leave the place. Paradoxically, they had just decided to settle permanently in Algeria: a few weeks earlier they had unanimously accepted Christian's final profession, and four who were still attached to French monasteries decided to take a vow of stability by which they would live in Algeria.*

*Brother Christian wanted Tibhirine to become fully autonomous with a superior elected by the community, so that its project could be truly adapted to Algeria's reality. This was accepted by the Abbot General in France. The only task that remained was to elect a Prior.*

*There was good support for Christian, but it was not unanimous. His bold positions on Islam and his style were off-putting for some of the brethren. But he was elected as Prior, and strengthened by the confidence of his brothers he could finally lead the small community towards its particular Christian vocation in the Muslim world. But he had to tame his impatience and his taste for the absolute. A few monks left Tibhirine because of his personality, or because his project did not correspond to their sense of their monastic vocation.*

Christian appealed to Cistercian monasteries elsewhere to send monks to reinforce his community, since it could not recruit locally. Between 1984 and 1989, five experienced and mature monks chose Algeria. Reassured about the future of the rejuvenated community, Christian de Chergè learned to become more human and fraternal. The members, from the oldest to the youngest, had chosen, like him, a fraternal and contemplative life in the heart of the Algerian people.

In 1988, when the construction of the village mosque was at a standstill, due to lack of funds, the monastic community lent the villagers a large room with direct access to the road. The proximity of Muslim and Christian prayer delighted Christian de Chergé.

In October 1993, the Armed Islamic Group issued an ultimatum to foreigners to leave the country. In community, the monks asked themselves: 'What are our community reasons for STAYING here now?' The idea of abandoning their neighbours to their fate did not satisfy anyone. Christian met with each of the brothers individually. He writes: 'There emerged this astonishing thing, of which I was the privileged witness. Each brother, one on one, told me: 'I am not at peace with the decision to leave.' The monks decided to stay put. One wrote to the Abbot General: 'The events which have brought us immensely closer have not erased any of our differences. But there is a 'we' that is moving forward, progressing in grace and wisdom.'

On the night of March 26, 1996, seven of the monks were abducted and beheaded. Two escaped and died later.[92]

## 3: The Evolution of a Religious Congregation
### The pedagogy of Esdac

We sketch here the transformation of a religious congregation thanks to the 'pedagogy of Esdac' as they call it, and above all thanks to their embedded practice of Spirit-led conversation at all levels, whether in exchanges during meals, in community meetings, in the work of various commissions or within the general council. The quality of these conversations makes each sister aware that she is truly important, loved by the Father and by her sisters; that she is a vital part of a body

---

92 The film *Of Gods and Men* illustrates the monks' journey of discernment in common.

and can contribute to making that body healthy and responsive to its mission.

As a result, the sisters have become more available to be missioned to places of greater needs, especially as these needs are detected through Spirit-led conversations at all levels, as happened for example during a meal when the sisters were casually talking about the education of children today and the education their parents had given them in their respective cultures.

What the sisters appreciate most about Esdac's approach is that it allows them to 'learn by doing'. Participating in the discernment of a Chapter animated according to the Esdac process can produce in delegates a very profound availability because they experience, in heart and body, through their resistances and impulses, that they are part of a common history and a common project.

How did these transformations take place in this Congregation? Slowly and steadily, as a small seed grows (Mt 13:31).

In November 2008, following a request from the General Chapter for a new mode of government, the General and her Council met with two Esdac facilitators. They wished to experiment with the Esdac method and asked to be accompanied up to and including the next Chapter. After a slight hesitation, because accompanying a Chapter was not then part of Esdac's routine, the facilitators accepted. They would first work with the Council, then animate its international Council, and finally propose a journey involving all the communities and national Chapters. In November 2009, three sisters took part in an Esdac training programme. They were deeply touched by the spiritual pedagogy they discovered and said to themselves, 'This is what our congregation really needs!'

Before the 2010 Chapter the pedagogy of Spirit-led conversation and discernment in common had already been well introduced into the procedures and especially into the ways of being, thinking and behaving of the delegates. They consented more and more to let themselves be led by the Spirit, with its disconcerting inspirations. An openness to change had progressively won over their minds and hearts, especially through re-reading their history which led to the acceptance of God's mercy. Experiencing this was very necessary, because as one remarked, 'There were corpses in the cupboards'. The two previous Chapters had left wounds that had not healed.

## New structures

Entering the 2010 Chapter the congregation had 432 members in 10 countries. A major concern was that there were not enough sisters capable of assuming leadership roles. The Chapter took the bold decision to abolish the provincial and regional levels of authority and to delegate to five General Councillors the office formerly held by a number of Provincials. These collaborate with the Superior General in a single government by practising Spirit-led conversation among themselves. When one knows the importance that each province can attach to their autonomy, and their concern to defend its singularity and its language, one can measure the strength and the audacity of this decision that Rome accepted as an experiment.

This change would obviously shake up all habitual procedures, especially as the Chapter closed without the members having had time to examine how the new structure was going to work in practice! To grasp what is at stake in the new mode of governance, it is necessary to understand two innovations: the General Council is now composed of sisters of differing mother tongues, and the Councillors are the delegates of the General tasked with the exercise of authority over territories whose culture and habits they may not know. The Council meets three times a year, for one month, at the General House. Each of the delegate general Councillors has a personal meeting with the General before the council meets.

## Belonging as a body

At the end of the 2010 Chapter, at least one thing was certain: the spirit of Spirit-led conversation and discernment in common was at work and it was necessary to open this spirit to all meetings and hearts across the congregation. The General and her Council set about this with determination. The call that the Lord addressed to the congregation was clear: to make a body, that is to say, to pass from the 'I' to the 'we', to help each of the sisters feel that they belonged to this body, to awaken to the missionary call and to make themselves available to go where the needs of the world were most urgent. A journey of conversion was designed, to accompany the change of structures, with Prayer Sheets and sharing that brought together sisters from different communities. Thus, in one way or another, all the sisters were involved in the new dynamic, including those who were living in pairs or alone or in a nursing home.

**Evaluation**
In 2013, a mid-term evaluation took place. And at this meeting, the criticisms were many:

- the decision-making level is too far removed from local realities
- power is in the hands of only a few.

While it became clear that the government was indeed centralised, it was accepted that this must go hand in hand with an increased participation of all the sisters. In time they realised that the power was really *in their own hands*.

The 2015 Chapter was prepared and facilitated with the help of a new Esdac team. It is interesting to note here that between 2010 and 2021, the congregation has called on Esdac several times, and each time new pairs – five in all – have been formed to respond to requests. The sisters therefore call on a pedagogy rather than on specific people. They say that they appreciate being accompanied by different teams, because each accompanier and each team has its own way of incarnating synodality. This diversity in the use of the same way of proceeding opens the door to more surprises from the Spirit.

**God of surprises**
Two major decisions had to be taken during the 2015 Chapter: whether or not to confirm the new mode of governance, and whether or not to accept the request from a Congregation of 120 sisters to merge with them. This Congregation was painfully poor in finances, but half of its members live in a country where vocations are plentiful! The 2015 Chapter concluded in great general consolation with the confirmation of the new mode of governance and the acceptance of the merger, which is transformative.

One of the facilitators observed that during the whole Chapter he had never once heard a sister deride another, whether at meals, in recreation or in the chapter assembly!

The congregation continued its journey with an Esdac-type approach to accompany the process of fusion and to move towards the next Chapter.

Esdac, say the sisters, has been much more than a methodology for them. It is a spiritual pedagogy that has enabled them to take two important decisions in serenity and communion: the change of structures and the merger. And this spiritual pedagogy has enabled Esdac to accompany the congregation over 12 years, through a spiritual animation which is based on prayer and Spirit-led conversation. The Esdac approach is bottom-up rather than top-down. It recognises that the Spirit speaks through each person. The new members are adjusting easily to this type of approach.

## *4: Finding God after Genocide*
### The request

The seven-day discernment process reported here took place in Rwanda in July 2019, twenty-five years after the internal genocide between April–July 1994 had claimed the lives of some 600,000, and during which over a million people fled the country. The requesting group was made up of a dozen Rwandans, women of prayer who represented a little less than half the sisters of an indigenous religious congregation. The original profile of this group was the combination of 5 young professed sisters with first vows and some older sisters – up to 79 years of age – among whom was the Provincial.

The request for accompaniment had been introduced by a sister of the congregation who had followed an Esdac formation and who felt that this type of journey could help her sisters to 'speak to each other in truth, in Jesus Christ': this was to be the theme of the process. The focus would be on Spirit-led conversation.

For various reasons, it was not possible for the group to be accompanied by a team of two facilitators. Therefore, in order to better discern what was happening in the group at strategic moments, the Esdac facilitator worked with the sister who had requested the accompaniment and who was participating in the retreat. She acted as an interpreter, which enabled her to reformulate certain issues in the local culture and language.

In the preliminary interview with the facilitator, the Provincial had expressed a strong desire that a real retreat must be offered, including meals in silence. She had pointed out the danger widespread in her country, of talking a lot but on the surface level only. She also shared her hope that this experience would renew in depth the spiritual guidance given by the older sisters to the younger ones. From various sides, warnings had been expressed about taboo subjects: among other topics that 'they should not speak about Hutus and Tutsis, nor say anything about politics, nor make any criticisms …'

## The process

The timetable for the Workshop was designed to resemble that of a retreat. The morning began at 8.30 am with a short prayer prepared by the sisters, followed by a 45-minute teaching. Over an hour was available for personal prayer as well as for sub-groups of four, of which there were three, with younger and older mixed. The morning ended with the Eucharist. The afternoon started again at 3.30 pm with an introduction to a Prayer Sheet, followed by a full hour of prayer, an hour of small-group time, and then an hour's plenary before the evening meal. This was the only plenary of the day.

On the third day, the History Line was discussed. To encourage people to speak without naming anything taboo by itself, and to deal with such different ages, the facilitator drew a line from 1940 – the year of birth of the oldest – to 2019, inviting the participants to put as many post-it notes as they wanted on three levels: the facts of the events, the facts of the congregation and the facts of their personal lives. In order to move from the facts to the feelings, the facilitator invited each one to choose only one event from the past and to express the feelings they had at the time of its occurrence and those they were still enduring in the retreat.

## The sharing

They all chose to focus on the 100 days of the genocide. They had fled to different countries, and a few months later the General Council had gathered them all for a crucial meeting: each had been given a whole day to express herself; sometimes it was by shouting and even pulling out their own hair. After this, the decision was taken together to return to the country, while leaving each one free to do so or not.

Now, as they contemplated their History Line, they were all impressed by the focus on the single event of the genocide, even those who had not directly lived through it because of their age, and who had no other memory of it than as a climate of terror. The genocide haunts Rwandans; it is like a leaden blanket, and it is very difficult for them to address it without increasing the flow of tears. But the reassuring framework offered by the Spirit-led conversation allowed unspeakable horror to emerge in various forms of communication.

Their stories revealed all the characteristics of a trauma, which is a situation whose magnitude exceeds the person's ability to manage it and which leads to a freezing of all their energy and then remains blocked in the body. Paradoxically, the freezing up appeared to be particularly noticeable among the youngest.

The harshness of the sharing led the facilitator to propose, on the fifth day, that the group might go to the heart of the Gospel, to the hour of Calvary, when darkness swept over the world. Only John and Mary remained at the foot of the cross (Mt 27:45–56). But in that hour, which seemed to be the hour of God's death, his presence was in truth signified in the highest degree: it was recognised by the Roman centurion and attested to by the tearing of the veil of the temple. This text left room both for doubt and for the most radical faith.

The afternoon was the real turning point and the crucible of this experience: each sister took her place with more ease, especially the youngers who emerged as increasingly free. The history of the old ones became common to all.

### The call

The personal review on the presence/absence of God had brought out two texts: the massacre of the innocents from which Jesus had fled in order to come back and save (Mt 2:13–23), and the sending of Moses because God had heard the cry of the enslaved people and promised to liberate them (Ex chs 3–14). The reception of these texts naturally gave rise to the central question of the three levels of consensus: 'To WHAT are we called today?'

Recognition of themselves as survivors saved by the power of God gently led the sisters to the desire to place themselves at the service of their traumatised people by helping them to rediscover their dignity and the presence of God in their lives. Participating among themselves in an experience of deep listening nourished their desire to offer the ministry of listening to others. As survivors, they could reach out to their people who today still silently carry within them a wound that is imaged as a huge untreated abscess.

## God's presence

In a document they wrote at the time, the sisters affirmed the following:

*Today, we all recognise ourselves as survivors of the genocide. But at the very heart of this tragedy, we have recognised the presence of God: in the midst of this history that has scattered us, the Lord has protected us and set us apart like Joseph and Mary who were forced to flee with the child Jesus to Egypt. We believe, because we have experienced it, that death does not have the last word, and that life is stronger than death.*

The whole retreat revolved around the phrase of Christian Bobin, posted on the first day: *'Perhaps paradise is being fully present, knowing that you are NOT going to be killed, it is being defenceless without feeling threatened.'* The Spirit-led conversation engendered this experience and offered a path of healing without blame or accusation.

## Reviewing the facilitation

From the beginning, the density of the exchanges was strong. The Provincial said that she had been afraid that she would not have a companion during the retreat, and admitted that she had first come to check the seriousness of the process. 'But I actually had three in my sub-group, including a novice!'. The young participants said that they had made more progress in their ability to share truthfully during these seven days than during their two years of novitiate.

Very quickly, it became clear to all that they were in fact living a retreat. There was no doubt that the Spirit was working strongly and sometimes more effectively than might have occurred in an individual retreat. They quickly felt the body being built up, and perceived that the sharing with each other was also the Word of God, the fruit of which was gathered in plenary in terms of freedom, authenticity, depth, union and mission.

They found that a path of healing is offered when a new word is both spoken in a collective setting and truly heard by each person. This word begins by revealing a part of the personal iceberg, is enriched by the authenticity of others, and then becomes truly new when the speaker does more than reveal what he or she has kept hidden, but says things that are discovered *in the very moment they are said*. Life is reborn, strengthened and deepened in a common identity and the desire to respond to the call of grace. Sharing brings people together and binds them to each other in order to build a better future together.

The question is often asked: 'Is Esdac truly the Spiritual Exercises of Ignatius or a process that is only vaguely inspired by them?' In the experience recounted here, Esdac did indeed propose the Spiritual Exercises with rigor, but centred on the group considered as a body: this did not leave room for individual accompaniment.

In this case, Esdac proved to be an original and effective approach to the treatment of a deep and entrenched wound around which were entangled relationships. The word 'entrenched' evokes a deep and dangerous disorder that is difficult to treat, while the word 'entangled' describes the extreme confusion and interplay of complex relationships. These deep wounds still cut off speech in Rwanda and break up relationships.

When God is directly invited to touch wounded hearts, the resulting fruit goes beyond what simple therapy can produce. This is even more true when a safe framework is put in place within a group to encourage a 'true conversation': this framework allows members to open up through each other, to healing and salvation.

The facilitator confided that he felt as much a part of this adventure as the group, because of his own history, as he himself had not been spared the heartbreak. The members had helped him to join them in shared suffering.

The simultaneous translation was more precious than cumbersome: it forced each person to slow down, to hear everything twice.

The Lord seems to be calling Esdac today in favour of this country: there is a great service to be rendered by the Church and a project to be planned to develop an unobtrusive methodology which would be applied with respect, love and compassion in response to so much suffering.

*Appendices*

### 5: A CLC World Assembly
*An Esdac team of three people (a Belgian, an Italian and a Spaniard) accompanied the 2018 CLC World Assembly in Buenos Aires, Argentina. Here is a synopsis of their report, which begins with the enthusiastic comment:* 'What an adventure, friends! God is great!'

**The requesting group**
The CLC, or Christian Life Community, is an international association of Ignatian inspiration, bringing together women and men, young people and adults, from all walks of life, who want to follow Jesus and collaborate in his mission. Members gather in small communities, about once a month, to share their personal reviews. CLC is governed by an international council: the Executive Council ('Exco')

**The request**
To help the World Assembly to find its 'name of grace' and also its vision for the next 5 years, while integrating Pope Francis' call to 'go out' to the peripheries.

To help the Worldwide CLC to become more united.

To make the Assembly live. Not only to write texts and amendments, but also to pray and practice together our spirit-led conversation by differentiating clearly the three rounds of sharing.

**The theme**
'How many loaves do you have? Go and see' (Mk 6:38).

**The grace asked of God**
'To live the CLC charism in a deeper and more integrated way in today's world.'

**The Assembly**
The 210 delegates from 73 countries were divided into 30 sharing groups, with an average of 7 people to each group. The languages used were English, Spanish and French.

The challenge around the plenaries was to make the sharing very visual, not too long and yet enough to allow the spokespersons for the small groups to communicate their thoughts, and then to enable the participants to express themselves individually.

## Duration
The Assembly itself lasted 10 days. Initially, the CLC Exco planned to entrust Esdac with 3 of these days. As the preparations progressed, the time devoted to discernment accompanied by Esdac was increased to four and a half days, which was seen as an excellent decision.

## The venue
The meeting took place at the Colegio Maxima in San Miguel (40 km from Buenos Aires), where Pope Francis, Jorge Bergoglio at the time, lived for many years. Before being accompanied by Esdac, a day of 'immersion' took place in these areas which carried us along.

## The celebration of mercy
We insisted that the Exco hold a celebration of mercy. It was a key moment to discern the name of grace in CLC. During a low point in this celebration, participants were invited to act out silently 'a museum of desolation'. This celebration touched many who were resistant to feelings and inner emotions, and created a turning point within the days of discernment.

## Discovering the name of grace
The four and a half days facilitated by Esdac to help clarify the name of grace ended with statements from each of the groups. They were reworked, rewritten by us and by a whole team, without a satisfactory formulation emerging. The Assembly ended with 2 days of business, governance, approval of the final text, finances, elections. The final report of this World Assembly was submitted by three people chosen as the drafting team. Before its approval, the re-reading of the final report by all the participants was accompanied by judicious remarks from several members. One said: 'But ... the name of grace is contained in your conclusion!' And it was absolutely true! The baby was there, before our eyes! It was born not during the days when it was accompanied by Esdac, but later! It was fabulous: we had already put the pen away

and God had taken it back, saying: 'I have not finished speaking.' Our hearts overflow with gratitude and awe at the action of the Holy Spirit.

## The name of grace

Short version: *To deepen – to share – to go out*

Long version: *We feel called to FURTHER develop our identity, through an inner conversion that allows us to be more faithful and more mindful of our charism in all its dimensions.*

*We feel called to humbly SHARE with others the gift of Ignatian spirituality as embodied in our vocation as lay people. We consider discernment and Ignatian tools and methods as precious gifts that we cannot keep to ourselves.*

*We feel called to GO OUT to serve those most in need and to plant seeds of mercy, joy and hope in the world in order to follow Jesus more closely and work with him in building the Kingdom.'*

## Our team of facilitators

Our team of three felt very close-knit. Our sharing was essential to creating communion between us. We felt so small. Sometimes in the morning, one of us would providentially arrive with a 'great' idea, explain it to the other two, and the idea was polished, translated into 3 languages and printed in 210 copies thanks to the support of a logistical team on site which pampered us with great generosity and friendship!

## No other way!

We were touched by this Assembly: clearly the group loved to pray, and loved the Exercises.

The Exco had put its trust in Esdac by taking great risks: 'Will we discover anything?' And many participants were completely lost in this method and wondered where we were going. Many people from all over the world prayed for the Assembly. The Holy Spirit was there, and the participants trusted us. It was absolutely overwhelming to experience this.

The Exco concluded with the words: 'There will be no other way to run a World Assembly.'

*Appendix 4: Discernment Journeys of Diverse Groups*

## 6: *The Birth of a Lay Association*
The discernment we are talking about here took place over a year and a half, i.e. six sessions in total, two of which were by Zoom. Two Esdac facilitators were involved.

### The request
A small group of women who had followed the same spiritual formation journey had each discerned a common call to the consecrated life. They called on Esdac to help them discern whether they were called to form a lay association. Coming from different backgrounds, with different origins, experiences and temperaments, were they called to become a group united by a common identity and mission? And if so, how?

At the end of three sessions, the call to continue the journey together was clear, but much remained to be done: to build fraternity, to explore the question of mission and to begin to organise.

Soon some other people from the same formation background joined them. The new group thus formed decided to continue the accompaniment with Esdac to lay the foundations of a structure, while waiting for recognition by the Church.

### The journey
*The first session (4 days)*
The programme included experimentation with spiritual conversation based on the experience of the Christmas feast; the expression of desires and fears around beginning a journey of discernment together; reviewing by each of the participants of their personal history with the Lord, including a training course they had followed together; the personal name of grace and the name of grace of the group; a celebration of reconciliation; the particular call to live as a group in the Church; concrete decisions and distribution of responsibilities for the period until the next meeting, and the revision of the 4 days spent together.

*The second session (2 days)*
It involved reviewing their experience since the last meeting, starting from the particular call of the group and with the help of a Prayer Sheet

sent in advance; fraternal life; the beginning of organisation with the handing over and distribution of responsibilities within the group.

*The Third session (2 days)*
There was sharing and celebration on the first evening, then an emphasis on the guidelines for spiritual conversation to help the group move forward in fellowship. Work was done on identity and belonging before tackling the theme of the mission of each one and the common mission.

*The Fourth session (2 days by Zoom)*
(Now with people from the second group). Governance and service of authority were addressed and organization began. The group agreed on the principle of three leaders.

*The Fifth session (2 days per Zoom)*
This took up the group's name of grace and sharing around the question: 'WHAT do we want to live out together?' Discernment followed on the form and timing of commitments, the modality of elections, the structure of the leadership team, and the duration of the mandate.

*The Sixth session (2 days)*
Each shared on their deepest desires. They prepared for the elections (searching for competencies and qualities, and for personal availability for election or not), and elected three leaders. Decisions and responsibilities were dealt with, and after a review of the series of Workshops there was a missioning celebration.

**Key moments**
*The fraternity under construction*
The question of fraternal life was part of the group's initial request. Tensions had arisen during a weekend that preceded the first meeting in which they were accompanied by Esdac. The instructions around Spirit-led conversation and the structure of the Esdac facilitation were felt to be a helpful framework, and a means of finding security within the group.

During the first Workshop, we proposed a Prayer Sheet on the group's sin and a celebration of mercy. The mediation of the facilitators was accepted, to help people to reconcile. The contribution around NVC (Non-Violent Communication) was beneficial. Peace returned to the group.

A Prayer Sheet was proposed on fraternal life and this was lived in its very concrete aspects during the sessions.

The group acquired a beautiful capacity to dare to express its difficulties, including its reticence and resistance, in a climate of truth and freedom, and mindful that this helps the group to build itself up and to move forward.

## Celebrations

The group experienced a number of celebrations that helped it to grow.

The first took place in the oratory, with each person being invited to choose the place and posture that best expressed her personal name of grace. In the same place, the group experienced a celebration of mercy, which marked a turning point in their journey.

The presence of a priest made it possible to experience Eucharistic celebrations in line with the group's living experience. The text of the group's particular call was used as the basis for a Eucharistic preface. The meetings began with a time of sharing prepared by a Prayer Sheet sent in advance, and then continued with the Eucharist. Similarly, the review of the meetings was integrated into the final Eucharist.

The celebration of the sending on mission was held outside, around a mandala, a collective creation made with elements from nature. Each person presented her personal mission to the group, which in turn prayed for her. This was an experience of sharing the mission, moving from 'I' to 'we': 'We are not a cooperative of individual projects, we are in solidarity with the mission of others.'

The final celebration was an opportunity to gather and offer all the fruits of the session at the moment of thanksgiving.

## Organisation and responsibilities

From the first meeting, decisions were made and responsibilities assigned according to the needs expressed by the group. At each subsequent meeting, a moment was devoted to 'going round the responsibilities', each one saying how she had experienced it, sometimes proposing improvements. Then the group distributed responsibilities for the next period. Two long plenaries were spent agreeing on concrete points of the group's life, including financial issues, to the great satisfaction of all. At the penultimate meeting, after reflecting and praying on the question of the service of authority, and by reliving personal experiences and comparing different models, the group chose a first form of organisation: a leader accompanied by two deputies who were elected at the final meeting.

*Evaluation by the facilitation team*
Once again, we have seen how much the Esdac approach and tools help the groups. These include the anchoring in the Word of God, the exercises of reviewing, the deep and attentive listening in the silence of prayer and in spiritual conversation, the experience of reconciliation as strengthening the bonds of charity and peace, free and true articulation, the expression of disagreements in a climate of benevolence and respect, the decisions taken in common and the sharing of responsibilities.

The group moved grew, built itself up, and showed capacity to say no to something that was proposed by the facilitators: thus, when these suggested setting up thematic groups to work on certain points, the participants instead chose to give priority to the election of leaders.

All were grateful for the help provided. The group noted in its final review, peace, joy, communion, hope; personal freedom to 'embark together' and commit to the group; awareness of spiritual struggle as an important issue; the discovery that they were forming a 'Church cell' with the desire to move towards recognition and statutes.

*7: Accompaniment in a Student Residence*
In a university town, Christian students are invited to share their life in a house which has an Ignatian spirit. There are five students, female and male. Their experience confirms that a small group is the ideal basic unit for growing in self-knowledge, openness to others and relationship with God.

The students live together and share the services of cleaning, washing up, cooking and eating on assigned days. A life-sharing meeting is held about twice a month, except during holidays and exam periods. In addition, there are two healing weekends during the year. Meetings and weekends are led by two facilitators, who teach through practice the art of Spirit-led conversation, the review of personal life, the sharing of these reviews, evaluation of their community life, and certain forms of prayer.

This formula of Christian living together makes it possible to accompany young adults for one or two years, at a time in their lives when crucial personal choices are being made.

One of the major difficulties encountered by all human beings is 'living together'. Being able to explore this issue in some depth, in the banality, intimacy and inevitable tensions of everyday life, prepares them for life as a couple, as a family, a community. The small size of the group requires and encourages honest speech, respectful listening and personal maturation. Several students said that in this five-person flat they finally felt 'at home'.

### 8: A Religious Community Meeting

*The agenda we are about to read was communicated a week in advance by the leader of a small religious community to the other 6 members, in the form of an e-mail.*

Dear companion,

We will be meeting on Monday evening from 8 to 9:30 pm for a consultative community discernment. Before our meeting, please take some personal time for silent reflection on the following.

**The question for discernment**
'Do we welcome Ahmed, an undocumented refugee, for two months?'

**Request for grace**
'Father, give us your Spirit. May the Spirit make us free from all repugnance, fear and prejudice, and give us light and strength'.

**Reference texts**
*(1) 'I was hungry, and you gave me food; I was thirsty, and you gave me drink; I was a stranger, and you welcomed me. Whenever you did it*

*to one of the least of these who are members of my family, you did it to me*' (Mt 25:35, 40).

*(2)* Re-reading thirty years later the great exploits he had done 'for the love of God', Ignatius recognises an ill-informed generosity, 'not knowing what humility was, or charity or patience, or discernment in regulating and balancing these virtues'.[93]

**Information**

Ahmed is 25 years old and originally from Africa. In Belgium since 2017. Undocumented. Sent by JRS (Jesuit Refugee Service), which remains his reference and which takes care of finding another living place after two months. The host community will provide a room, food and some pocket money. A person is delegated by JRS to accompany him in administrative procedures. It is agreed that Ahmed will not invite anyone to the house without our agreement. He will also inform us of his absences.

**Method**

During the meeting, the 'time keeper' will be chosen, who will ensure that everyone is given the opportunity to speak and that we finish on time. In the first round of sharing, each person will speak in turn, possibly holding an object that signifies that they 'have the floor'. Then there will be a short time of silent reflection during which each person will look over what has been shared and ask themselves: 'What do I feel? Peace, joy, breathing easy? Worry, unease, tension? What promotes life for me in what has been shared? What do I feel is blocking it? What are my aspirations and how does what was said satisfy them or not?'

Next everyone will share what touched them most in what others say. It may be that a consensus quickly emerges. If not, we will note together the advantages and disadvantages of receiving him. If it turns out that the answer is yes, we will note all the conditions required for such a welcome to go well.

---

93 Ignatius, *Personal Writings*, p. 19.

### 9: A Family Prayer

Here is a way of praying as a family, based on the fact that it is possible to pray about one's own experience as one would pray about a Gospel story.

The leader invites the members to gather in a circle, sitting on the floor, with a feather in the centre, and explains: 'The American Indians invented this way of doing things. These are the talking circles. For them, the feather is an eagle feather (for us, a pigeon feather will do). The eagle flies high and is closest to the Divine Spirit. The one who wants to speak takes the feather in hand to signify that they will try to speak from the depth of their heart. As long as one of you has the feather in his hand, they have the floor and the others listen in silence. When the feather is returned to the center, someone else takes it, speaks, then puts it back, etc. This helps to listen well ... and to dare to say what you want to say.'

Before starting the sharing, the leader invites people to take one or two minutes to calm down and to listen to their breathing.

Then one or more sentences can be read out, such as:

- *'Where two or three are gathered in my name, I am in their midst'* (Mt 18:20),
- *'The essential is invisible to the eyes, one can only see well with one's heart'* (from *The Little Prince* by Saint Exupéry). And so on ...

The leader can address Jesus as follows: 'Jesus, help us to listen with respect and to speak frankly', and then give some instructions:

- 'Now each person is going to think about something beautiful that they have experienced (today or this week) and write it down in two or three words on a piece of paper, so that they won't forget it. In this way, each of us can better listen to the speaker, without being preoccupied with what we're going to say.
- The person who prefers to remain silent says: 'I'll pass'. If they want they can speak at the end or remain silent.
- If someone remains in silence with the pen in hand, don't become impatient; give them time to find the right words. If they cry, the tears are welcomed, calmly'.

When everyone has expressed what they have written down, the leader says: 'Now we take a moment to think about what someone else has said that we find beautiful.'

Whoever wants to, takes the feather and says: 'What X said touched me because …'

When all those who wish have spoken, the leader asks: 'Say in one word what you are feeling now' and the feather is passed round in a clockwise direction. It is possible that the first one says: 'happy', the second one: 'at peace', the third one: 'happy'… If someone says 'tense' or 'sad', the leader can question them by asking, for example: 'Tense' because you would have preferred to watch the football on TV?' 'Sad because you didn't manage to explain yourself well?' The aim is for everyone to feel listened to, understood and at peace before going to sleep.

Close with a song of thanksgiving: *'Alleluia'* or *'Magnificat'* or …

## 10: Classroom Retreats

Esdac runs retreats for 16- and 17-year-olds. For years the leaders have found themselves in the presence of young people who are more and more allergic to being talked at about God. A new form of retreat was therefore developed, the aim of which is to invite all the students in a class to experience *'real talk'* and *'respectful listening'* together. The leaders are convinced that when this goal is reached, the students have an experience that brings them closer to God, prepares them to open their hearts and helps them to experience the benefits of freely giving themselves to others, because such sharing is what life is about.

The exercises proposed are diverse. For example, cooperative games are followed by a time of personal and then collective reflection. Pupils are also invited to reflect on the interpersonal relationships that matter to them. A story, a parable from the Gospel, a situation from everyday family life is acted out and gives rise to a personal review, followed by a sharing of these reviews, using the three rounds of Spirit-led conversation.

In the plenary, the 25 or 30 young people are in a circle; a ballpoint pen is passed around on the floor. The instructions for Spirit-led conversation regulate speaking and listening. It is not a requirement to name God: it is sufficient to refer to the golden rule of the great religions: 'Whatever you would have others do for you, do it for them too' (Mt 7:12 etc.). Two other rules are fundamental: 'Be quicker to accept the contributions of others than to rubbish them', and 'Do not put anyone on a pedestal'.

In practice, there were up to four classes led by Esdac for three days in one place, each class having two facilitators. These prepared the retreat activities together and during the retreat met in the evening to discuss what had happened in their classes. They then prepared the next day together and celebrated the Eucharist, during which they could give thanks for all that they had received and intercede for the students.

By the end of this type of retreat, the facilitators will have made the students aware they have co-operated to how much success of the experience because they have become better at following the instructions that make it possible not to feel threatened in a group. The pupils often admit to being surprised: they had never before spoken to each other so frankly and deeply. While they may not understand it until years later, they may hear the following message: *'The one who has enabled you to communicate in depth with one another is the Holy Spirit, the Love which, while uniting the Father and the Son, maintains each of them in their singularity. You have experienced this Love among yourselves.'*

## *11: Brief Communal Discernment*

Here is a concrete example of what this Manual is about: it illustrates a three-hour communal discernment as it took place. Ideally a discernment process lasts as long as is necessary, but when time is strictly limited one has to cut corners while retaining the essence of the process![94]

### Introduction

A busy parish had been debating an important project for some time without coming to agreement. The issue was: *Does this project make the*

---

[94] Adapted from Brian Grogan, *Making Good Decisions: A Beginner's Guide* (Dublin: Veritas 2015), pp. 242–247.

*best use of our limited financial resources at this time?* The Parish Pastoral Council members were unsure; the Finance Committee was in favour; the Parish Priest was keen to go ahead, but the Bishop was cautionary, due to the cost involved.

I was asked to facilitate a discernment process between the PPC and the Finance Committee and was given three hours, no more, because of time restrictions on the twenty participants, all busy people. Whatever the outcome, it would be accepted by the PP, who stayed outside the room, so that each participant could speak freely without being held accountable.

In the days before the meeting I prayed a good deal about it, and gathered prayer support from various sources, including parish members and a nearby community of cloistered nuns.

## Opening the meeting

We met for 10.00am in a large airy room; chairs in a circle; no tables, central décor and candle lighting. Each person was welcomed, offered tea/coffee and given a name-badge: these gestures helped to bond the participants, who already knew one another at various levels, but some of whom were nervous about what might be asked of them. Humour helped to create a relaxed atmosphere! (10 mins). [We had only the one room: ideally there would be a chapel and or group rooms. A gong was used to mark time.

The PP formally welcomed everyone, and sketched the history of the project and its Pros and Cons. This meeting, he said, would be the last on the issue: he would accept the outcome. He stated that a 2/3 majority either way would be accepted: he checked that all had read the material distributed and then clarified points as needed. (10 mins)

## Facilitation

As facilitator I introduced myself, then welcomed the group, saying: 'You may well be asking yourselves, *'Why am I here?'* It can be a shock to know that the decision about our project lies with you. We have talked the talk: now with the help of God let's walk the walk! What *you* decide is the way things will be. We are here, not as rival groups, but as a collaborative:

whether we are aware or not, the Good Spirit is with us and will help us to find consensus. As Carl Jung says, *'Bidden or unbidden, God is present'.* We can add, 'and God is involved!' With God's help we will pray our way together to a decision. Only you, not I, will be voting!' (10 mins)

Silent moment followed by Prayer*: 'Our Father… Then, 'O God, from whom all good things come, grant that we, who call on you in our need, may at your prompting discern what is right, and by your guidance do it. We ask this though Christ our Lord, Amen.' (5 mins).*

*(35 mins total. From here on the facititator leads)*

### Ice-breaker

- To build us into a collaborative community for this morning, we begin with an Ice-breaker.
  I ask you first to move toward someone you don't know well and share on the question: 'How did you get involved in the parish and the project?' (7 mins)
- I invite you now to sit and to notice your image of this group – Pilgrims at a crossroads? A football team, ready to go? A herd of sheep? Lost like the Hebrews in the desert? Get your imagination going! Now share your image with the person beside you. Brief plenary sharing. Funny images help! (3 mins)
- Now ask yourself: 'What can I contribute to this meeting?' Share with someone you don't know well.' (5 mins)
- Now a silent pause. Ask yourself, 'How might I spoil the good working of this group?' Is there anyone here I don't like or trust? Pray for them! Am I biased or free in regard to the project? Can I trust God to show us the way forward? Can I keep an open mind until I vote?' (10 mins). [No sharing].

(25 mins total)

### Pray and share

- Pray for a listening heart. The Spirit is in the group looking around for people who are paying attention to what God may want. 'The still small voice' (1 Kg 19). Ask to listen well. Prayer: *'Come, Holy Spirit…!'* (5 mins)

- Next, in silent reflection and prayer ask yourself, *'Does this proposed project enhance our parish Vision?'* [A word to refresh the group on the Vision statement] (10 min).
- Now form 5 groups of four, and share briefly (3 mins each: I will be Timekeeper), on what has come to you from the silent prayer (15 mins).
- Now share again, this time on something said by someone in the group that struck you as important: this may be the nudge of the Spirit! (10 mins)
- Then agree on the main point you want to bring to the plenary group. (10 mins).
(45 mins total)

## Plenary

The sharing from each group may hint at consensus; but we won't rush to a vote! We will write on the flipchart all the bullet points we can think of FOR the project; then all the points AGAINST. We will look at the two lists in silence – as Quakers do in their decision-making. We take a BREAK! (Plenary and short Break: 40 mins).

(40 mins total)

## Voting

- Now I will lead a short time of prayer during which I invite you to ask God to direct your heart to what seems wisest and best for all who will be affected by the decision. Imagine the Three Divine Persons herein this room and chatting on what best to do and hoping we get their prompting. *Story from Introduction to this book: Be like the cook who has to go upstairs to ask the lord of the manor what he wants for dinner! No amount of chatting in the kitchen will do*! So in imagination, go upstairs and sit and chat with the Trinity! (10 mins). At least say: 'God, help us chose well!'
- Now comes the vote, which will be secret. Write Yes or No on your voting slip. I will not be voting but I will gather up the slips and call them out. (5 mins)
[The vote was 7/1 in favour].

## Appendix 4: Discernment Journeys of Diverse Groups

**Consensus secured!**
- We will wrap up the morning by thanking God for bringing us to our decision. Prayer/Hymn. Next comes Implementation, so can we have volunteers to help the PP later on that? (5 mins)
- [If no concensus] I invite the minority to indicate their reservations, and/or what modifications would enable them to support the majority. (10 + mins)
- If still no decision, recall the group as early as possible. (In a Papal Conclave there can be 4 votings in a day)
- Finally I invite you to chat on what you have learnt from this morning (5 mins)
(35 mins total)

**Closure**
A final word from the PP on Confidentiality, his thanks, and then a little celebration!
Grand Total: 180 mins!

# Acknowledgements

**For *Pratique du discernement en commun*, 2022**
We warmly thank Father Arturo Sosa SJ for his preface. On his appointment as Superior General of the Society of Jesus in 2016, he made a strong gesture of support for communal discernment by naming a General Councillor for Discernment and Planning.

We are grateful to the members of the ISECP team (Ignatian Spiritual Exercises for the Corporate Person): Jim Borbely SJ, John English SJ, George Schemel SJ and Judith Roemer, who trained the pioneers of Esdac in Scranton, USA. Special thanks to Jean Charlier SJ who discerned in the ISECP methodology a promise of renewal for the Church, and to the members of DICAP (Discernment in Common for Apostolic Planning), especially in the area of planning.

Our gratitude extends to the groups and individuals who have participated in Esdac Workshops. Thanks to their trust, our experience has been enriched and expressed in today's words. Thanks also to the Jesuit Editors, Bernard Bougon SJ and Bertrand Hériard-Dubreuil SJ, whose encouragement gave us the energy to rewrite rather than to reprint the initial Esdac book of 2006, *'Pratique du discernement en commun'*.

Thanks to Geneviève de Taisne, psychoanalyst, for the critical and friendly observations she gave us after reading a first draft of the present book. And gratitude to the anonymous reviser or censor who has made the current text more theologically and spiritually sound.

Finally, thanks to those who provided advice and suggestions for the final drafts of this French edition, 2022; notably Franck Janin SJ, Annick Bonnefond, Françoise Uylenbroeck, Syviane Bouillon and Cécile Gillet. Special thanks to Céline Doutrepont who proofread and edited the manuscript.

**Acknowledgements for the current book, *Communal Discernment: A Lamp for Our Synodal Journey*, 2024**
Deepest thanks to Michel Bacq SJ, who conceived the project of an Engish edition, and shepherded it with high professionalism, sensitivity

and patience; to Moira McDowall rlr and Mary O'Connor, who fine-combed successive drafts and made valuable suggestions based on their own experience with Esdac; next to Phyllis Brady, Joe Greenan, Martin Hyde, Anne Lyons, Michael Smith SJ, Colleen Wong and my community in Dublin for contributing their varied perspectives; and finally thanks to God who saw this work through to completion.

Brian Grogan, SJ,
Jesuit House of Writers,
Dublin, May 2024.

# Bibliography

Note: A fuller bibliography is given in the French edition. This list offers books mainly accessible in English.

Arbuckle, G., *Refounding Religious Congregations* (New York/London: Mahwah Paulist Press, 1988).

——— *Refounding the Church, Dissent and Leadership* (Montreal: Bellarmine, 2001).

Borbely J., and others, *Ignatian Spiritual Exercises for the Corporate Person*, vol. 1, 3 (Scranton: ISECP, 1990).

——— *Facilitators' Manual for Ignatian Spiritual Exercises for the Corporate Person*, vol. 2 (Scranton: ISECP, 1991).

——— *Understanding Group Spiritual Life*, vol. 3 (Scranton: ISECP, 1999).

——— *Ignatius of Loyola, the Founder of the Jesuits* (Paris: Le Centurion, 1979).

Cobble, J. and Elliott, C., *The Hidden Spirit: Discovering the Spirituality of Institutions* (North Carolina: C.M.R, 1999).

Dhotel, J-C, *Discerner ensemble: guide pratique du discernement communautaire* (Paris: Éditions Jésuites, 2013).

Dunn, T., *Graced Crossroads: Pathways to Deep Change and Transformation* (St Louis, 2020).

English J., *Spiritual Intimacy and Community – An Ignatian View of the Small Faith Community* (London: Darton, Longman and Todd, 1992).

——— *Spiritual Freedom: From an Experience of the Ignatian Exercises to the Art of Spiritual Guidance* (Chicago: Loyola, 1995).

Pope Francis, *Evangelii Gaudium* (Vatican: The Holy See, 2013).

——— *Laudato Si'* (Vatican: The Holy See, 2015).

——— *Amoris Laetitia* (Vatican: The Holy See, 2016).

——— *Querida Amazonia* (Vatican: The Holy See, 2020).

——— *Fratelli Tutti* (Vatican: The Holy See, 2020).

Futrell, J. C., *Making an Apostolic Community of Love* (St Louis: Institute of Jesuit Sources, 1970).

Greenleaf, R. K., *Servant Leadership: A Journey into the Nature of Legitimate Power and Greatness* (Mahwah: Paulist, 2002).

Grogan, B., *Alone and on Foot: Ignatius of Loyola* (Dublin: Veritas, 2008).

——— *Making Good Decisions: A Beginner's Guide* (Dublin: Messenger Publications, 2015).

———— with P. Brady, *Meetings Matter: Spirituality and Skills for Meetings* (Dublin: Veritas, 2009).

———— *Pedro Arrupe: A Heart Larger than the World* (Dublin: Messenger Publications, 2022).

Haers, J., 'A Synodal Process on Synodality: Synodal Missionary Journeying and Common Apostolic Discernment', *Louvain Studies* 43, 2020, 215–238.

Halík, T., *The Afternoon of Christianity: the Courage to Change* (Notre Dame: University of Notre Dame Press, 2024).

Hopkins, G. M., *Poems and Prose* (London: Penguin, 1963), edited by W. H. Gardner.

Ignatius of Loyola, *Personal Writings* (London: Penguin, 2004), edited by J. Munitiz SJ and P. Endean SJ.

Ivens, M., *Understanding the Spiritual Exercises* (Leominster: Gracewing, 2004).

Kolvenbach, P. K., 'Letter on apostolic discernment in common', in *Acta Romana Societatis Jesu, (ARSI)*, vol. XIX, fasc. III, anno 1986, Rome, 1987.

Laloux F., *Reinventing Organizations: The summarised and illustrated version of the phenomenon book that invites us to rethink management* (Paris, 2017).

Lonergan B., *Insight* (London, 1957).

Nepper M., 'Conversation spirituelle', in *Dictionnaire de spiritualité*, II (Beauchesne, 1953), col. 2212–2218.

Peck, M. Scott, *The Different Drum: Community-Making and Peace* (London: Arrow, 1987).

———— *A World Waiting to Be Born: Civility Rediscovered* (New York: Random House, 2009).

Puhl L., *The Spiritual Exercises of St Ignatius* (Chicago, 1951).

Rahner, K., *Discourses of Ignatius of Loyola to the Jesuits of Today* (Paris: Centurion, 1983).

Roemer J., *The Group Meeting as a Contemplative Experience* (Typofile Press, 1982).

Rogers C., *Freedom to Learn*, 4th ed (Dunod, 2013).

Rosenberg M., *The Art of Reconciliation: Respecting One's Own Needs and Those of Others* (Geneva, 2010).

———— *Nonviolent Communication, a Language of Life*, and *The Spiritual Basis of Non-Violent Communication* (Encinitas, CA: PuddleDancer Press, 2015).

Scharmer O., *Theory U: Leading from the Future as it Emerges* (San Francisco: Berrett-Koehler, 2016).

———— *Theory U: Renewing Leadership: Collectively Inventing New Futures* (Gap, 2016).

Schemel G., *Focusing Group Energies – Common Ground for Leadership, Organization, Spirituality*, vol. 1 (Scranton: ISECP, 1992).

Schemel G. and Judith A. Roemer, 'Communal discernment', first published in *Review for Religious*, 40:6, Nov.–Dec. 1981, revised July 1992.

Schiffers N., 'Authority, Power' in *New Dictionary of Theology*.

Sosa A., 'On discernment in common', in *ARSI* XXVI, Fasc. II, 2, 2018, 756–765.

Tetlow, J., 'The most Postmodern Prayer: American Jesuit Identity and the Examen of Conscience, 1920–1990', in *Studies in the Spirituality of Jesuits*, 26:1, 1994.

Vatican II, *Gaudium et Spes* (Vatican: The Holy See, 1965).

# Index

Abuse 141, 161
Action 123
Aspirations – longings, needs, desires 64, 68, 98, 107
Authority 79, 87

Basic Human Aspirations 68
Bibliodrama 152
Body language 64
Body sensations 131
Brief Communal Discernment 246

Change 88
Circle 41
Collaborators 29
Commitment 44
Communal Discernment (throughout)
Communication 55
Confidentiality 58
Consensus 84, 93, 97, 113, 122
Consequences 62
Consolation 128, 134, 140
Conversion 90

Decision-making: Three moments 118
Delegates 83, 177
Desolation 133, 138
Discerning Together 43, 89
Discernment of spirits 128

Emotions 64, 68, 131
Empathy 156

Energy Cycle 69
Esdac 22, 24, 165
Evaluation 165
Examen 74

Facilitation 145, 156, 163
Feelings 64, 68, 106
Follow up to Workshop 180
For/Against 120
Freedom, Inner 7, 9

Games 107, 153
Grace, personal 99
Group grace 100
Group power 65

History Line 105
Holy Spirit 25, 165

Ice Breaker 247
Ignatius 130
Incarnation 90
Inner weather 62

Joy 133
Joy, False 142

Leader 82, 176
Life-Death-Resurrection cycle 93
Listen 159
Logo 41

Mercy (celebration) 111
Mission 19

## Index

Non-affiliated 215

One-to-one accompaniment 162
Plenary Session 60
Power 65, 69, 81
Personal Review 74
Prayer, personal 48
Prayer, prayer sheets 49, 148, Appendix 3

Recommendations 47, 70
Rounds, sharing 43

Sadness 138
Shared governance 79
Signs of our times 19
Sin: cf. Graces resisted 198–200
Small group 43, 53
SMART 122
Spirit (good and bad) 130, 140

Spirit-led conversation 37
Spiritual Exercises of
   St Ignatius 21
Stories of groups Appendix 4
Supervision 166
Synodality 46, 168
SWOT analysis 116

Theory U 72
Thoughts 52, 132, 140
Three good moments for decision 118
Three hour discernment 246

Unanimity 85, 126

Weather reports 62, 67
Who-What-How 105, 115
Wolf 12
Workshop design Appendix 1 & 2